Applications of Soft Systems Methodology for Organizational Change

Maryam Ebrahimi
Independent Researcher, Germany

A volume in the Advances in Business Strategy and Competitive Advantage (ABSCA) Book Series

IGI Global
PUBLISHER of TIMELY KNOWLEDGE

Published in the United States of America by
IGI Global
Business Science Reference (an imprint of IGI Global)
701 E. Chocolate Avenue
Hershey PA, USA 17033
Tel: 717-533-8845
Fax: 717-533-8661
E-mail: cust@igi-global.com
Web site: http://www.igi-global.com

Library of Congress Cataloging-in-Publication Data

Names: Ebrahimi, Maryam, 1980- author.
Title: Applications of soft systems methodology for organizational change / by Maryam Ebrahimi.
Description: Hershey : Business Science Reference, 2020. | Includes bibliographical references and index. | Summary: "This book provides a theoretical foundation and practical practice of soft systems methodology in organizations"-- Provided by publisher.
Identifiers: LCCN 2020000289 (print) | LCCN 2020000290 (ebook) | ISBN 9781799845041 (hardcover) | ISBN 9781799852506 (paperback) | ISBN 9781799845058 (ebook)
Subjects: LCSH: Organizational change. | System theory.
Classification: LCC HD58.8 .E247 2020 (print) | LCC HD58.8 (ebook) | DDC 658.4/06--dc23
LC record available at https://lccn.loc.gov/2020000289
LC ebook record available at https://lccn.loc.gov/2020000290

This book is published in the IGI Global book series Advances in Business Strategy and Competitive Advantage (ABSCA) (ISSN: 2327-3429; eISSN: 2327-3437)

British Cataloguing in Publication Data
A Cataloguing in Publication record for this book is available from the British Library.

Advances in Business Strategy and Competitive Advantage (ABSCA) Book Series

ISSN:2327-3429
EISSN:2327-3437

Editor-in-Chief: Patricia Ordóñez de Pablos, Universidad de Oviedo, Spain

MISSION

Business entities are constantly seeking new ways through which to gain advantage over their competitors and strengthen their position within the business environment. With competition at an all-time high due to technological advancements allowing for competition on a global scale, firms continue to seek new ways through which to improve and strengthen their business processes, procedures, and profitability.

The **Advances in Business Strategy and Competitive Advantage (ABSCA) Book Series** is a timely series responding to the high demand for state-of-the-art research on how business strategies are created, implemented and re-designed to meet the demands of globalized competitive markets. With a focus on local and global challenges, business opportunities and the needs of society, the **ABSCA** encourages scientific discourse on doing business and managing information technologies for the creation of sustainable competitive advantage.

COVERAGE

- Joint Ventures
- Ethics and Business Strategy
- Competitive Strategy
- Co-operative Strategies
- Balanced Scorecard
- International Business Strategy
- Differentiation Strategy
- Core Competencies
- Globalization
- Value Chain

IGI Global is currently accepting manuscripts for publication within this series. To submit a proposal for a volume in this series, please contact our Acquisition Editors at Acquisitions@igi-global.com or visit: http://www.igi-global.com/publish/.

The Advances in Business Strategy and Competitive Advantage (ABSCA) Book Series (ISSN 2327-3429) is published by IGI Global, 701 E. Chocolate Avenue, Hershey, PA 17033-1240, USA, www.igi-global.com. This series is composed of titles available for purchase individually; each title is edited to be contextually exclusive from any other title within the series. For pricing and ordering information please visit http://www.igi-global.com/book-series/advances-business-strategy-competitive-advantage/73672. Postmaster: Send all address changes to above address.

Titles in this Series

For a list of additional titles in this series, please visit:
https://www.igi-global.com/book-series/advances-business-strategy-competitive-advantage/73672

International Perspectives on the Youth Labor Market Emerging Research and Opportunities
Samir Amine (Université du Québec en Outaouais, Canada)
Business Science Reference • copyright 2020 • 217pp • H/C (ISBN: 9781799827795) • US $170.00 (our price)

Open and Innovative Trade Opportunities for Latin America and the Caribbean
Pablo Alberto Baisotti (University of Costa Rica, Costa Rica)
Business Science Reference • copyright 2020 • 255pp • H/C (ISBN: 9781799835035) • US $215.00 (our price)

Cases on Performance Improvement Innovation
Darlene M. Van Tiem (Capella University, USA & University of Michigan – Dearborn, USA) and Nancy Crain Burns (Crain Burns Associates LLC, USA)
Business Science Reference • copyright 2020 • 377pp • H/C (ISBN: 9781799836735) • US $195.00 (our price)

Handbook of Research on Entrepreneurship Development and Opportunities in Circular Economy
Neeta Baporikar (Namibia University of Science and Technology, Namibia & University of Pune, India)
Business Science Reference • copyright 2020 • 696pp • H/C (ISBN: 9781799851165) • US $265.00 (our price)

Digital Transformation and Innovative Services for Business and Learning
Kamaljeet Sandhu (University of New England, Australia)
Business Science Reference • copyright 2020 • 282pp • H/C (ISBN: 9781799851752) • US $235.00 (our price)

Development and Implementation of Adaptive Trade Policy in the Era of Digital Globalization
Vardan Mkrttchian (HHH University, Australia) and Yulia Vertakova (Financial University Under the Government of the Russian Federation, Kursk, Russia)
Business Science Reference • copyright 2020 • 300pp • H/C (ISBN: 9781799831341) • US $215.00 (our price)

For an entire list of titles in this series, please visit:
https://www.igi-global.com/book-series/advances-business-strategy-competitive-advantage/73672

IGI Global
PUBLISHER of TIMELY KNOWLEDGE

701 East Chocolate Avenue, Hershey, PA 17033, USA
Tel: 717-533-8845 x100 • Fax: 717-533-8661
E-Mail: cust@igi-global.com • www.igi-global.com

Table of Contents

Preface

OVERVIEW

Currently, people despite their authority and awareness do not perceive each other properly. In many cases, we ourselves accuse others of malice which is often at the root of misunderstanding. Finding common ground with other people provides a pathway for understanding. Science makes a response to the needs and interests of the societies including providing a tool for better understanding. Viewing the world on the basis of a mental model which is mostly in accordance with what we physically see is inclined to cause an oversimplified understanding that touches the surface of the real-world. Systems thinking as a way of thinking about is recognized as a language for understanding and describing. Systems thinking can boost our understanding of the complex system realizing that a system of interrelations is much more than the sum of its components. It broadens our thinking and supports us to illustrate issues in new and different ways. It helps us to explore problems in a larger system or from a wider perspective. According to this approach of interconnecting worldview, a different process for problem solving becomes known. Edwards W. Deming (1900-1993) said: 94% of problems in business are systems driven and only 6% are people driven.

Checkland has been trying to develop the systems thinking for more than 30 years since 1970s. Obviously, the most considerable contribution of his work is his Soft Systems Methodology (SSM). The purpose of the SSM is to improve the system and the result of its usage is beyond a solution to the original problem situation. Problem solving for the sake of the improvement in human activity systems (HAS) is a continuous process with never ending. The SSM interprets the concept of system as subjectively created by humans who have the interaction and interdependence with the problem situation rather the objective entities in the world. On the contrary, hard system methodologies are not suitable to address the complexity and ambiguity of social systems like organizations. The SSM can be explained in respect of seven stages: (1) the analysis of a problem situation, (2) building a rich picture of the situation, (3) the preparation of root definition of relevant systems to the problem situation, (4) the construction of conceptual models of the defined systems in the root definitions, (5) the comparison of what perceived as the existing real-world and the conceptual models, (6) the determination and agreement on feasible and desirable changes, and (7) the implementation of those changes.

The SSM has triggered great academic debate as a result of its practical applications in a broad set of situations by people, who has lack of technical knowledge. It has been used by those who have some relevant previous experience. This book aims to provide the theoretical foundation and practical practice of the SSM in varoius case studies. SSM in the information systems (IS) development has a key role, and it has been extensively applied for business analysis and information management. In addition, it is recognized as an appropriate tool to perceive insights for the change optimization. Organizational change can be a situation where SSM can be applied due to its use for sharing vision and team learning which is beneficial to bridge the gap between the present world and conceptual world. SSM deals with cultural issues including of conflict, and mutual understanding.

Technology management (TM) which is considered as a hard operations research (OR) can be combined with SSM to further develop the multi-methodology. SSM as a problem structuring tool can be aggregated to multiple-criteria decision analysis (MCDA) and SSM in the assessment of energy efficiency initiatives. The term multi-methodology refers to the combination of more than one methodology often from different paradigms such as the multi-methodology of the SSM and simulation methodologies.

The SSM approach contributed to various areas of studies such as human resource management (HRM), education management, and project management (PM). Managers work is a complex system whereby an increasing variety and number of human functions could be reproduced. HRM interacts closely and constantly with all other sub-systems of an organization and SSM gives the manager to see the organization as a whole and as a part of the larger external environment. It also provides an opportunity for managers to consider abstracted viewpoints of each stakeholder. SSM gives a deeper understanding of the processes of educational systems, such that appropriate action can be taken to improve them. Additionally, the SSM views PM through the principles of holism and more importantly involves the HAS early on in the analysis.

APPLICATIONS

SSM has proved its effectiveness in respect of an organized method of defining and taking action to improve problematical situations. It is a systematic approach to challenges of transition through identification of and taking counsel from the people involved in the definition of the action to be taken. The analysts using the SSM want improvements in what is taken to be a problem situation. SSM has been used to various kinds of studies pursuing different purposes. It has practical applications in organizational and industrial analysis. It allows for the proposition of new ideas and change of perceptions. SSM is perceived as a flexible tool which can be applied to create individual knowledge and understanding.

There are many possibilities for the combining of more than one methodology. For instance, the combination of methodologies using SSM and simulation methodologies including discrete event simulation (DES), system dynamics (SD), and agent based modeling (ABM) as representations of hard systems thinking. DES models provide a complete representation of a system in comparison with other simulation techniques and are tightly fitted for an analysis with the aim to improve the system capacity, resource utilization or queuing time. The DES-model was used during later SSM-steps to identify possible areas of improvement. In SD, system behavior is conditioned by its structure. The combined usage of SSM and SD gives an opportunity to eliminate of some limitations of SD related to conceptualization phase and the identification of the issue that should be considered. ABMs are useful for capturing emergent behavior in which interaction between agents is highly complex. The combination of SSM and ABM refers to adding the two fundamental elements of ABM to SSM which are attributes and rules of interactions.

Additionally, TM is positivistic and functionalist. It assumes the system can be effectively engineered and finally is goal seeking. Therfore, it is considered to be a hard OR method. It means planning, developing, and implementing technological capabilities to form and achieve the strategic and operational objectives of companies. In this regard, SSM as a soft OR tools and techniques can be incorporated into each phase of TM. Decision makers have three main objectives including creating knowledge relevant to the context of a problematic situation and its usage for problem definition, and planning systemically for action. SSM as a tool for problem structuring can encompass development of a decision support based on MCDA.

Information technologies (IT) are considered as a reason of organizational change which needs the extensive amount of work prior to design. Regarding IS development methodologies, SSM belongs to the systems paradigm. Products of SSM are identified problems within the system, root definitions, and desired changes. It deals with a wider context including overall IS strategy, purpose, and planning, rather than just a particular system. Each systemic tool such as technology should be used in a harmonized and thoughtful manner to create the best possible result. SSM with its pragmatic and open system approach not only allows for the inclusion of subjective information but also enables the incorporation of objective facts. SSM is not to be used in a linear manner or like a range of stages during the analysis process but as a holistic tool of a broader cultural scope.

SSM has been applied in various phases of project management such as project definiton, risk management, business process reengineering, and etc. It looks to gradually develop relationships within projects to make it possible for better decision making. SSM to the discipline of management views organizations as unified and purposeful systems having interrelated parts. HRM like other social systems changes over time and SSM as an approach for developing decisions and practices related to human resources gives the foundation of a better understanding of the system and provides the basis to make more meaningful decisions. In addition, this approach gives the opportunity of more obviously capturing the change that is essential to provide the ideal processes of educational systems that will satisfy the relevant people

TARGET AUDIENCE

This book is a collective resource with comprehensive knowledge in the field of Soft Systems Methodology in theory and practice. It is a qualitative methodology that applies systems thinking to non-systemic situations and is viewed as a learning system as well as problem solving approach which might cause change in the world. It has wide application in system design, and organizational and industrial analysis. Therefore, it can assist in the analysis, design, and evaluation of complex systems. Analysts, designers, managers use soft systems methodology to solve problems by looking at the situation rather than the issue. Target audiences are practitioners (business and system analysts and designers, experts in systems thinking, managers of organizations), academics (researchers, lecturers and advanced students) and professional institutions (professional bodies of systems thinking).

ORGANIZATION OF THE BOOK

The book is organized into 10 chapters. A brief description of each of the chapters follows:

Chapter 1, 'An Introduction to Soft Systems Methodology', describes SSM as soft systems thinking and the required techniques including rich picture, CATWOE analysis, root definition, and conceptual modeling. It reviews and cattegorizes practical applications of SSM in organizational analysis and the industry sector.

In Chapter 2, 'Soft Systems Methodology in IT-Related Organizational Changc', particular attention is on IT as a reason of change in an organization. It considers the position of SSM in other information systems development (ISD) methodologies according to a 7-element framework and reviews some case studies of SSM in IT-related organizational change.

Chapter 3, 'The Use of Soft Systems Methodology for Change Management', seeks to develop new knowledge, which will show the use of SSM as an interventionist action for optimizing change. It reviews some case studies that have highlighted issues in in the process of change.

Chapter 4, 'Soft Systems Methodology for Organizational Culture Analysis', reviews concepts of organizational culture, factors affecting organizational culture, and presents a model of organizational culture, cultural aspects of SSM, and explains an SSM application in a case study of corporate ethical culture analysis.

Chapter 5, 'Multi-Methodology Approach: Using Soft Systems Methodology and Simulation Modeling', reviews the combination of methodologies using SSM and simulation methodologies including discrete event simulation (DES), system dynamics (SD), and agent based modeling (ABM). Additionally, it convinces the difference between SD, ABM, SSM, a synthesis of SSM and SD named as soft system dynamics methodology (SSDM), and an integration of SSM and ABM referred to as soft systems agent based methodology (SSABM).

Chapter 6, 'Soft Systems Methodology in Technology Management Practices', explains five processes of technology management and refers to SSM as one of the soft operations research (OR) tools and techniques that could be incorporated into each phase. It reviews case studies regarding application of SSM in policy making for the commercialization of new technologies and technology scenario planning in an R&D organization as well.

Chapter 7, 'Soft Systems Methodology as an Approach to the Management of Education', reviews applications of SSM to the process of teaching and learning, the educational planning, analysis of the examinations department, an educational context for enhancing students' perception and understanding, the cheating problem in the national exam in Indonesia, and personalized learning environment.

Chapter 8, 'Application of Soft Systems Methodology to the Real-World Processes of Human Resource Management', reviews various applications of SSM in human resource management such as employee participation, group creativity, HR development, HR maintenance, and knowledge worker productivity.

Chapter 9, 'Project Management: The Use of Soft Systems Methodology', explains two studies about the use of SSM in funds allocation planning among major development projects, and feasibility study of industrial projects based on sustainable development principles.

Chapter 10, 'Using Soft Systems Methodology for the Analysis of Sustainable Energy Initiatives', explains four studies which applied the aggregation of multiple-criteria decision analysis and SSM in the assessment of energy efficiency initiatives.

This book presents different case studies about applications of SSM in the areas of change management, technology management, human resource management, education management, project management, and energy efficiency initiatives assessment. It provides a realistic understanding of the business environment and allows for the practice that impacts on business results. Therefore, it helps managers and decision makers make better decisions for systems improvement.

SSM is considered as a methodology for structuring complex real world problems and to determine and create feasible and desirable changes in a miscellaneous group of actors. It specifically contributes to concern different worldviews. It can be used throughout the entire process of co-creating knowledge, from problem analysis to make results come into being. Since SSM makes the need of change in a situation more comprehensible, it provides practitioners and researchers in buisness/ system analysis the major factors that lead the change. It enables them to trace from the real-world to feasible, realistic well-defined and desirable systems, and stipulate how to change a problem situation. Worldviews are the basis of the forming of problems and possible solutions. SSM applies techniques for developing models in order to question the real-world situation. This gives analysts a systematic structure to dispute or argue about both the situation and the way of its required change. Through the discussion worldviews will come to the surface and ideas of change and improvement will be produced. This improvement will lead to a change in a problematical situation and a cycle of learning is a continuous process.

In selecting a methodology for problem solving, SSM as a soft systems thinking or soft OR can mixed with hard systems thinking such as system dynamics or hard OR like MCAD. Multi-methodologies are discussed in this book in the forms of the combining of simulation methodologies and SSM in addition to MCAD and SSM. The chapter 5 assures the difference between SD, ABM, SSM, SSDM and SSABM with their ontological, epistemological, and methodological assumptions underpinning their correspondent paradigm. SSM as a problem structuring tool can be used flexibly with MCDA, as a precursor or in an integrated manner. In chapter 10, four studies have been reviewed which applied SSM to the field of energy efficiency as an aspect of sustainable energy. All of them encompass aggregation of MCDA and SSM in the assessment of energy efficiency initiatives.

The application area for SSM is very wide. Chapter 2 explains uses of SSM in the world of IS and IT, where it is much used. Organizations are social systems in which task, technology, people, and structure are interconnected and mutually adapting. In this chapter studies were conducted to explain SSM as an ISD methodology. Additionally, it provides practitioners and researchers in system analysis and design some case studies of applications of SSM in IT-related organizational change. TM is a set of management disciplines that make companies to manage their technological fundamentals for the creation of competitive advantage. It is also percieved as a tool to accelerate research and development (R&D). Regarding multi-methodology, TM was viewed as both a problem structuring and management framework that was possible to be combined with SSM. In each phace of TM such as identification of technologies, rich pictures, root definitions, conceptual models, or the SSM itself can be used which lead to develop a common dialogue between stakeholders involved. Chapter 6 explains applications of SSM in policy making or scenario planning for the technology development and commercialization. It helps practitioners and researchers analyze complexities of R&D organizations for a better management of their dynamics.

Obviously, there has been a gap in knowledge relating to SSM and organizational change management. Chapter 3 has tried to develop new knowledge, which will show the use of SSM as an interventionist action for change optimization. In this case, culture as one of the organizational properties besides strategy, structure, technology/process, and leadership can be changed to be fitted with both external and internal contingencies. Although, the needed endeavors to change each property differs from one to another. Culture analysis is very complex, but at the same time SSM gives practitioners and researchers the chance to the cultural analysis and change.

SSM is a powerful approach for the improvement of inter-subjective understanding which is necessary to develop and progress groups effectively. It can create in depth participation to enhance reciprocal understanding in groups by determination of problems and acquisition of knowledge or skill of bringing improvements. SSM can be applied to go along with goals, give an explanation of managers' expectations and actions, and provide feedback on individuals' performance. Considering that many people and factors are involved in the process of organizational creativity, the decision in this regard is one of the real and complex issues of the real world. SSM as an approach for developing HR-based information has the potential to overcome the complexity of HR-related decision making. Chapter 8 reviews various applications of SSM in HRM such as employee participation, group creativity, HR development, HR maintenance, and knowledge worker productivity. It refers to the issue of current HR development because of the shortage of arguing the central role of SSM in it. In addition, it explains the problem situation of low knowledge worker productivity using SSM.

Chapter 7 focuses on education system using SSM as an action research process. SSM can be used for self-analysis of teaching and learning methods used by a lecturer and self-audit of the teaching. SSM for eduactional practitioners and researchers gain a deeper understanding of the processes of educational system, such that appropriate action can be taken to build an ideal system.

Making use of the existing organizational structures and resources, PM seeks to manage the project through using a set of tools and techniques, without unfavorably interfere the regular operation of the company. SSM is being developed for project managers due to the fuzzy aspects of PM. SSM can clarify relationships within projects to enable better decisions to be made. Chapter 9 focuses on utilizing SSM in sustainable development-based feasibility study and funds allocation planning.

Since SSM is a soft systems thinking for problem solving and system improvement, it has a great importance for system/business analysts and managers. This book presents an in-depth description of theories and applications of soft systems methodology in organizations. The objective of this book is to create a comprehensive coverage of all important areas of business and enterprise from the perspective of SSM. Universities and industries are interested in this book for their related learners and experts.

Chapter 1
An Introduction to Soft Systems Methodology

ABSTRACT

Soft systems methodology (SSM) is the outcome of a real-world action research program that uses the idea of systems to improve poorly defined, so-called soft problem areas. Theory and practice of SSM arouse interest and encourage discussions from various backgrounds by academics and practitioners. In order to introduce SSM for use in the real world, this chapter begins with different definitions and methodologies of systems thinking. Then, SSM defines the seven technical analysis steps, including the soft systems thinking and the necessary techniques such as rich picture, CATWOE analysis, root definition, and conceptual modeling. SSM has organizational analysis and practical applications in the industry sector that are reviewed and classified.

INTRODUCTION

We have recognized that as human understanding of reality is developed, this reality can be seen as an integrated system network. This network involves the hierarchy of systems, subsystems, and elements ranging from the universe to the components, so that we can grasp the reality as an integrated system of separate components. Although we have found out that the physical world can be defined in terms of systems, it can also be of the cognitive world. In this sense, it can be seen that the cognitive world has more effects on human behavior than the physical world. For example, in a business environment,

DOI: 10.4018/978-1-7998-4504-1.ch001

human behavior assumes a complexity level that is currently impossible to predict precisely.

Using a set of skills called systems thinking, we can expect to further identify the deep roots of the complex behavior in the world to better predict the behavior and eventually, correct its consequences (Arnold and Wade, 2015). There are various ways to rationally interfere with human affairs according to systems thinking: to grasp the complexity of real world through the ideas of systems. Systems thinking addressed the ways of thinking about the problems and solutions via the "whole system" viewpoints (Behl and Ferreira, 2014).

Mathematics presents a general language that is commonly applied to the so-called "hard" problems. The elements of the unstructured or "soft" problems may be conflicting goals, ambiguous or complex information flows, people with different attitudes and perceptions, and so on. When such factors are involved, it is difficult to assess the suitability of a mathematical language. This chapter examines the development of systems thinking and emphasizes the soft systems methodology (SSM) as one of the systems approaches. SSM was designed by Checkland (1981) and developed by Checkland and Scholes (1990) as a tool to explore the unstructured problems.

This chapter starts with the systems thinking definitions mainly obtained from the literature review. Throughout the history of systems thinking, there are many different systems thinking methodologies. It is argued that the soft systems thinking is more relevant in the completely poorly defined conditions where human beings and cultural considerations are involved. In addition, SSM is described along with its techniques.

SYSTEMS THINKING DEFINITIONS

Jay Forrester (1994) mentioned that there is no clear definition or use of systems thinking. Systems thinking is sometimes used interchangeably with system dynamics (SD). Systems thinking means much less than thinking and talking about systems, and recognizing the importance of systems. Rather, the relatively superficial general awareness of systems is considered in systems thinking. In Table 1, the systems thinking definitions are compared.

Systems thinking revolves around trying to understand how the things are related to each other. Formal thinking, which includes the most scientific thought and actually the most academic effort, mainly aims to gain understanding about something by making it separate. Focusing on the relationship reveals the way something works and how it impacts its surroundings. According

Table 1. Comparison of systems thinking definitions (Arnold and Wade, 2015)

Author	Wholes rather than parts	Dynamic behavior	System as the cause of its behavior	Interconnections/ interrelationships	Stock and flow relationships	Delays	Non-linear relationships	Feedback loops	System structure generates behaviors
Richmond (1994)	✓	✓	✓					✓	✓
Senge (1990)	✓			✓					
Rouse	✓			✓					
Sweeney and Sterman (2000)		✓	✓		✓		✓	✓	
Hopper and Stave (2007)	✓	✓	✓	✓	✓			✓	✓
Kopainsky, Alessi and Davidsen (2011)							✓	✓	
Squire, Wade, Dominick and Gelosh (2011)		✓		✓					

to such understanding, when a situation is considered as a whole, instead of concentrating on the components, there are only features that cannot be simply observed from the features of the components.

Additionally, system approaches begin with the complexity and uncertainty of whether an accepted part of the problem should be determined, and whether there is a single "right" resolution. Therefore, the systems language is not about the problem and its solution (problem solving), but rather about problem resolution and situation (situation improvement) (Reynolds and Holwell, 2010).

HARD AND SOFT PROBLEMS

The "problem" concept also turned out to be inappropriate. The concept of problem identification indicates that there may be a solution that addresses the problem. For the problem spectrum, it is rational at the "hard" part, but does not occur at the "soft" part so that problems are easily separated. It is more common to find highly interactive problem sets and it is more suitable to explore the "problem situation" rather than the problem; that is, it is perceived as a problem (Wilson, 1984).

Identifying the problem situation (modeling language) should be appropriate to the considered problem nature. As the distinction between "soft" and "hard" implies the extreme spectra of a possible problem, the modeling language can be seen with respect to the extreme points.

When choosing a method for solving a problem, it is important to distinguish between "soft" and "hard" problems. A "hard" or structured problem is a problem that only deals with the "how" questions. Such problem falls within the scope of the design engineer who tries to find economic and effective answers for the "how" question. A "soft" or unstructured problem is a problem that is described as a combination of both "how" and "what" questions. Such problem exhibits with a feeling of restlessness, but it cannot be articulated until it arises to over-simplify the situation. Obviously, the "hard" systems thinking and most operational research are related to the structured problems (Checkland, 1981; Wilson, 1984).

The systems thinking is about a new system of learning, a new learning method and coping with experience. Coping with complex situations does not often allow for the final results or answers that naturally depend on this viewpoint. Considering the engineered system of the world (hard facts) illustrated by the name of the world as an assumption is even more concerned with the search for goals when entering a complexity that cannot be identified with a system not far from an abstract intellectual system. Therefore, the

Table 2. Comparison of "soft" and "hard" traditions of systems thinking (Hoffmann, 2019)

Soft systems thinking	Hard systems thinking
Orientation to learning	Orientation to goal-seeking
Assumes the problematic nature of the world, but can be investigated using the models of system	Assumes the systems existing in the world which can be "engineered"
Assumes the intellectual constructs of the system models (epistemology)	Assumes the models of system as the world models (ontology)
Talks the "accommodation" and "issue" languages	Talks the "problems" and "solution" language
Advantages	
Available to both problem owner and professional practitioner; keeps contact with the human contents of problem situation	Allows the powerful methods to be used
Disadvantages	
Does not provide the ultimate answer	May require qualified practitioners
Accepts the never-ending nature of the inquiry	May lose contact with the features beyond the problem situation logic

Figure 1. The "hard" systems practice (Checkland, 1999 cited in Hoffmann, 2019)

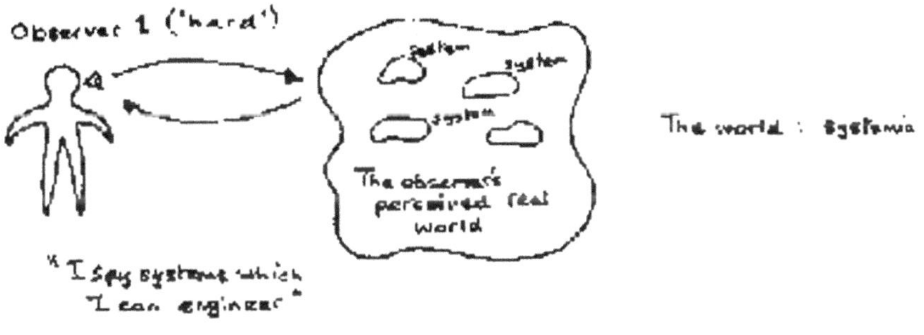

discrimination between "hard" and "soft" systems was made by different authors, and for illustration, the Hoffmann's (2019) table (Table 2) is used to identify the differences and requirements of this discrimination.

This does not lead to the assumption that the "hard" systems thinking is suitable for the definite technical problems presented in Figure 1 where the limits and proportions of everything are specified.

The "soft" systems thinking is more relevant in completely poorly defined situations where people and cultural considerations are involved. The figure (Figure 2) presented by Checkland (1999) illustrates where the 'system' is used when stating what the definition means, which is from the systemic attribution.

While performing the project, since the systems thinking is often confused in practice ("soft" and "hard") and also defines a particular system, the system picture will be affected by how an interviewee provides the information based on his priorities, point of view and world view ("weltanschauung").

Figure 2. The "soft" systems practice (Checkland, 1999 cited in Hoffmann, 2019)

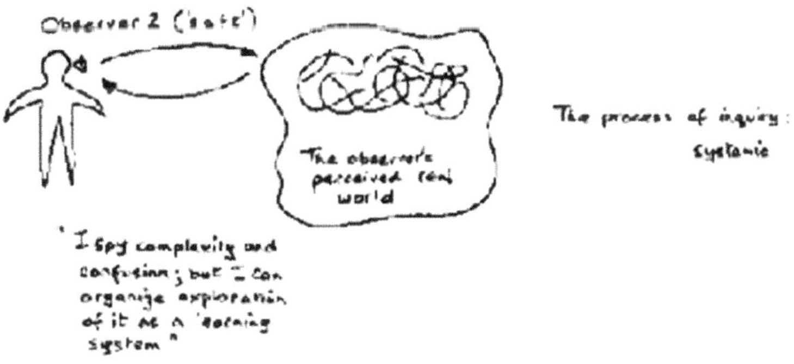

Table 3. Principles forming basis of soft systems approach (Cavaleri and Obloj, 1993)

Principles of Soft Systems Approach
Experience and perception are subjective and dependent on different interpretations.
Problems arise by the perception and conditioning of people.
It is essential to identify general problems in the complex messy situations.
No permanent solution exists except the improvement.
System is the projection of the mind rather than real things.
The improvement of system is based on the accommodation and learning and not the optimized results.

The different backgrounds of the researchers and the "preconditioning" in the environment where they come from will affect at least the approach to the system analysis.

Since the soft systems thinking postulates that people have different opinions about the problem situation considering their mental models, there may not be one correct answer to satisfy every participant. Cavaleri and Obloj (1993) indicated that the soft systems thinking can be used to well achieve the most proper solution to the complex messy problems. They also summarized the six principles underlying the approach to soft systems distinct from other approaches shown in Table 3.

SYSTEMS THINKING METHODOLOGIES

In his book "Systemic Intervention: Philosophy, Methodology and Practice", Midgley (2000) makes a distinction between three 'waves' in the systems thinking history according to the major shift in thoughts.

The three waves along with the corresponding methodology are shown in Table 4.

In 1954, there was only one type of systems thinking on the table: development of mathematically expressed general system theory. This was thought to offer the meta-level languages and theories so as to express and solve the problems in many different disciplines. In this way, it was expected that this would help enhance the science unity as the aspirations of the pioneers. However, when we look back from 1999, it is seen that the project was not successful (Checkland, 2000a).

The first wave was mainly concentrated on the quantitative techniques of mathematical modeling. The focus of second wave was shifted from

Table 4. Various types of tradition or wave of systems thinking (Reynolds and Holwell, 2010)

Waves of Systems Thinking	Selected systems approach
First Wave of Systems Thinking (Hard)	General systems theory (Bertalanfy, 1956) Classical (first order) cybernetics, 'mechanistic' cybernetics (Ashby, 1956) Operations research (Churchman et al., 1957) Systems engineering (Hall, 1962) Socio-technical systems (Trist et al., 1963) RAND-systems analysis (Optner, 1965) System dynamics (Forrester, 1971; Meadows et al., 1972)
Second Wave of Systems Thinking (Soft)	Inquiring systems design (Churchman, 1971) Second order cybernetics (Bateson, 1972) Soft systems methodology (Checkland, 1972) Strategic assumption surface testing (Mason and Mitroff, 1981) Interactive management (Ackoff, 1981) Cognitive mapping for strategic options development and analysis (Eden, 1988)
Third Wave of Systems Thinking (Critical)	Critical systems heuristics (Ulrich, 1983) System of systems methodologies (Jackson, 1990) Liberating systems theory (Flood, 1990) Interpretive systemology (Fuenmayor, 1991) Total systems intervention (Flood and Jackson, 1991) Systemic intervention (Midgley, 2000)

the quantitative modeling to the considerable knowledge of perceptions and relationships. The models were used to direct debates and arguments rather than being viewed as the representation of reality. The third wave of systems thinking encompasses the conflicts and power relations and encourages the methodological pluralism. The third wave is referred to as "critical systems thinking" (Midgley, 2000). The purpose of this wave was to develop methodologies by including power issues and expanding the way the methodologies were used, rather than replacing the methodologies of the previous waves.

In the second wave methodologies, SSM is classified as one of the widely used approaches. Systems Thinking, Systems Practice (STSP) (Checkland, 1981), though successful when exploring the natural phenomena, identifies the systems thinking aiming to prevent the reductionism of natural sciences. It reveals the first experience of attempting to implement 'systems engineering' beyond the technical field in which it was developed, the first form of SSM developed as a seven-step inquiry process by rethinking the 'systems thinking' where early experience is necessary (Checkland, 2000a). Soft Systems Methodology in Action (SSMA) (Checkland and Scholes, 1990) includes the application of the developed SSM in the public and private sectors both in the wide-ranging and limited situations. It goes beyond the "seven-step" methodology model (Checkland, 2000a).

Nevertheless, it is important to know that the third wave of systems thinking aims to provide direction on the way of improving the use of methodologies. Thus, in the third wave of systems thinking, SSM is utilized as part of the Creative Design of Method described by Midgley (2000) as developing an ever-changing set of interconnected questions, showing the intentions of intervention evolving with time, which they may be required to be resolved using different methods or part of method. Contributing to the third wave of systems thinking, he preferred the SSM use in various case studies and used SSM as part of the systemic intervention methodology (Midgley, 2000).

Great efforts have been made to analyze, develop and improve methodologies for problem situations (Flood and Carson, 1988). "Reductionist" actions explored certain methodologies. The assessment of a holistic approach to methodology is equally important, where different methodological approaches are connected or integrated to form a system that represents a wide range of possibly existing situational classes. Such approach is useful in joining methodical approaches appropriate to problem situations. Some real guidance will be provided to choose from methodologies (Flood and Carson, 1988).

SSM Paradigm

The position of SSM paradigm is more evident than that of SD. SSM adopts an interpretative point of view (Checkland, 1981; Checkland and Scholes, 1990; Wilson, 1984). To put it briefly, according to Checkland, the world of life is the dynamic flow of ideas and events, and to "manage" means to react to this flow. We take measures, assess and perceive, which are part of the flow that leads to further perception and assessment and more measures. It is concluded that SSM postulates that this flow will be differently assessed and perceived by different actors of the situation, which poses problems that the manager has to deal with. SSM here provides the system administrators with a useful weapon to deal with problem situations that arise from the problems. The outside world appears to be highly connected to make a whole. Hence, the 'system' concept seems to help deal with the perceived interconnected reality.

Need of a "Soft" Methodology

For an action research program based on the situations in the real world, Checkland (1981) developed a methodology currently referred to as the Checkland methodology or Soft Systems Methodology (SSM). The question "what methodology should be utilized?" arises when considering a number of methodologies. Flood and Carson (1988) found no general acceptance with any of the studied approaches. Alternatively, Wilson (1984) maintained that the compilation of systems concepts (methodologies) should be apt to the situations and to the special analyst personality.

PHILOSOPHY OF SSM

Checkland (1981) argues that generally systems thinking are based on two pairs of ideas: "emergence and hierarchy" and "communication and control". The pair of emergence and hierarchy implies a systematically complex general model where the complexity is described as a hierarchy of levels. A whole with hierarchical arrangement and the evolving features can essentially survive in a dynamic environment if there are communication and control processes that allow it to adjust in reaction to the environment shocks.

This brings the basic SSM philosophy closer to the functionalist sociological traditions. The position of traditional functionalist is, in essence, that the social structures can be studied by creating a kind of boundary to the system environments, isolating or separating them into systems dominated by causal relationships. The system function can be defined which is proportional to the environment and the consistent function in the system. Functionalism tries to describe the systems in a functional or teleological manner so that they could protect themselves and have a higher goal. The system maintenance or survival is its superior principle, and the system events can be defined as the function existing for the principle. Although Checkland admits that some similarities may exist, he disagrees and goes against the "functionalist" label.

Of course, some similarities exist, since they are required due to the general framework of structural functionalism, but there are different objectives for the sociologists and the solvers of system-oriented problems, which make the use of methodology different from the functional analyses. The sociologists demand the most exact, probable and testable definition of the social systems. The systems that use the methodology want to improve what is considered the problematic situation. Considering these goals, the functionalist sociologists need the richest model one can possibly obtain, including the clear and hidden functions. The system analysts require the systems thinking to be evident and consistent as much as possible to lead to explicit discussion, and thus, make their possible systems model.

The Checkland's opposition with falling the SSM in the functional-structural tradition category of sociology looks quite simple:

1) The accusations are based on the initial facts that only one conceptual model and root definition exists. Thus, there may be a variety of contradictory root definitions that reflect different weltanschauung, and the discussion then basically refers to contradiction and change (to which the functional-structural tradition of sociology does not pay proper attention).
2) Using the SSM, the real world is modeled as a system, but it is not claimed to be a system. Seeing the world in terms of system differs from stating that the world contains systems. It is completely reasonable that a researcher states, for instance, that he considers the provision of education as a system, but it greatly differs from stating that as a system. It looks scrupulous, but it is a mistake that disturbs the systems thinking and creates a lot of confusion in the systems literature. It may be useful to choose to think of the world as a system, but this widely differs from the argument that views the world as a system. This position assumes the knowledge that no one can possess.

SSM can be regarded as the 'learning system'. It is a significant change from the optimization [hard systems thinking] to the learning of concepts that people who share a human condition aim to understand. This is a learning system as a whole, and it may be possible to utilize the system models (although, in principle, it is possible to add other models). Importantly, the models do not potentially describe parts of the world. As an abstract logical machine, they can pursue a purpose defined as the stated worldviews that can create a perceptive discussion when they stand against potentially decisive actions in the real world.

Checkland maintains that SSM, in fact, is more similar to the phenomenological traditions in the social sciences and that it speaks of a formal approach to clearly identifying and comparing different kinds of typification of people for the structures and events in the real world, which are phenomenologically high. In addition, Checkland found a considerable consistency between SSM and critical theory. The methodology of Checkland seeks to reach a consensus which examines other worldviews and its success criteria is the benefit for the actors rather than the analyst validity. For this reason, the implicit nature of the SSM social reality is expressed as the dynamic result of social processes where people are constantly negotiating and building their interpretation and perception of the outside world with others as well as the addressing rules. The SSM process can be viewed as a system of learning, a process that learns the approach to the concepts characterizing an organization. The organization in this process can be considered the readiness required for the members of organization for the conceptualization and their internal and external relations in a certain manner. Such readiness is actually the existence condition of the abstraction, namely organization. Obviously, the change over time may be incrementally made or may be done in a revolutionary manner, like the change of perception and membership.

NATURE OF SSM

Checkland strongly focuses on seeing SSM as a learning system (Checkland, 1983; 1985a; 1985b; Atkinson and Checkland, 1988), summarized in Checkland and Scholes (1990), as it was born of systems engineering and practically shifted from an approach aiming to optimize the system to an approach grounded on expressing and implementing the systemic learning processes.

In addition, the meanings of seeing SSM as a learning system are twofold: to learn a particular system of human activity which is the project's center of attention, and to learn methodology. Another duality exists regarding the SSM, because in addition to improving the situation of problem, the methodology modifies the people attitudes and values in the problematic situations (Atkinson, 1986).

Also, Checkland (1985a) attributes SSM to the appreciative system concept developed by Vickers (1986). In this concept, the objective-oriented behavior model is rejected which prefers the viewpoint of maintaining the relationships. Checkland outlines that the appreciative systems are a cultural mechanism which tries to maintain the desirable relationship and eliminate the unwanted one. This is a cyclical process as follows: previous experience has created some norms or standards, mainly implicit (in addition, values at a more common level, which are the more common concepts bad and good from a human perspective). Values, norms and standards result in the readiness for only recognizing the specific characteristics of a situation. They specify the appropriate 'facts': the perceived facts are compared with the norms, and this process leads us to take regulatory measures and change the standards or norms to differently evaluate the future experiences.

Davies and Ledington (1991) argue that the SSM mainly aims to improve communication. Also, Checkland (1985b) underlines that the model development through SSM prepares the ground to widely discuss the intervention of problems, which are appropriate for the improvement of the system, but are likely to be culturally enforceable. Atkinson (1986) discusses the concept of communication when explaining the conceptual models as not being enforcing, but as appropriate for starting discussion.

The requirement of SSM to become a really participatory approach has developed through the use of methodology and is currently recognized by numerous users as an essential SSM element. Using a facilitator for managing the workshop-style participatory session contradicts previous methods where the interviews were conducted with the stakeholders and the analysts inconspicuously developed the models (Galliers et al., 1994).

The purpose of intervention is to provide the participants with the approach in the problematic situations, to have them use the approach and to keep their abilities for its future use. McLoughlin (1986) highlighted the repetitive features of SSM presented in all works of Checkland, and essentially considered SSM as a cyclical process in which the methodology organizes the problem situations rather than considering the problem as mentioned above.

Creativity of SSM

Checkland and Holwell (1998) argue that SSM can be considered a 'sense-making device' and that it is a creative and flexible methodology in essence. It was stated that the principles of SSM enable such principles to be creatively used which is related to specific methodology users, specific participants and specific situations.

SSM allows the new ideas to be proposed and the perceptions to be changed (Attwater, 1999), and makes people more open to new concepts. Also, when SSM is used to consciously organize a process, it enables the production of insight and commitment (Checkland, 2000b).

The rich picture is an innovative element in SSM, and according to Checkland (2000a), it is a better tool for the expression of relationships relative to the linear writing and can be considered as a whole to promote the holistic thinking about a situation instead of the reductionist one. Checkland also views the picture as an invaluable element that can be shown as a point for starting the explorative debate in problematic situations. In a research, the rich pictures used in the intervention of SSM raised some critical (and yet unexplained) problems (Luckett et al. 2001). Certainly, the last statement truly reflects the experiences of first author when using the SSM as both facilitator and participant for several years. We think that the construction of a conceptual model is another innovative element of SSM.

Learning and Thinking Aspects of SSM

An important feature of SSM benefits to generate creative ideas is the capability of facilitating the learning. Jackson (2000) argues that the cyclical learning process of SSM elucidates the natural management processes occurring in organizations, which makes it possible to propose alternative actions and ongoing change. SSM is viewed by Davies and Ledington (1991) as a framework used for directing the learning.

The aim of directing the learning has a special position to make SSM work in practice. By opening the thinking 'door', this methodology allows systematic understanding to take place, and thus helps to find solutions that consider the entire system, including the complex political, cultural and sociological factors that may affect the proposed solution. In this regard, Checkland and Scholes (1990) stated that SSM is perceived as the regular application of systems ideas in the methodologies to learn how to take measures for improving a problematic situation.

The ability of SSM used for facilitating the learning is improved by the flexibility emphasized by Kane and Del Mistro (2003) who considered SSM as a flexible tool for generating personal knowledge and understanding. In the SSM process, Taylor and DaCosta (1999) stated that the learning direction is altered while building the models and more questions are raised about the problem situations. According to Sinn (1998), the SSM flexibility can be demonstrated by its use as a guideline for thinking and can be included in other methodologies of systems as an exploration tool.

In order to produce creative outputs, it may be required to facilitate creative thinking in the group. According to Kane and Del Mistro (2003), SSM presents the tools of thinking to help explore and interpret a complex socio-political or human situation. For the SSM development, one of the major achievements is to articulate the natural process of systemic thinking, which is thought to give the participants the meticulousness to their mental processes and enables them to describe their work.

Fuenmayor (2000) states that SSM can provide the context to think about a lot of comments that have an effect in the problem situations. Thus, the methodology makes space for creative thought, and Fuenmayor (2000) states that the soft systems thinking of Checkland is an advanced type of instrumental thought for such sequence of ideas at a higher level.

SSM 'limitations'

Flood and Jackson (1991) set the limitations of SSM. Basically, they stated that SSM cannot be viewed as a 'problem-solving methodology' due to its interpretive support, and may upset and disturb the practitioners. The methodology of SSM is based on exploring the real world, and the SSM models are not normative as they do not describe the real world (SSM has a firm belief that it is difficult to understand the real world), and are the 'ideals' loyal to a specific worldview. SSM has limitations particularly in the modeling despite being successful when used in the complex management situations in the real world. This is because it has not provided a technological tool to assist in understanding the results and outcomes of the proposed cultural and applicable models. Thus, the analysts were not aware of the actual effects of the proposed changes. With the combination that can establish a proven useful framework, A variety of perceptions can be identified and addressed for those involved in the complex problematic situations of the real world both qualitatively and quantitatively.

DESCRIPTION OF SOFT SYSTEMS METHODOLOGY

As a seven-step analysis process, SSM can utilize the notion of a system of human activity as a tool to gain information about the situation and to take measures for improving the situation. This process is shown in Figure 3. A sequence should be chronologically obtained ranging 1-7 where it is most appropriate to describe the logical sequence, but it should not be used to follow it.

In fact, this represents an activity pattern. The analysts can begin with the activities and advances in the desired directions and can use considerable repetitions at any step. In a real-world research, the thinkers of the most effective systems will work at different details in numerous steps at the same time (Checkland, 1981). It should be the case, as this methodology can be viewed as a system, and the changes at any step affect the other steps. The methodology involves two types of activities. Steps 1, 2, 5, 6 and 7 are the activities in the real world involving those faced with the problematic

Figure 3. Seven stages of analysis with SSM (Checkland, 1981)

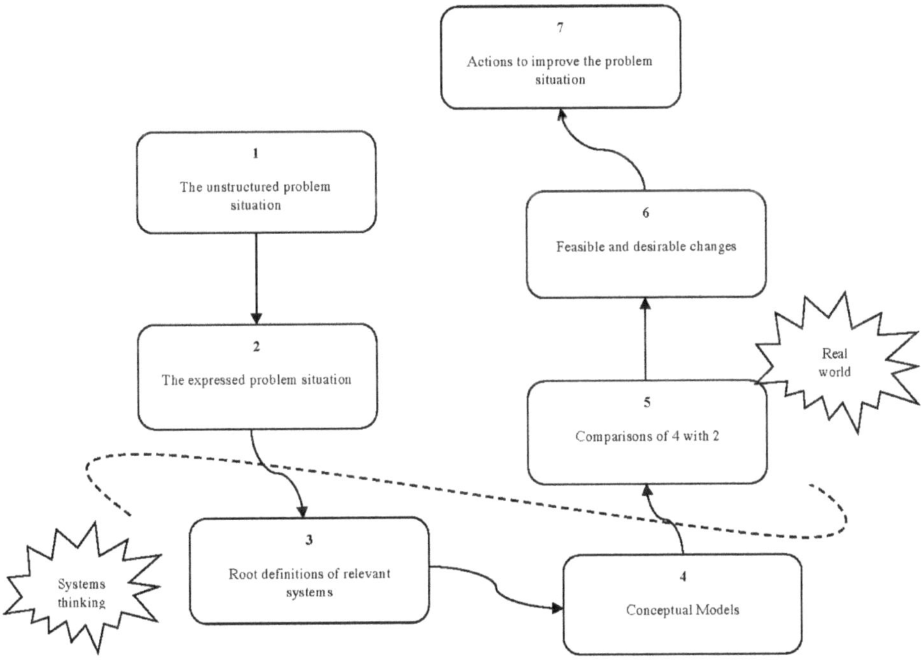

situations. Steps 3 and 4 involve the activities of systems thinking and can include those in the problematic situations subject to the research conditions.

Generally, the languages of previous steps are the usual languages of the problematic situations whatsoever; steps 3 and 4 are the systems language, because the complexity of real world is resolved in such steps and identified by translating into the systems language at higher levels (Checkland, 1981).

During the evolution, the SSM process model appeared and the major steps of the process are presented in Table 5.

Table 5. Key steps of SSM

Step	Objective
1 and 2	Try to create the picture of situation as rich as possible.
3	Tries to express the nature of selected systems.
4	Provides a conceptual model for the specified systems.
5	Compares conceptual models with real situations for holding discussion with stakeholders.
6	Describes likely changes that are favorable and plausible.
7	Includes taking measures according to step 6.

Basic Elements

To serve the purposes of this study, the main results of the action research for the use of methodology are summarized by Checkland (1981):

Initially, the SSM approach tries to identify the real-world situations that some stakeholders consider problematic. The situation is described in order to diagnose the current situation and identify the participants and the nature of the problem. The graphical representation of the considered problem is the most frequent strategy. The graphical presentation is referred to as "rich picture" and involves the stakeholders as a whole and their relationships for providing an overall view of the problems. The SSM approach generates the conceptual model in steps 3 and 4. This indicates that there is a proper interpretation of the modeled system, referred to as the root definition, and the model generation has to be directed to include these six components: Customers, Actors, Transformation process, Weltanschauung (worldview), Owner, and Environmental constraints (CATWOE).

The conceptual model is simply developed from the root definition to perform the transformation mentioned in step 3. The model consists of a series of activities that are perceived as the process of transformation and linked through the logical dependences. Thus, the conceptual models should be verified by comparing with formal systems. The formal systems should have six elements: Purpose/mission; Performance measure; Decision-making process; Subsystem; Interaction with environment; Physical and human resources; Continuity. Also, to evaluate the effectiveness, efficiency and efficacy of the system, the model should incorporate the control and monitoring activities.

After developing the model and moving to the situations of real-world problems, the SSM approach compares the model with the real world in step 5. In the comparing step, the stakeholder engagement is crucial to discuss about any changes that may be likely made for improving the situation. According to the comparison, it is possible to determine the proposed changes in step 6 which is required for introducing the actual structures and processes of the system for the implementation in step 7. The successful implementation requires the proposed changes to be favorable and plausible.

Rich Picture

Examining the rich picture diagrams developed as part of previous SSM research shows that using a few numbers of symbol and cartoon-type characterization (mainly funny) for the situation of the problem has been increased. No single strict rule can be applied for drawing rich picture diagrams, as they are unique, reflecting the special meaning attributed by their creators to the characters drawn. This is in part the reason why the instances of rich picture diagram are usually removed from the description published for the SSM use; it may be possible that the readers can be misled by their inclusion and think that the shown rich picture is 'true', and may be encouraged for imitating the pictures in the works they do. The question of 'what should the rich picture diagram show and how should it be presented?' has possibly a single answer that 'what looks important to you in handling the situations and help you use SSM'.

The freedom can be frightening for the methodology beginners. Although many examples are provided for using the diagram during the methodology application, there are a limited number of examples for traditional rich pictures which may be used for the reference of students - perhaps the loss of new thinking about SSM. The frequently asked question of the students that 'what picture is rich?' has the stock answer of 'it is a meaningful picture and can be made as rich as possible'. However, their views make sense, as there is a limited number of good instances of the rich pictures for the novices. What is needed by the rich picture is not a lot, but the schematic representation of types of analytic collection and interpretation of information continues at the phase of the appreciation of the problem. The tendency to standardize the form of diagram can be inevitably displayed in the later generations of SSM users asking for direction from the previous research and several instances of rich picture diagrams published.

The humor introduced into the rich picture diagrams in some cases and presenting topics in a new method that encourages open and illuminating discussions may be useful. The deliberate humorous representation of situations has drawn attention to a non-threatening controversial issue, and in this way, has led to a useful discussion that may not have happened otherwise. However, it is a waste of time to try to add humor to the rich picture diagrams for their own sake and often fail to do so.

There is also a clear tendency towards the not explained symbolic representations of some features of the situations of problem. It is particularly dangerous, as using the symbols and pictorial metaphors can cause uncertainty, especially when the diagram has no key. Obviously, the symbols have cultural dependence, and it is of interest to predict what problems may occur when the problem-solving team members have no common iconography or cultural background.

Possibly, there are a large number of suggestions for using some sets of standard symbols to resolve the problem of uncertainty. It is interesting to use the standard symbols when not considering oneself 'artist' or when preparing the diagram in a quick manner by means of the packages of graphical software is sought. Still, there are some drawbacks. A tendency may exist to attempt to articulate the delicate and complicated features of the situations in a very simplistic way (for example, slightly different views may be seen in the same manner as wild opposite views), and can also cause the diagrams to be highly stylized and non-original.

In addition, one reason for defending the standard symbols is based on the misinterpretation of SSM as a series of methods the external analysts use for the problematic situations to facilitate the reading of a rich picture diagram. In this sense, the analyst's need to convey his appreciation to problem owners may offer some arguments to use standard symbol languages. However, SSM is principally a method of learning through participatory actions, where stakeholders, customers and problem owners can be among the problem-solving group that work in case of problems. A standard set of symbols is less needed when it is used in this way; every application of SSM produces its symbols, and for those involved in the investigation case in question, it is meaningful.

For instance, in a company's organizational project management study, Figure 4 shows the problems of current situation in the rich picture.

Primary Task/Issue-Based Root Definitions

There is a useful difference between the "primary task" and the "issue-based" root definitions which should be kept in mind during the systems selection for the modeling.

CATWOE Elements

For the systems described in the root definitions, since the conceptual models are controlled according to the features of the formalized model in every system of human activity, the well-formed root definitions should have features that are related to the formalized model of system and allow for the control process.

In a satisfactory root definition, there should clearly exist five elements; otherwise, there should be a good rationale behind the elimination of each of the elements. These elements are as follows: The "transformation" process (T) is the basis for a system's root definition; the tool for converting the defined

Figure 4. Rich picture of an R&D organization

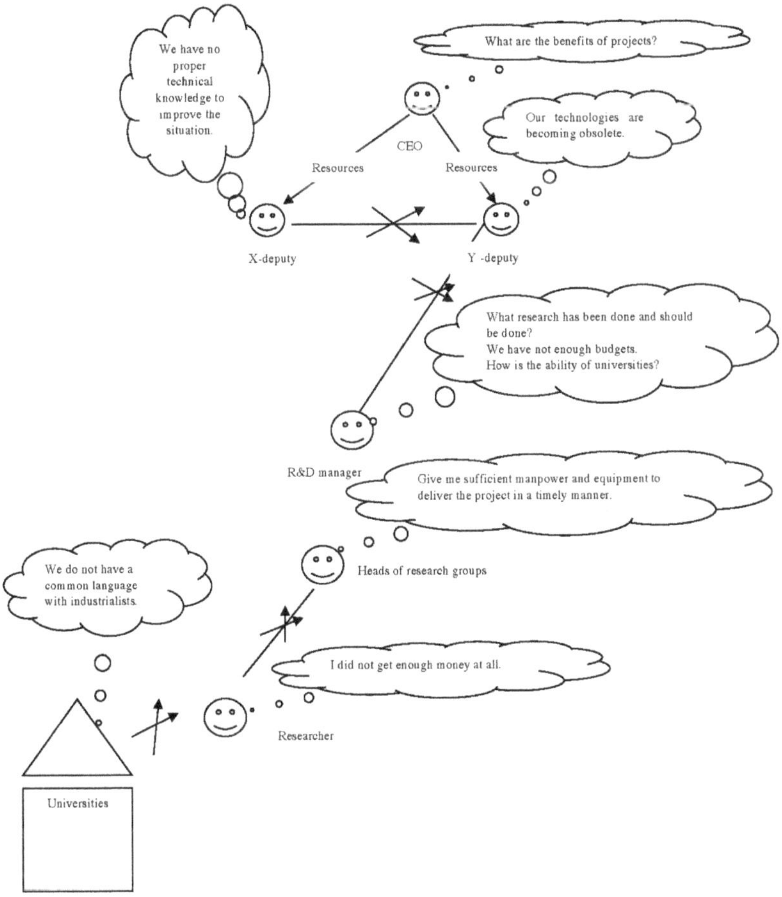

input to the defined output. This transformation then includes the direct object for the verb of the principal activity needed for the system definition.

The system will have "ownership" (O); some institutions are primarily concerned about the system and about the absolute power to end its existence. The system owner can talk about it. In the system, there are "actors" (A), who are the agents that perform or make the main activities of the system, particularly the main transformation, to be performed.

There are system 'customers' (C) in the presence or absence of the system, the beneficiary or victim influenced by the activity of the system. Customers are the indirect object for the main verb used for describing the systems. The "environmental constraints" (E) upon the systems, the aspects of the environment of the systems or broader systems which should be taken as given.

The sixth element added to these five elements and naturally having a rarely explicit root definition but to be included is "Weltanschauung" (W), the image, framework or viewpoint which causes a certain root definition to be significant. For the mnemonic, the six elements are referred to as CATWOE.

For instance, the aircraft landing system of Checkland includes the following elements of CATWOE:

- (Transformation) the aircraft is approaching from a distance and altitude. The purpose is to land safely on the runway.
- The pilot is the actor (people and cars), and the air traffic controllers, ground personnel, crew, passengers and those living beneath the runway are the customers.
- The owner consists of airline agents (managers) and owners
- Environment: airways, geographical features and traffic conditions, control of take-off and landing areas at airports, other competing airports.
- Weltanschauung may include the increase of passenger traffic, competition between international airports, dwelling environment of airport, high security concerns, and hi-tech operations.

Table 6. Root definition - CATWOE

C: Customer – direct beneficiary or victim of system outcomes. Who has been the system worked for? Who are the victims or beneficiaries of the transformation system?
A: Actor – those engaged in the transformation, that is, those performing any activity in the system. Who performs the activities related to the transformation process? If there are more than one set of people, this usually means two or more transformations are confused.
T: Transformation – the basis for the system of human activities where input is converted to output and presented to customers. In such transformation process, each actor plays a role. Which single process converts the inputs to the outputs? Defining a single (uncomplicated) transformation is necessary. When there is more than one verb, this usually means two or more transformations are confused.
W: Weltanschauung (worldview) – viewpoint that identifies the developed root definitions. Which view makes the transformation valuable? The identification of this element informs the true system intentions from this point of view.
O: Owner – a person or group responsible for the system proposed. They are able to change and even stop the system and overlap with other actors of system. Who is able to tell if the system will be operated? (Who is authorized to contribute to the change?)
E: Environmental constraints – systems of human activities operating under certain restrictions placed by the environment outside as ethical, physical or legal constraint. Which restrictions (constraints) can stop the system operation? What do you need to know about the operating conditions of the system?

Conceptual Models

Conceptual models are system models of human activities and, therefore, they consist of the activities observed by separating every verb suggested by the root definitions. The verb list should be organized in a consistent manner and there should be a model for each of the root definitions. The system can be modeled as an independent entity by combining 7+2 activities arranged based on the logical dependences. This number is due to the fact that the human brain is only capable of coping with such number of concepts at the same time. Every activity in the model can be the source of root definitions that will be extended at the next level of resolution. The conceptual model aims at achieving what was specified in the root definitions. Therefore, conceptual models are the models of root definition and not those of other things (Checkland and Scholes, 1990; Wilson, 1984). Although conceptual model is organized according to logic, there may be some inconsistency. The performance measurement method is applied to resolve this issue. It only requires combining the needed activities to convert inputs to outputs, and ensuring that every activity needed by other elements of CATWOE is considered. The activities should be connected to figure out if there is any dependence on other activities.

Conceptual model can provide the context for the modeling of information systems and suggestions for the improvement of the system of human activities. Hence, it is necessary for the both users and developers of the information systems to grasp the conceptual model, even though it is very complex. It should be noted that the models represent the real-world complexitics. While complexities can complicate the modeling, it may be useful to use the more complex models, as they can contribute to the discussion if the models are compared with the reality. The disadvantage of model complexity is that increasing the complexity may lead to models being considered as a real entity and not those related to the debates about the real-world improvement (Checkland and Scholes, 1990).

One of the methods for the analysis of the activities is to derive a conceptual model, which should be done for the clear definition what an actor should do to ensure transformation. Try to exclude any activity performed by others except those actors cited in the root definition (and restrict the actors to a group of individuals if possible; it is very complex to monitor the activities when there are two or more groups). Moreover, it is necessary to organize the thinking; record any activity required to accomplish the system goals. In

Figure 5. Conceptual model-the 1st level for the system

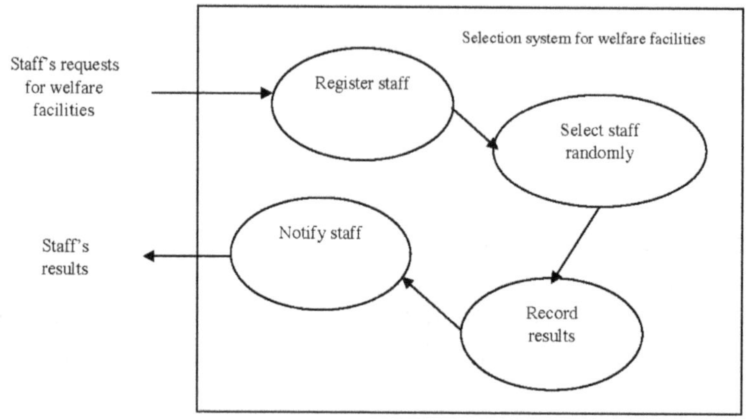

Figure 6. Conceptual model- the 2nd level for the system

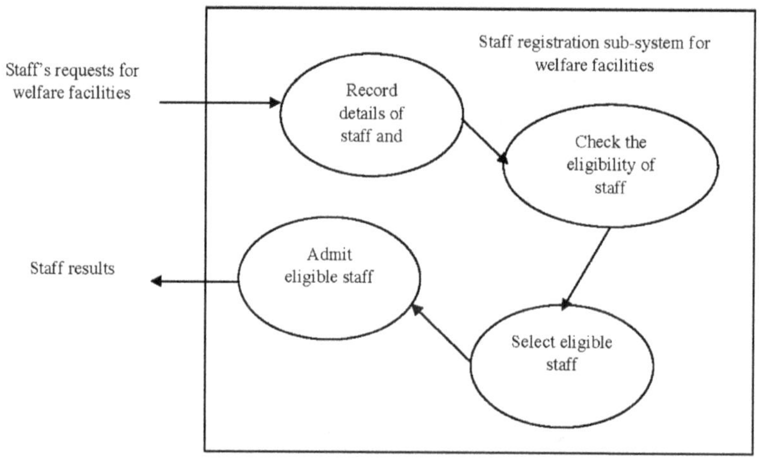

order to efficiently perform the system activities, including the activities for monitoring the system and results of feedback is of great importance. The questions that should be asked include: What does determine how successful is the system? how the success can be measured? what should be done by the actors for measuring the success?

Figures 5 and 6 show, for instance, the conceptual model of a system at two levels for the personnel demanding the welfare facilities.

The feedback loop is one of the important elements of conceptual model. Every conceptual model usually contains two feedback loops:

- Internal feedback loop, enables actors from the modeled system perspective of human activities to regulate the way they do their own work (in this case, there is a loop between the "Determine" and "Assess" activities).
- External feedback loop, between input and output of the model of activity system. It allows managers to evaluate and control the entire activity system (The loop is shown in the model by dotted lines).

Discuss Feasible and Desirable Changes

Models are only generated as a tool to serve a purpose. They provide the basis for the consistent and reasoned debate about the way of improving the situations that are thought to pose problem. This debate is arranged to compare the models according to various world views with the perception of the problematic situations in the real world. It aims at finding the adjustments among diverse interests in the problematic situations instead of improving the models. Such adjustments should include the improvement in the initial situation of problem (Checkland and Scholes, 1990). The problematic situation should be compared with the conceptual model along with the engagement in the problematic situations. The aim is to initiate the discussion about the feasible and favorable changes that can be made in the problematic situations to make the improvement happen.

There are four comparison methods that are often used: model overlay, historical reconstruction, formal questioning, and informal discussion (Checkland and Scholes, 1990; Wilson, 1984). These methods generally assist in assuring of the intentionality, rationality and justifiability of the comparisons. It can be used to take any of the comparison approaches or to make comparison by means of different techniques. The informal discussion method deals with the general discussion of the model nature. This type of discussion tends to raise strategic issues, since the questions raised related to current activities naturally revolve around why they are primarily carried out. Thus, it is relevant to see this comparison method as a basic approach and to investigate which feature of the conceptual models specifically differs with the real world and why it is different (Wilson, 1984).

Formal questioning is the most widely used comparison method. In this method, the models provide the basis for the real-world inquiry. Giving answer to questions provokes the debate to be appropriate for each particular situation. The debate can be done at a time in a place by a group of people or through the interview with one person while distributing the conversations in a time period. The core in this kind of inquiry with the specified models is to fill a matrix (Checkland and Scholes, 1990). This can be viewed as the question-asking process. Is there any activity? How is the activity currently being conducted? Who takes the responsibility for performing the activities? How well is done the activity? Is there any relationship? What form do they take? (Wilson, 1984). The discussion of change is provided using the system models in which, the questions are systematically answered after being written. It is useful to enlighten the perceived situation of the problem. The historical comparison technique requires the reconstruction of a series of past events based on the conceptual models. The sequence of events is established on paper or in a mental manner and its goal is to consider a scenario that would be compared to the activities in the real world. This method is among those that should be treated with caution. It may entail the risks if it criticizes the previous performance and not a method to learn from, and, in this way, it may cause dissatisfaction with those involved (Checkland and Scholes, 1990; Wilson, 1984).

As the last comparison method, the model overlay requires that the conceptual models to be structured to clearly reflect what is actually present. With the actual overlay of the model on the conceptual model for what is available in the reality, the transparent papers can be used to immediately reveal any conflict. The technique of directly overlaying a model on the another one clearly reveals the inconsistency in the both. Such inconsistency could directly stimulate the discussion of probable variations (Wilson, 1984). The comparison is made aiming to provoke discussion on the changes that can be potentially made in case of perceived situations of the problem. The discussion should form a set of suggestions for the changes. But it is not very realistic to expect any change would be accepted. The change should be desirable in a systematical manner and should be approved by the specific culture of the problematic situations. The change is called 'culturally feasible' if approved in this way (Wilson, 1984). This comparison allows discussing the possible variations of the three types in which the combinations can be suitable in a given situation. The possible changes may require the modification in structures, procedures or attitude. It is relatively easy to understand and implement the both procedural and structural variations. Such variations, if made, can have unexpected impacts in the organization, but the implementation design can be done at least as a certain task. The third type of attitude change is more difficult to achieve. In principle, it is likely to deliberately attempt to assume the change of attitude in the organization. In practice, however, exactly achieving the desired results is difficult. The debate about the desired and applicable changes should be accompanied by those in the problematic situations who are concerned with the perceived problems and want to act in this respect.

Laws of Procedure

There are two laws of procedure that should be considered: (a) "conceptualization law", which specifies not to define and model a system serving another until there exists a definition and model for the served system; and (b) "model-building law", stating that the model of the systems of human activities should be composed of organized verb groups defining the activities that the actors can directly perform.

Measures of Performance-Three E's

It is a mechanism for the control and monitoring that measures the performance of the systems designed according to the established objectives and criteria defined in the root definition. The transformation concept can simply be judged as being successful or unsuccessful by transforming the inputs to the outputs according to the three parameters as follows.

E1: Efficacy – Do the tools or systems operate? Does the needed transformation take place?
E2: Efficiency – measuring the efficiency of the valuable system through the comparison of the obtained outputs with the needed resources as inputs.
E3: Effectiveness – Can the system attain its objectives in the long run according to the goals specified in the Z of the root definition?

It should be quite easy to generate the conceptual models given that the arrangements are made in the CATWOE and root definitions.

APPLICATIONS

SSM has been utilized in various research to serve different purposes including the design of systems, historical analyses, and concept explanation (Checkland, 1981, Wilson, 1984). Currently, SSM has practically applied to the organizational analysis (Atkinson, 1989; Patching, 1990) and industries (Youssef and Jackson, 1989; Checkland and Scholes, 1990). Checkland and

Scholes (1990) used the methodology for the National Health Service in the UK at the community level. However, Smallwood (1990) applied the soft systems approach to the issues related to transferring the information of patients and the communication models among the nurses.

SSM is a general system analysis method developed from the concepts of systems engineering. Neves et al. (2004) organized the issue of evaluating the initiatives for promoting the efficiency of energy using the SSM. Ngai et al. (2012) employed SSM for identifying the management support opportunities to rationally use the energy in the textile industry. Also, the application of SSM in the planning problems for the urban energy was studied by Coelho et al. (2010). Using the literature review, inspections, and SSM, some sparse features were developed which were originally regarded as potential considerations and measures to evaluate the incentives and plans for the promotion of innovation in electricity technology, and it was required to be organized (Antunes et al., 2016).

Mingers and Taylor (1992) presented the findings obtained from a study that explored how much SSM is actually used. Based on the findings, SSM was further identified as a questioning process or a system of learning which can change the perceptions and knowledge of people without making any immediate, problem-driven change. It is also seen as a methodology for solving the problems, which can cause the interventions and changes to be made in the world.

The SSM uses reveal a wide range of applications presented in Table 7.

The authors described the advantages and disadvantages of SSM use, as shown in Table 8.

CONCLUSION

Seeking for developing a good theory and practical use in sciences and engineering has enabled many people in society to assess the value of seeing the facts in terms of the systems. Much advances have focused on the application in the field of hard systems. The hard systems have accurate mathematical representations and can be predicted. However, the advances in the soft systems have been hampered without accurate mathematical representations. Nevertheless, the soft systems problems are the most widely used, most crucial and most complex ones in the business. The soft systems methodology (SSM) offers an efficient catalyst for eliciting the actions required to reach the considered transformation.

Table 7. Application range of SSM (Mingers and Taylor, 1992)

Organizational design	· Role restructuring · Designing new organization · Creating new organization culture
Performance evaluation	· Performance indicators · Quality assurance · Monitor an organization
Information systems	· Defining information requirements · Formulating IS strategy · Knowledge capturing · Initial scoping/players · Evaluating impact of computerization
Education	· Determining training needs · Course design · Causes of truancy · Analysis of language teaching
General problem solving	· Understand complex situation · Clarify initial problem
Diverse subjects	· Project management · Business strategy · Risk management methodology · Case for industrial tribunal · Personal life decision

Table 8. Major advantages and disadvantages in use of SSM (Mingers and Taylor, 1992)

Advantages	
Intervention management	· Providing structure/framework for study (highest score) · Giving overall/broad/holistic view · Proper means of communication · Improving study speed
Process of thinking	· Clarification of thought/organized thinking (highest score) · Promoting shared thinking, gathering people · Releasing from current situation · Enforcing explicitness · Promoting creativity and provoking thinking
System of problem content	· Organizing situations that are complex/messy/have much information, and generating understanding of perception and perspective of other people (highest score) · Focusing attention on problems and organizational culture · Not making assumption about situation
Disadvantages	
Methodology	· Time consuming · Requiring extensive experience
Organizational situation	· Organization has its own standard methodology · Getting right people involved · Language/jargon of SSM putting off some managers · SSM needs interactive methods and engagement of users
Problem content	· Power and policy problems

In order to introduce SSM for use in a real world, this chapter first began with different definitions and methodologies of systems thinking. First of all, it was stated that the systems thinking is related to enhancing the understanding through viewing how things are related. Second, systems approach begins with the complex and uncertain situations in which an accepted part of a problem is the establishment and acceptance of the problem nature, and no single "right" solution can exist. Then, it described SSM as soft systems thinking and the required techniques including rich picture, CATWOE analysis, root definition, and conceptual modeling to do its seven stages of analysis. The SSM process can be considered a system of learning, the process that has identified the meaning and characterizes an institution. It enables suggesting new thoughts and the change in perception, and if the process has a conscious structure through using the SSM, it has the ability to gain insight and commitment. However, there are limitations, especially in the modeling step, since it does not provide a technological tool to assist in understanding the results and outcomes of the proposed cultural and applicable models. SSM has organizational analysis and practical applications in the industry reviewed and classified.

REFERENCES

Antunes, C. H., Dias, L., Dantas, G., Mathias, J., & Zamboni, L. (2016). An application of Soft Systems Methodology in the evaluation of policies and incentive actions to promote technological innovations in the electricity sector. *Energy Procedia*, *106*, 258–278. doi:10.1016/j.egypro.2016.12.121

Arnold, R. D., & Wade, J. P. (2015). A definition of systems thinking: A Systems Approach. *Procedia Computer Science*, *44*, 669–678. doi:10.1016/j.procs.2015.03.050

Atkinson, C. (1989). The use of Soft Systems Methodology in designing a job. In R. L. Flood, M. C. Jackson, & P. Keys (Eds.), *Systems Prospects: The next ten years of systems research*. New York: Plenum Press. doi:10.1007/978-1-4613-0845-4_30

Atkinson, C. J. (1986). Towards a plurality of soft systems methodology. *Journal of Applied Systems Analysis*, *13*(6), 19–31.

Atkinson, C. J., & Checkland, P. B. (1988). Extending the metaphor 'system'. *Human Relations*, *4*(10), 709–724. doi:10.1177/001872678804101001

Attwater, R. (1999). Pragmatist philosophy and soft systems in an upland Thai catchment. *Systems Research and Behavioral Science*, *16*(4), 299–309. doi:10.1002/(SICI)1099-1743(199907/08)16:4<299::AID-SRES252>3.0.CO;2-N

Behl, D. V., & Ferreira, S. (2014). Systems thinking: An analysis of key factors and relationships. *Procedia Computer Science*, *36*, 104–109. doi:10.1016/j.procs.2014.09.045

Cavaleri, S., & Obloj, K. (1993). *Management systems, A global perspective*. Wadsworth Publishing Company.

Checkland, P. (1999). *Systems thinking, systems practice*. John Wiley & Sons, Ltd.

Checkland, P., & Holwell, S. (1998). *Information, systems and information systems*. Chichester, UK: John Wiley & Sons.

Checkland, P. B. (1981). *Systems thinking, systems practice*. Chichester: John Wiley & Sons.

Checkland, P. B. (1983). O.R. and the systems movement: Mappings and conflicts. *Journal of the Operational Research Society*, *34*(8), 661-675.

Checkland, P. B. (1985a). From optimizing to learning: A development of systems thinking for the 1990s. *The Journal of the Operational Research Society*, *36*(9), 757–767. doi:10.1057/jors.1985.141

Checkland, P. B. (1985b). Achieving 'desirable and feasible' change: An application of Soft Systems Methodology. *The Journal of the Operational Research Society*, *36*(9), 821–831.

Checkland, P. B. (2000a). Soft systems methodology: A thirty year retrospective. *Systems Research and Behavioral Science*, *17*(S1), S11–S58. doi:10.1002/1099-1743(200011)17:1+<::AID-SRES374>3.0.CO;2-O

Checkland, P. B. (2000b). The emergent properties of SSM in use: A symposium by reflective practitioners. *Systemic Practice and Action Research*, *13*(6), 799–823. doi:10.1023/A:1026431613200

Checkland, P. B., & Scholes, J. (1990). *Soft systems methodology in action*. Chichester: John Wiley & Sons.

Coelho, D., Antunes, C. H., & Martins, A. G. (2010). Using SSM for structuring decision support in urban energy planning. *Technological and Economic Development of Economy*, *16*(4), 641–653. doi:10.3846/tede.2010.39

Davies, L. J., & Ledington, P. W. J. (1991). *Information in action: Soft systems methodology*. London: Macmillan. doi:10.1007/978-1-349-12698-9

Flood, R., & Jackson, M. (1991). *Creative problem solving: Total system intervention*. Chichester: Wiley.

Flood, R.L., & Carson, E.R. (1988). *Dealing with complexity*. New York: Plenum Press.

Forrester, J. W. (1994). System Dynamics, Systems Thinking, and Soft OR. *System Dynamics Review*, *10*(2), 1–14. doi:10.1002dr.4260100211

Fuenmayor, R. (2000). A brief crack of light? *Systemic Practice and Action Research*, *13*(6), 757–772. doi:10.1023/A:1026427512292

Galliers, R. D., Pattison, E. M., & Reponen, T. (1994). Strategic information systems planning workshops: Lessons from three cases. *International Journal of Information Management*, *14*(1), 51–66. doi:10.1016/0268-4012(94)90095-7

Hoffmann, B. (n.d.). *Soft Systems Methodology: a tool for handling and developing complex systems*. Retrieved May 13, 2019, from: http://s24770edd2ba60829.jimcontent.com/download/version/0/module/6678402684/name/SSM%20B%20Hoffmann%20Vortrag%20Innsbruck.pdf

Jackson, M. C. (2000). Checkland, Peter Bernard (1930--). *Systems Research and Behavioral Science*, *17*(S1), S3–S10. doi:10.1002/1099-1743(200011)17:1+<::AID-SRES380>3.0.CO;2-Z

Kane, L., & Del Mistro, R. (2003). Changes in transport planning policy: Changes in transport planning methodology? *Transportation*, *30*(2), 113–131. doi:10.1023/A:1022562125856

Luckett, S., Ngubane, S., & Memela, B. (2001). Designing a management system for a rural community development organization using a systemic action research process. *Systemic Practice and Action Research*, *14*(4), 517–542. doi:10.1023/A:1011360204102

McLoughlin, P. (1986). Soft Systems Methodology - Its role in management services or finding a nut to fit the spanner. *Management Services*, *30*(8), 16–20.

Midgley, G. (2000). *Systemic intervention: Philosophy, methodology and practice*. New York: Kluwer Academic / Plenum Publishers. doi:10.1007/978-1-4615-4201-8

Mingers, J., & Taylor, S. (1992). The use of Soft Systems Methodology in practice. *The Journal of the Operational Research Society*, *4*(4), 321–332. doi:10.1057/jors.1992.47

Neves, L. P., Martins, A. G., Antunes, C. H., & Dias, L. (2004). Using SSM to rethink the analysis of energy efficiency initiatives. *The Journal of the Operational Research Society*, *55*(9), 968–975. doi:10.1057/palgrave.jors.2601763

Ngai, E., Chester, K., Ching, K. V., Chan, L., Lee, M., Choi, Y. S., & Chai, P. (2012). Development of the conceptual model of energy and utility management in textile processing: A soft systems approach. *International Journal of Production Economics*, *135*(2), 607–617. doi:10.1016/j.ijpe.2011.05.016

Patching, D. (1990). *Practical soft systems analysis*. London: Pitman.

Reynolds, M., & Holwell, S. (2010). Introducing systems approaches. In M. Reynolds & S. Holwell (Eds.), *Systems Approaches to Managing Change: A Practical Guide* (pp. 1–23). London: Springer. doi:10.1007/978-1-84882-809-4_1

Sinn, J. S. (1998). A comparison of interactive planning and soft systems methodology: Enhancing the complementarist position. *Systemic Practice and Action Research*, *11*(4), 435–453. doi:10.1023/A:1023098025076

Smallwood, S. (1990). *The District nurse and patient assessment* (Master thesis). Department of Information Science, The City University, London.

Taylor, M. J., & DaCosta, J. L. (1999). Soft issues in IS projects: Lessons from an SME case study. *Systems Research and Behavioral Science*, *16*(3), 263–272. doi:10.1002/(SICI)1099-1743(199905/06)16:3<263::AID-SRES257>3.0.CO;2-W

Vickers, G. (1986). *Value systems and social process*. London: Tavistock.

Wilson, B. (1984). *Systems: concepts, methodologies, and applications*. Chichester: John Wiley & Sons.

Youssef, F. A., & Jackson, M. C. (1989). Using systems ideas to explore the problems of the textile public sector in Egypt. In R. L. Flood, M. C. Jackson, & P. Keys (Eds.), *Systems prospects: The next ten years of systems research*. New York: Plenum Press.

Chapter 2
Soft Systems Methodology in IT-Related Organizational Change

ABSTRACT

Any organization needs information technologies (IT) to attain efficient process and make effective decisions. The main discussion of this study is focused on IT as a reason of change in an organization. Besides providing a definition for information systems (IS), this chapter aims at explaining soft systems methodology (SSM) as an IS development methodology. Considering seven elements of philosophy, model, techniques and tools, scope, output, practice, and product, it clarified the SSM position in other methodologies. In this concern, it revealed the main concern of using SSM in the development of information systems (i.e., meeting the real needs of the organization through generating meaningful information based on the available data) as represented in five case studies of SSM in IT-related organizational change.

INTRODUCTION

Organizations are increasingly applying strategies to enhance their capabilities to survive in the global competitive market. In this context, they improve the decision making process through advancing their agility level, performing efficiently and effectively to meet the successive fluctuations of the market. Achieving this important goal, many modern organizations, either mid or

DOI: 10.4018/978-1-7998-4504-1.ch002

large sized, made attempts to invest and adopt new management information systems components (Jalal Karim, 2011).

Information systems development is a long and complex process involving various elements from the beginning to the end. System development projects require widely financial, technical and human resources, and are implemented using various techniques and tools. Therefore, using specific and appropriate methodology will guarantee planning and successfully managing such projects. A development methodology is mainly used to have control over the development process. The selection of this methodology is largely led by the IS professionals (Gasson, 1995).

Interests in the use of soft systems methodology (SSM) in working with computer-based information systems (IS) have been growing in recent years. Playing an important role in the development of information systems, SSM also differs from other technical approaches. Due to its nature, it is widely used in 'information management', 'information strategy' and 'business analyses'. It focuses on 'social', 'cultural' and 'political' factors (Memon, 2011).

This chapter is focused on information technologies/ information systems (IT/IS) as one of the causes for the organizational change. Such change requires a large amount of work prior to design since it must be self-motivated. Besides, institutionalization and incorporation of a system to its organizational context is hard to apply; otherwise, the system will continue working when the designer/consultant leaves the scene. It is also difficult to put the goals in use and determine the criteria for achieving success. This study provides a definition for IS and focuses on system development methodologies and clarifies the position of SSM in other methodologies regarding a framework described by Avison and Fitzgerald (2006), which includes seven elements.

In the end, five relevant case studies are reviewed. The first one is the work by Lockett et al. (2006). They used SSM to develop an implementation process for the installation of the applications of customer relationship management (CRM) in small to medium-sized enterprises (SMEs) in the UK mail order sector. The next one is the study by Williams (2000) who provided an analysis of the flow of communication and the use of information technology in ABC & Co through SSM. Md Saad et al. (2012) worked on four case studies conducted within Malaysian Public Institution of Higher Education (PIHE) context to discuss about the application of SSM as a basis for formulating knowledge management system (KMS) strategy. The fourth case study was conducted by Bhattacharjya et al. (2006) to investigate what effect SSM has on conducting a strategic information systems planning (SISP) process in a non-profit organization. Finally, Al-Zhrani (2010) studied the application of SSM to the issues and obstacles the Saudi government organizations were faced with in an attempt to manage ICT to their advantage.

INFORMATION SYSTEM

Information systems development (ISD) can result in generating many terms including 'information and communication technology' (ICT), 'information systems applications' (ISA), IT or IS (Small, 2007). Various Information Technologies (IT) such as computers, software, databases, communication systems, the Internet, mobile devices and many others are involved in IS. These technologies are used to perform specific tasks, interact with and inform various actors in different organizational or social contexts (Boell, 2015).

The technical and computational aspects of IT are not primarily involved in the IS field. IS target finding the ways to appropriate and instantiate technology to enable the realization of IS that provide various actors – such as individuals, groups or organizations – with the fulfillment of their information needs and requirements on specific goals and practices (Boell, 2015).

Computer specialists generally assume it apparent that the central role of IS in decision making is undeniable. Leavitt (1965) classified the organizations as a diamond; in this classification, Task, Technology, People, and Structure

Table 1. An overview of definitions for IS (Boell, 2015)

View	Definition
Technological View	The system makes use of computer hardware and software, manual procedures, analyzing models, planning, control and decision making and a database. The emphasis is on incorporated information technology in organizations.
Social View	An information system is, in fact, a social system, which is embedded in information technology. The influence of information technology is rapidly increasing. But this does not mean that the overall information system cannot be a social system; in fact, an information system can be effectively designed with significant amounts of embedded technology only if it is treated as a social system.
Socio-Technical View	Besides investigating the technological and social systems separately or in combination, The IS field examines the phenomenon emerged from the interaction of two systems
Process View	An information system is a work system intended to regard the processing information through capturing, transmitting, storing, retrieving, manipulating, and displaying information.

are interrelated and mutually adjusting, indicating the complex nature of social systems. Any change in technology causes adjustment in other components to modulate the innovation impact. Coordinating planning and improving management control, IS are often intended as coupling devices. In many instances, the new IS are considered to be a direct threat to the people or units in organizations who have control over information, and thereby get influence and autonomy. Therefore, they have their own backlash accordingly (Keen, 1981).

The application of the IS cannot be wholly determined in technical terms as they are part of social systems (Memon, 2011). ISD may be regarded as technical change. A technical solution can be proposed, evaluated, and implemented only for a single well-defined problem. However, where ISD involves broader social and organizational change, a societal change will occur. ISD is developed from a new social system and supported by computer-based technology (Gasson, 1995).

INFORMATION DEVELOPMENT METHODOLOGIES

According to Maddison et al. (1984), methodology can be defined as a collection of philosophies, phases, procedures, rules, techniques, tools, documentation, management and training recommended for developers of information systems.

Considering this definition, we suggest that the components of a methodology find answers to (Avison and Fitzgerald, 2006):

- What tasks are to be carried out at each stage;
- What outputs are expected to be produced;
- When, and under what circumstances, methodologies are to be carried out;
- What constraints are to be applied;
- Who the concerned people are;
- What strategies should be applied to manage and control the project;
- What supporting tools may be utilized.

In addition, a methodology is required to determine the training needs of the users of the methodology. The critical issue of philosophy should be also specifically addressed in a methodology. An information systems development methodology goes therefore beyond a series of techniques and software tools.

Avison and Fitzgerald (2006) used these ideas and beliefs to define a methodology:

A system development methodology is a recommended means that applies a set of rationales and an underlying philosophy by which it is enabled to support, justify, and make coherent such a recommendation for a particular context in order to achieve the development, or part of the development, of IS. The identification of phases, procedures, tasks, rules, techniques, guidelines, documentation and tools is also included in the recommended means. Recommendations on the management and organization of the approach as well as the identification and training of the participants might also be included.

However, the possibility of a post-methodology era was another topic of discussion by Avison and Fitzgerald (2003), which was started in the late 1990s and is characterized by a serious revaluation by researchers and practitioners on the concepts and usefulness of the earlier methodologies. They concluded that some organizations continue to adopt different (perhaps newer) methodologies and approaches, while others have given up methodologies altogether.

The statement about 'development or part development' included in the definition indicates that some methodologies are more comprehensive than others and, as mentioned above, it is not always clear what 'rationales and underlying philosophy' are applying but they always exist and are the key to understanding a particular methodology. The statement of 'a particular context' in the definition demonstrates that methodologies apparently are not universal in their applicability, in spite of some methodology authors' assumption. Together the philosophy and the context make clear the assumptions made by the authors of the methodology and hence, there is no clear cut reference to 'assumptions' in the definition. In practice, many methodologies, especially the commercial ones, are a bundle of products that may include: manuals, education and training (such as videos), consultancy support, tools and tool sets, pro forma documents, model-building templates, and so on.

Jayaratna (1994) asserts that methodologies contain models and reflect, based on a set of philosophical paradigms, particular perspectives of 'reality'. A methodology should help you find the answers to the questions of 'what', 'how', and most importantly 'why' on the adopted steps in that particular order.

Distinguishing between the two terms, Checkland (1981) says that a methodology consists of a set of principles of method and has to be reduced to a method uniquely suited to a particular situation. According to Checkland (1985), ISD must be treated as a form of enquiry in the context of the general model of organized enquiry, consisting of three components: an intellectual framework, a methodology, and an application area. This suggests a hierarchical system of elements to enquiry.

The firs element is intellectual framework made up of the ideas used to make sense of the world. This is described as the philosophy that guides and imposes constraints to the enquiry. It consists of two ontology-based and epistemological assumptions. The ontology-based assumptions are the beliefs about the essential nature of the physical and social world and the way it operates. Epistemological assumptions refer to the theory of the method or grounds of knowledge. The second element is the methodology by which the intellectual framework of ideas is operationalized into a set of prescriptions or guidelines for investigation that requires, or recognizes as valid and particular methods and techniques. The third element is the application area; that is, some part of the real world that is considered to be problematic and worthy of investigation. The intellectual framework is the element that is often ignored in methodologies or not explicitly articulated.

Categories of Rationale

Three main categories of rationale are a better end product, a better development process, and a standardized process through which analysts are expected to adopt a particular methodology (Avison and Fitzgerald, 2006).

A Better End Product

People are trying to use a methodology to improve the end product of the development process. In other words, they require better IS. This may be confounded with the quality of the development process, which is discussed in the following. The quality of IS, which is produced as a result of using a particular methodology, cannot be easily assessed. The following items represent the attempt to address some components of quality of an information system (Avison and Fitzgerald, 2006):

- Acceptability: it indicates the system satisfactory and fulfillment of information needs of the people who use it. It includes business users and managers and their requirements.
- Availability: it shows the accessibility of the system when and where required.

- Cohesiveness: it refers to the interaction between components (subsystems), through which IS and the associated manual and business systems are integrated.
- Compatibility: it demonstrates the adjustment of the system and other systems as well as other parts of the organization.
- Documentation: it examines the presence of good documentation contributing to communications between operators, users, developers, and managers.
- Ease of learning: it examines whether the learning curve is short and intuitive for new users.
- Economy: it shows the effectiveness of system in terms of costs and whether it is within resources and constraints.
- Effectiveness: it demonstrates the performance and operations of the system in the best possible manner in order to meet its overall business or organizational objectives.
- Efficiency: it refers to the application of resources by the system to get the best advantage.
- Fast development rate: it determines whether the time needed to develop the project is quick, relative to its size and complexity.
- Flexibility: it specifies whether the system can be modifies easily and whether components can be easily added or deleted.
- Functionality: it demonstrates providing the requirements by the system.
- Implement ability: it shows the possibility of changing the system from the old to a new form in technical, social, economic, and organizational senses.
- Low coupling: it determines whether the interaction between subsystems is poor that they can be modified without affecting the rest of the system.
- Maintainability: it specifies the required effort by the system to keep running satisfactorily and continuing to meet changing requirements over its lifetime.
- Portability: it specifies whether the information system can run on other equipment or in other sites.
- Reliability: it refers to the possibility of minimization of the error rate as well as the consistency and correctness of outputs.
- Robustness: it determines whether the system is fail-safe and fault-tolerant.
- Security: it shows the robustness of the system against misuse.

- Simplicity: it refers to the possibility of minimization of ambiguities and complexities.
- Testability: it determines the possibility of testing the system to minimize operational failure and user dissatisfaction.
- Timeliness: it specifies whether the information system operates successfully under normal, peak, and every condition, giving information when required.
- Visibility: it determines whether it is possible for users to find out why certain actions took place.

These criteria cannot be maximized. Indeed, some actually work against each other. Ideally, the most appropriate ISD methodology can be chosen and then tuned. In this context, choosing criteria that are of great importance in the problem situation can be more emphasized. Methodologies, however, rarely regard such tuning or even any consideration of tuning.

A Better Development Process

Controlling the development process and identifying the outputs (or deliverables) at each stage is considered to be important requirements, resulting in improved management and project control. Using a methodology can enhance productivity; that is, the same results can be achieved through either using specific resources or using fewer resources to build systems faster. It is sometimes also argued the level of required skills for the analysts can be reduced by using a methodology, resulting in reduced cost and hence, improved development process.

For some, quality standards that are popular in manufacturing and industrial processes can improve the problems of developing IS. The quality of processes, rather than that of the end product, is guaranteed by using these standards, and this sometimes leads to emphasis on conformity to the standard irrespective of any effect on the quality of the system.

The traditional manufacturing process and the process of developing software products are mainly different. For example, the product of software is the result of a one-off replication of a design. There are schemes that identify these difficulties and attempt to interpret the standards in methods that are applicable to software development. Despite limited impacts, either in terms of coverage or improved quality, such standards contribute to raise the issues and level of debate concerning quality in the development of IS.

A Standardized Process

A common approach throughout an organization determines the needs associated with this category. This means that high system integration can cause decreased rollout and deployment costs, and thereby staff can easily change from project to project without any requirement for retaining, and a base of common experience and knowledge can be achieved. In short, all the normal benefits of standardization can be realized, including the particular benefit of easier maintenance of systems.

THE BASIS TO COMPARE METHODOLOGIES

The comparison of methodologies becomes easier through a framework including seven elements described by Avison and Fitzgerald (2006), which is not fully comprehensive. However, it is a very difficult task.

Philosophy

Due to underscoring the other aspects of a methodology, the question of philosophy is an important aspect of a methodology. Methodology determines the choice of the areas covered by it, the systems, data, or people orientation, the bias or otherwise toward a purely IT solution, and other aspects. Though explicit in some methodologies, the philosophy is implicit in most methodologies. In fact, a methodology is composed of philosophy that is defined as set of principles. The four factors of paradigm, objectives, domains, and applications, as a guide to philosophy, are discussed.

a) Paradigm

There are two paradigms of relevance. The first is the science paradigm; it characterizes most of the hard scientific developments of the latest times. The second is the systems paradigm, which is characterized by a holistic approach.

b) Objectives

The stated objective or objectives can be regarded as one fairly obvious clue to the methodology philosophy. In some methodologies, the objective is to

Table 2. Comparison of the science paradigm and system paradigm

Science Paradigm	System Paradigm
The science paradigm concerns hard thinking.	The system paradigm concerns soft thinking.
It has a long and successful history.	The history is much shorter and less successful.
It focuses on complexity and copes with it through reductionism, breaking things down into smaller and smaller parts for examination and explanation.	Human activity systems include emergent properties (i.e. the whole is greater than the sum of the parts.). These systems perform differently as a whole or as a part of a system than when broken down to their individual components.
Realism: objectively given, immutable objects and structures are the components of the universe.	Nominalism: reality is not given invariable 'out there', but it is socially constructed. It is the product of human mind.
Positivism: The available causal relationships can be investigated using scientific methods.	Interpretivism: There is no single truth can be proven by such investigation. Different views and interpretations can be potentially used and the way to progress is to accept the differences and seek to gain insight by a deep understanding of such complexity rather than to discover one correct view.

develop a computerized information system while others take a wider view and lead their attention to achieving solutions or improvements regardless of the implications. Such improvements might entail manual, procedural, managerial, organizational, educational, or political change. This is a paramount difference since it determines the boundaries of the area of concern. Regarding the logic of the business, the problem with focusing on aspects to be computerized is that this is an artificial boundary. The question why the solution to a specific problem should reside only in the area that can be automated is unanswered. The problem requires more likely to be examined in a broader context. A thorough analysis and redesign of the whole problem area are needed.

Obviously a methodology with main concerns on itself solely by providing an IT solution and the methodology that does not concern it is quite different. The answer to the question: 'could the use of this methodology cause to the implementation of an absolutely organizational or non-IT solution? can contribute to the selection and understanding a methodology. It is interesting to note that the answer of many most widely used commercial methodologies to this question would be "no".

c) Domain

The third factor on philosophy is the domain of situations addressed by methodologies. It is often found that the systems and problems are interrelated and the solution to a number of interrelated problems differs from the sum of the solutions to the individual problems in isolation, leading to a number of methodologies with a different development philosophy. Solving individual problems, the following steps are necessary: analyzing the organization as a whole, devising an overall IS strategy, sorting out the strategic requirements of the business, and in this way ensuring that the IS are designed to support these fundamental requirements.

d) Target

The last aspect examined through philosophy is the applicability of the methodology. Some methodologies are specifically targeted at specific types of problem, environment, or type or size of organization, while others have a general purpose.

Model

The second element of the framework is concerned with an analysis of the methodology model. The model is the basis of the methodology's worldview; it abstracts or represents the important factors of the information system or the organization.

The working levels of the model are: first, as a means of communication; second, as a way of capturing the essence of a problem or a design, and hence, it can be translated or mapped to another form (e.g. implementation) without loss of detail; and, third, as a representation providing insight into the problem or area of concern.

There are 4 distinct types of models: 1) verbal, 2) analytic or mathematical, 3) iconic, pictorial, or schematic, and 4) simulation. The third type of models almost exclusively form the models concerned in the field of IS methodologies because of the perceived importance of using the models as a means of communication, particularly between users and analysts. Models of ISD have a further important aspect that is ensuring that the required information to be able to develop a working system is captured at the appropriate stage.

Techniques and Tools

The identification of the techniques and tools used in a methodology is considered as a key element of the framework.

Scope

The next element in the framework is the scope of a methodology. Scope indicates the stages of the life cycle of ISD covered by the methodology. Further, an analysis of details of addressing each stage is useful. Since there are methodologies that do not follow a life cycle, it may be not possible to use the stages of the life cycle as a basis for the examination of scope. These methodologies may adopt a more iterative, evolutionary, or spiral model. Nevertheless, the usefulness of an examination of the scope of a methodology in relation to the life cycle is undeniable.

Outputs

The next element in the framework is concerned with the outputs from the methodology. It is important to know what methodology is producing based on the output at each stage and particularly the nature of the final output. This can cover an analysis specification to a working implementation of a system and all its related procedures.

Practice

The next element of the framework is the practice. It is measured in accordance with the following items: 1) what the methodology background is, in terms of commercial or academic; 2) what the user base is (including numbers and types of users); 3) who the participants in the methodology are (e.g. does it need professional analysts to be undertaken), and what skill levels are required. An assessment of difficulties and problems encountered, as well as perceptions of success and failure should be included in the practice. This is possible by considering the experiences of prior users of the methodology. Depending on who is consulted, it will inevitably be subjective, but it can be a revealing exercise. The degree to which the methodology can be, and is, altered or interpreted by the users according to the requirements of the particular situation should be considered in the process of examining the process. It is of great importance to assess any differences appeared between the practice and the theory of the methodology.

Product

The last element of the framework is the product of the methodology. The product refers to what purchasers actually get for their money, including software, written documentation, and agreed number of training hours, a telephone help service, consultancy, and so on.

SSM

SSM is a part of systems paradigm. It is considered to be the planning, organization, and the strategy type. In other words, it is in pursuit of representing the general planning, organization, and the strategy of information and systems in the organization as the domain addressed by the methodology. It is mainly focused on the understanding of wider issues and the context of the problem situation. The term problem situation in SSM refers to an ill-defined problem. It is to identify the underlying issues contributing to the understanding of the problem situation, including the purpose of the organization. In the following stages of the methodology, feasible and desirable changes are assessed and actions required to improve the situation are recommend. The results can be the development of IS. SSM targets to be applicable in human activity situations where very complex problem situations exist.

The models in SSM are process-oriented and data flow diagrams are not used. In SSM, the rich picture as a model of the problem situation is in part, a model of processes, structures, and their relationships. There is no mention on tools in SSM. In the analysis of scope, strategy is applied to indicate whether the methodology addresses any aspect of an organization-wide context. It also deals with overall IS strategy, purpose, and planning, rather than just that of the particular system or area of concern. SSM deals with the wider context. The next stage is feasibility; that is, the economic, social, and technical evaluation of the concerned system. SSM focuses on changes that are feasible and desirable. The analysis stage including user requirements analysis is incorporated in SSM. However, SSM does not cover the logical design stages. Other stages, including programming, testing, implementation, and maintenance, are not considered in SSM.

Identified problems within the system, root definitions, and desired changes are the outputs of SSM. SSM has academic background, at least in part. Nevertheless, this does not mean that it is not a commercial methodology. It has a broader range of involved stakeholders, in particular, from the business

Figure 1. The concepts of serving system and served system (Checkland and Holwell, 1998)

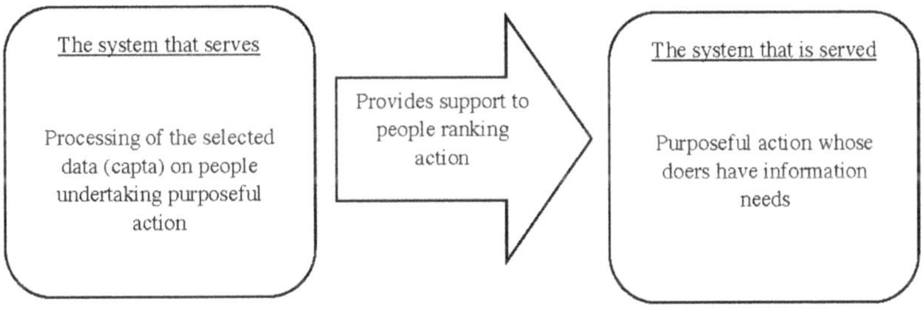

side as well as the professional system developers. A set of papers and a book can be the products of SSM.

SSM AND IS

In order to meet such challenges and issues in real world for "messy" and "ill-structured" situations, where especially the social and cultural factors are concerned, SSM is the appropriate and best fitting choice. Using SSM in the development of information system, the main concern is to meet the organization's real needs by generating meaningful information based on available data. The successful IS are created, not designed, for any organizational real needs based on purposeful "human activity systems", which depends on the concepts of "serving system" and "served system" (Memon, 2011).

Usually computer-based IS are considered to be "serving" systems, whereas purposeful human action is taken as the served system; it is being served by information system in the organization. Therefore, designing an information system that satisfies the needs of the organization and fully understands the purposeful human action through human activity system concept is considered to be necessary. This will lead to the selection of proper data and information based on human activity systems in organization to develop and create the relevant system.

Checkland and Holwell (1998) introduced a new term "capta" for data, and hence declared a clear distinction between data and information. Capta means choosing the relevant and appropriate data based on some "criteria" to process by converting into meaningful information. "IT-based" IS are capta processing systems that serve people who take actions, and SSM that is used to design the system is used in sense of human activity systems concerning the organizational development (Memon, 2011).

Purposeful Human Activity

In a real-world situation, people who are trying to take purposeful actions in the face of ambiguity, uncertainty, disagreement and conflict to constitute a whole as a new kind of system that is known as human activity system. Such purposeful actions are meaningful to them for achieving their objectives in a systematic way of activities linked with each other. The idea of modeling purposeful human activity systems was formed. The purposeful activities of organization, which are meaningful to the people, are modeled in the conceptual models with the people in the organization, through comparing such activities with the current action. The political arena receives such debate in real-world organization to pursue different conflicting interests and their accommodation, leading to the development of meaningful human activity system models more specific to the organization (Memon, 2011).

Processes for Organizational Meaning (POM) Model

According to Memon (2011), the overall model of "organizational meanings" of "social process" is the processes for organizational meaning (POM) model. In this model, people take "purposeful action" in support of IS. The IS, which are supposed as capta processing systems, have an important and vital role to meet the organizational meanings and serve people in their purposeful activity. The whole process consists of seven elements. The 1st and 2nd elements are concerned with the people who are in groups or individual and perceive, through their various taken-as-given assumptions, the data-rich world selectively. In a discourse which will consist of inter-subjective creation of meanings, this perception can be exchanged, shared, challenged, and argued over, which will result in capta processing and generating information, as mentioned in elements 3rd and 4th. Element 5, where conflicts and battles take place and are settled as part of politics, should be encouraged to enable assemblies of related meanings, intentions, and accommodations between conflicting interests. This is one of the complicated social processes, which ultimately leads to the persuasion of purposeful action as mentioned in element 6. The last and most important element (7th) of this POM model is the organized information system that is the basic building block to support organization and people to achieve their objectives through supporting human activity systems and finding accommodations. This information system that is developed and designed

Figure 2. Processes for Organizational Meaning (POM) Model (Checkland and Holwell, 1998)

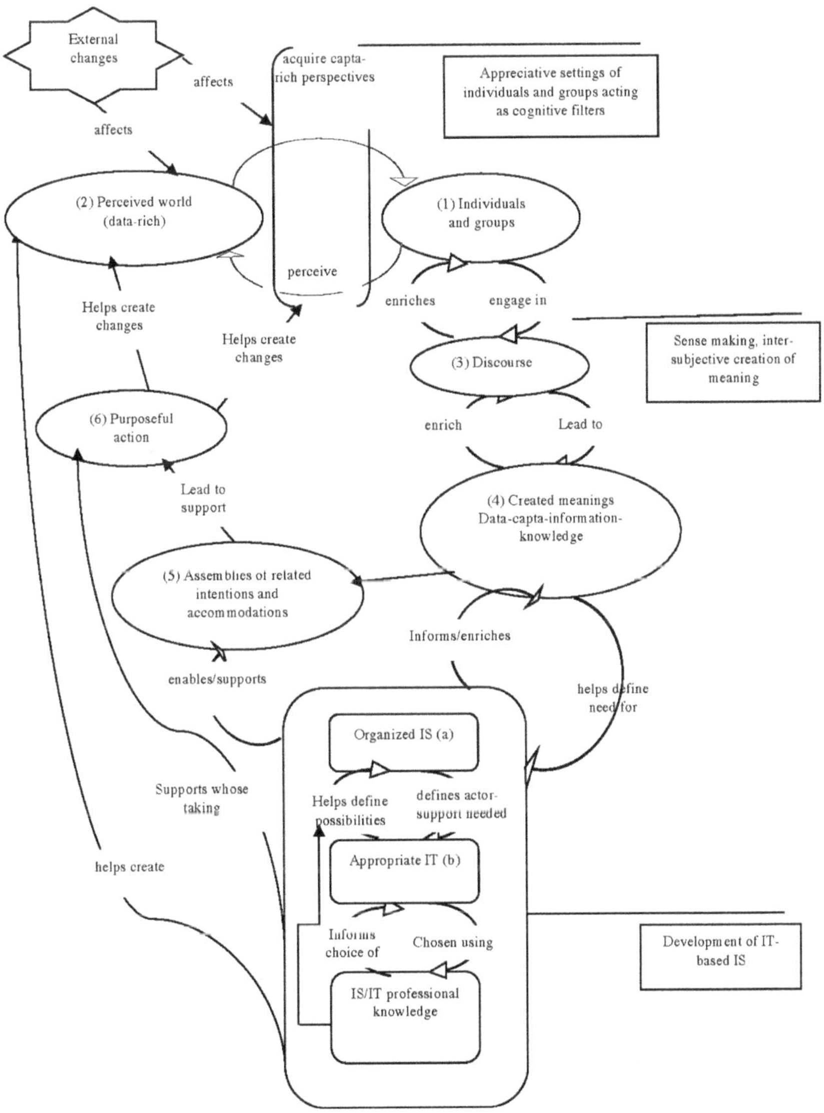

for each requirement of the real world for capta processing is on the basis of proper use of the information and communication technologies. These technologies support the IS infrastructure with the latest trends of the computer and IT since the designed information system is a kind of social system through which people in organization can interact to take purposeful action, and it is not only a part of software but a social practice. Specialized professional knowledge is needed to design, develop, maintain, control or change the system or technology.

SSM IN IT-RELATED ORGANIATIONAL CHANGE

Lockett et al. (2006) used SSM to develop an implementation process for the installation of CRM applications in SMEs in the UK mail order sector. This project that is an action research was undertaken by a Knowledge Transfer Program associate (the Associate) working in an independent software vendor (ISV) with the support of University academics. The Associate was first to express the problem-situation as rich picture diagrams. The rich picture diagrams were presented to the management team of the ISV to specify issues and opportunities in the problem-situation form the perspectives of employee and customer. The Associate presented and communicated the current problem-situation of the ISV, their main stakeholders and the issues around not only the implementation of their CRM application, but also issues regarding communication within the company itself by using the rich pictures. The Associate made sure participants were aware that this was only a representation the employees and customers' perspective of problem-situation, not that of the organization.

Following the SSM workshop and based on this primary task, the root definition was developed as a system to manage the implementation process for the ISV's products and services with a new customer. The aim was providing a sustainable business model. The associated CATWOE for the root definition was:

- Customer=Client
- Actor=Implementation team
- Transformation =Need for ISV product/service
- Worldview=ISV product/service benefits customer
- Owner=ISV (Operations Director)
- Environment=Multi-channel business solutions.

Using the root definition, a conceptual model of purposeful activity was developed and performance measures were determined (efficacy, efficiency and effectiveness).

Williams (2000) provided an analysis of the flow of communication and the use of information technology in ABC & Co, a wholesale book and goods seller by using SSM in a flexible and individualistic manner. The flow of communication in ABC & Co. between the company's internal and external entities were illustrated by the rich picture. The responses by staff and service providers demonstrate the areas of concern such as threat from electronic commerce, scarcity of warehouse space, flow of communication between retail and wholesale, lack of stock experienced by retail and wholesale department, expansion of the operations to interstate, and competitors' strategies. Based on the root definition, ABC & Co. is a privately owned, a commercial system with a limited liability, which imports Christian books, church goods and religious material from suppliers of foreign countries (in line with government regulations) and sells and deals out these goods to churches, schools, and individual customers in Western Australia through its retail outlet ABC Christian shop. The conceptual model indicates the main functions of ABC & Co. which include planning, importing, selling, administration, and evaluation.

The discussion in the study by Md Saad et al. (2012) was about the application of SSM as a basis for formulating KMS strategy in four case studies performed within Malaysian PIHE context. The holistic view of formulating KMS strategy by combining both technical and non-technical issues including business processes and human activities within an organization is presented by this approach. They demonstrate the likenesses and dissimilarities to discover the conventional patterns of activities in a conceptual model for implementing KMS initiatives. Six activities of this conceptual model are revealed:

- Gain awareness and appreciation of KMS initiatives by top management. It is crucial for creating more formal and attentive efforts to implement KMS initiatives at the university level.
- Identify and assign KMS champions to lead the KMS initiatives. It is important to be considered as the university's top management that can strongly provide the opportunity to the selection and assignment of KMS champions.
- Establish a strategy for the KMS initiatives. It is considered to be so crucial that would serve as a platform to effectively conduct the overall implementation of KMS initiatives.

- Identify the necessary IT support for the KMS initiatives. It is concerned with the efforts of making decisions and preparation of the necessary IT solutions to support the desired KMS initiatives' objectives. It consists of IT infrastructure and platform, knowledge repository, system application development, network performance and reliability.
- Prepare support programs for the KMS initiatives. It is considered to be another prime stage to address in the process of implementing KMS initiatives. It is comprised of motivation and commitment of KMS champions, and motivation and commitment of participating departments.
- Management activity dealing with monitoring and controlling the implementation of the KMS initiatives. It is also considered a main activity in SSM. In fact, it has become indispensable to monitor and control with the issues that prevent effective KMS initiatives.

Bhattacharjya et al. (2006) investigated the adaptation and usage of SSM to carry-out a SISP process in a non-profit organization. According to systems thinking, SISP is a flexible methodology can be adapted to a distinct organizational situation. It is able of considering the internal and external social and political contexts of an organization. Rich pictures were found to have a more appeal for participants to represent the problem situation since they use various symbols rather than just text and arrows in these diagrams. CATWOE was explained as BATROE with C (Customers) in the original mnemonic that was replaced by B (Beneficiaries), as it was considered culturally more suitable for a Non-profit organization (NPO), and W (Weltanschauung) that was replaced by R (Reasons for desires to make the transformation). In initial working documents, the term/technique 'system definition' was used instead of 'root definition' because participants were found to communicate better to the former. Prior to the meetings, informal discussions with management team members declared that CATWOE/BATROEs would be easier to read and present at the meetings than root definitions. The CATWOE/BATROEs were used as useful discussion tools. A comparison between the proposed activities in conceptual models is showed in the comparison tables. These tables and the current activities as well appealed to participants better than the graphical conceptual models themselves.

Al-Zhrani (2010) studied the application of SSM to the issues and obstacles the Saudi government organizations were faced with in an attempt to manage ICT to their advantage. Four actors play role in drawing a rich picture: organization management bodies, IT managers, staff, and customers. All these actors are considered as problem owners. External parties were also identified. In addition, other concerns include ambiguous goals and strategies, tight budgets, lack of training, conflicts in the internal and external communications.

In this work, root definitions of the systems were selected by considering the above expressed problem situation. These definitions are:

- Network steering committee -based system,
- Monitoring- and maintenance-based system,
- Communication-based system, and
- Education- and training-based system.

The following overall root definition of the computer-based information system can be presented:

A computer-based information system is owned by a government to fulfill its required function of managing an information network system. This system provides access nationally and internationally to coordinate an electronic information system in order to provide an electronic communication channel for staff through which they can use the information easily to improve the Saudi organization's products based on the standards set by the government.

The following CATWOE elements present the elements of the root definition of the computer-based information system for Saudi organizations:

- **C:** Saudi organization staff, IT managers, chief information officer (CIO), information network users and public users.
- **A:** CIO, IT professionals.
- **T:** The need to change the traditional way and making transformation in distracted or disorganized information to coordinated information units with interconnected services.
- **W:** The need for a sufficient electronic computer system offering and exchanging information and experience in order to meet users' needs, and thereby to improve the public organization.
- **O:** Public organizations and funders in Saudi Arabia.
- **E:** Government regulation, Saudi culture, organization policy, human resources, funds, technical and political issues, network infrastructure, hackers, viruses and technological change.

The conceptual models made in the fourth stage is to build based on the root definitions.

CONCLUSION

The IT was used as a main tool for achieving corporate competitive power over the past few years. The main evidence for the organizational change is the integration of IT/IS in the business process and activities. In this sense, the IT create complex framework in order to structure the working operations and support the people attempts in doing their tasks.

In this chapter, soft systems methodology (SSM) was presented as a methodology for information systems development (ISD) through conducting studies. In this context, the features of ISD methodologies were considered according to a 7-element framework (including philosophy, model, techniques and tools, scope, output, practice, product) described by Avison and Fitzgerald (2006). Each feature was described in SSM arising the main concern of using SSM in the development of information system, i.e. meeting real needs of the organization by generating meaningful information based on the available data. The data were presented in five case studies of application of SSM in IT-related organizational change. This change causes a wider transformation in an organization because any change in technology causes adjustment in other components including task, people, and structure which are interrelated and mutually adjusting modulate the impact of the IT-related organizational change.

REFERENCES

Al-Zhrani, S. (2010). Development of a soft system model to identify information and communications technology issues and obstacles in government organizations in Saudi Arabia. *Journal of Theoretical and Applied Information Technology*, 93-104.

Avison, D., & Fitzgerald, G. (2003). Where Now for Development Methodologies? *Communications of the ACM*, *46*(1), 79–82. doi:10.1145/602421.602423

Avison, D. E., & Fitzgerald, G. (2006). *Information Systems Development: Methodologies, Techniques and Tools*. New York: McGraw-Hill Education.

Bhattacharjya, J., & Venable, J. (2006). *Adapting Soft Systems Methodology for Strategic Information Systems Planning: An Action Research Study in a Non-Profit Organisation in Australia*. The 17th Australasian Conference on Information Systems, Adelaide, Australia.

Boell, S. K. (2015). What is an Information System? *The 48th Hawaii International Conference on System Sciences*, 4959- 4968. 10.1109/HICSS.2015.587

Checkland, P. (1981). *Systems thinking, systems practice*. Chichester: John Wiley & Sons.

Checkland, P. (1985). From optimizing to learning: A development of systems thinking for the 1990s. *The Journal of the Operational Research Society*, *35*(9), 757–767. doi:10.1057/jors.1985.141

Checkland, P. B., & Holwell, S. (1998). *Information, Systems and Information Systems*. Chichester: Wiley.

Gasson, S. (1995). The role of methodologies in IT-related organizational change. In *Proceedings of BCS Specialist Group on IS Methodologies, The 3rd Annual Conference, The Application of Methodologies in Industrial and Business Change*. North East Wales Institute.

Jalal Karim, A. (2011). The significance of management information systems for enhancing strategic and tactical planning. *Journal of Information Systems and Technology Management*, *8*(2), 459–470. doi:10.4301/S1807-17752011000200011

Jayaratna, N. (1994). *Understanding and Evaluating Methodologies, A Systemic Framework*. New York: McGraw Hill.

Keen, P. G. W. (1981). Information systems and organizational change. *Communications of the ACM*, *24*(1), 24–33. doi:10.1145/358527.358543

Leavitt, H. J. (1965). Applying organizational change in industry, structural, technological and humanistic approaches. In J. G. March (Ed.), *Handbook of organizations*. Chicago: Rand McNally.

Lockett, N. J., Brown, D. H., & Sissons, A. (2006). Soft Systems Methodology in IT Project Management: Implementing CRM in SMEs. *Proceedings of the Twelfth Americas Conference on Information Systems.*

Maddison, R., Baker, G., Bhabuta, L., Fitzgerald, G., Hindle, K., Song, J., ... Wood, J. (1984). Feature Analysis of Five Information Systems Methodologies. In T. Bemelmans (Ed.), *Beyond Productivity: Information Systems Development For Organizational Effectiveness*. Elsevier Science Publishers, North Holland.

Md Saad, N. H., Kasimin, H., Alias, R. A., & Abdul Rahman, A. (2012). *Soft Systems Methodology: A Conceptual Model of Knowledge Management System Initiatives. International Joint Conference on Knowledge Discovery, Knowledge Engineering, and Knowledge Management*, 377-392.

Memon, S. (2011). *Designing examinations information system management: a comparative case study application of soft systems methodology*. Lap Lambert Academic Publishing.

Small, A. (2007). *The exploration and adaptation of soft systems methodology using learning theories to enable more effective development of information systems applications* (Master thesis). School of Computing, Engineering and Information Sciences, Northumbria University.

Williams, M. C. (2000). A soft systems case study investigating the information system of a small business and demonstrating the usefulness of rich pictures. *The 1st International Conference on System Thinking in Management*.

Chapter 3
The Use of Soft Systems Methodology for Change Management

ABSTRACT

Due to the gap in our knowledge of soft systems methodology (SMS) and organizational change management, this chapter seeks to develop new knowledge that explains the use of SMS as an intervention measure in optimizing change. Using SSM, leaders are able to see the big picture, consequences of their measures in a larger environment, and provide effective, long-term, and sustainable solutions. Here are some case studies on subjects related to issues of stakeholder selection and management, communication assumptions in SSM, the facilitator's ambiguous role, and the impact of highly politicized problem environments on the methodology effectiveness in the change process.

INTRODUCTION

Today, we are confronted with an environment characterized by constant change along with the growing relevance of the elements contained therein (Robbins, 1990). The nature of change in today's world is more revolutionary, not evolutionary. Regardless of the impact of interventions and changes on the larger system in which they work, leaders often anticipate success in their team or department, and thus their desired change may not be sufficiently effective. Conversely, successful leaders utilize a systems approach to see

DOI: 10.4018/978-1-7998-4504-1.ch003

the business or organization as a complete system, and thus can even see the impact of small activities, interventions or changes in one sector on that sector and on the whole organization. The systematic approach is based on two principles. Firstly, no single thing can change without affecting every part of the system to which it belongs. Secondly, change in any part of a system affects every other part (Javidi, 2003).

Similar to living systems, organizations also experience a variety of gradual and incremental changes during stages corresponding to growth, maturity and decline stages (Miller, 1978). Furthermore, organizations experience some kind of oscillatory change due to the feedback mechanisms to achieve a steady state or homeostasis (Bertalanffy, 1973; Skyttner, 2001). However, in case that the environmental changes exceed the permitted level achievable by homeostatic mechanisms, the organization as a system must adapt itself to a new form fitted with a new environment. Therefore, one can expect some dramatic change here (Leifer, 1989).

Leaders have the opportunity to see the bigger picture and adjust to the underlying trends, patterns, and consequences of actions in the larger environment using a systematic approach. Such an approach enables them to use systems integration and provide effective, sustainable and long-term solutions to them. Observing events or data, identifying behavioral patterns overtime, and display basic structures are often used in systems thinking to guide events and patterns. Understanding and changing structures, that are incompatible with the needs of the company, will facilitate the expansion of options and lead to more satisfactory and long-term solutions to problems.

This chapter seeks to create new awareness of the use of soft systems methodology (SSM) as an intervening measure to create optimal changes. In this regard, some case studies have been examined related to stakeholder selection and management, relationship assumptions in SSM, facilitator's ambiguous role, and the impact of highly political problem environments on the methodological effectiveness in the change process.

ORGANIZATIONAL TRANSFORMATION

According to Rouse (2005), organizational transformation relates not only to changing practices, but also to fundamentally changing organizational relationships in one or more key areas, such as customers, employees, suppliers, and investors. Hence, new value propositions can be offered by transformation in terms of products and services, the way of delivering and supporting them, and/or way of organizing enterprise to provide these propositions. It can also include providing old value propositions in completely different manners.

Company status and business process are two key components of the transformation that, according to Rouse (2005) inputs include demand, competition, investment, people, technology, income requirements with limited regulations influence both business processes and company status. Input sources, for example, also influence the way of doing the job and how well it is done. Outputs include products, services, market share, innovation, jobs and income. In his view, the concept of status is at the core of enterprise transformation theory. Constructs such as double-loop learning and organizational learning are included in Transformational processes (Argyris and Schon, 1978; Senge, 2006). Therefore, it can be said that transformation can be the integral part of normal business processes and maybe as Rouse (2005) believes, as a routine.

In some cases, for example shift from products to services, needs changes in the organizational structure, marketing strategies and stakeholder relationship. However this is not a simple change or innovation, but requires a radical change in thinking because of formulating different goals (e.g. new market opportunities, sustainable lifestyles, new jobs, etc.). Also, reaching goals is not an insignificant task as multiple goals can influence each other in different positive or negative ways. Because of the barriers resulted from the organizational status, trade-off decisions among goals is essential.

TOOLS FOR SYSTEM CHANGE

Using the management systems model (MSM), it is possible to manipulate complex systems such as organizations (Cavaleri and Obloj, 1993). Here are five systemic tools or factors in MSM that managers can use to control or manipulate organizations in their own way:

1) Strategy,
2) Structure,
3) Procedures (technology/process),
4) Culture,
5) Leadership.

According to this model, as each tool or factor would yield a different systemic result, it should be used in a harmonious and wise way in order to yield the best possible results. Leadership and strategy are generally tools for imposing change and disrupting organizational stability, while cultures, practices, or technology and structure are considered systematic tools for imposing stability or regulation on the organization. In addition, the organization dynamic behavior is resulted from the interaction between these endogenous factors and the environment as well as among the factors themselves (e.g. the interaction among strategy, leadership, structure, procedures and culture). Each of these factors can be seen as an organizational property that can be changed to match with internal and external conditions rather than as a tool for manipulation. However, in order to change any property, a certain level of effort is needed. In superficial or adaptive change, for instance, changing one or more of an organization's properties (e.g., procedures, technology, strategy, and structure) is common to adapt to the changing environment and this in turn requires effort and energy, even if less effort and energy is needed compared to transformational change situations. On the contrary, a great deal of energy, resources, and effort is needed to change the organizational culture and political network when it comes to transformational (deep) change (Svyantek and DeShon, 1993).

In order to make a change in the organization, a system interface and a hierarchy of efforts are required. The interface between the subsystems and the organization environment is required for successful performance in the particular environment. For example, organizational strategy is one of these interfaces (Cavaleri and Obloj, 1993). The area of interaction between technology, process, and structure for organizational operations is the next layer in which variables and factors are more sensitive to external and internal resource turbulence and it is less difficult to manage and change it compared to the inner core. Through a process called adaptation, this whole group of variables can be modified with a certain level of effort to align with the environment. Although to varying degrees, all elements of both zones are exposed to the environment (for example, the production line is affected by fluctuations in demand and supply of a given material).

Finally, organizational culture, as a critical element of the survival and performance of an organization, is at the core of this chart (Peters and Waterman, 1982; Handy, 1995; Hofstede, 1997). By controlling people's shared beliefs and values and the possibility to transfer it from generation to another, the impact of culture on the organization is very inclusive. Changing the culture to adapt to a changing environment is not easy without a lot of energy, effort and time, and it is more than a simple adaptation mechanism (Svyantek and DeShon, 1993). Therefore, cultural change is considered as a profound change. Consequently, in this model, only transformation as a tool of systemic change can have a deep impact on the organization's culture. In this regard, leadership is considered as an essential factor affecting change in other variables or factors. As a source of power and authority needed to bring about change at different levels, leadership provides a linkage between the external environment, strategy and internal factors in both zones. Powerful leadership, according to Tushman and Romaneli (1985), is necessary especially for the reorientation or transformational phase of change. This is because not only must the organization have a clear vision, but also adequate power and authority is needed to alter dysfunctional political networks and overcome resistance to change. Successful implementation of change in an organization is not possible without a strong leadership.

As organizational politics, power, and control are related to self-awareness in systems, organizations are considered as natural open systems with political relationships and interaction as the characteristic of their collective behavior. Such a system, acting as political groups or networks, is clearly irrational in maintaining control over its own scope rather than the mission and goals of the organization. If the organization area of interest is under control, the existing situation is unlikely to change and this is the cause of resistance to change. Organizational culture with such a characteristic is potentially ineffective and requires transformational change. However, the psychological aspect of self-awareness in systems is not included in this model.

The change in the adaptation level simply requires adapting certain characteristics of the organization (e.g. strategy, structure, procedures or technology and size) to the environment. However, cultural change goes beyond adaptation and involves profoundly changing individuals' beliefs. Adapting the organization to a drastically changing environment requires transformation, which is a more fundamental and pervasive form of change, involving the of cultural and the political network to ensure the organization's survival.

ORGANIZATIONAL DEVELOPMENT

For more than 50 years, the field of organizational development knowledge (OD) has been studying planned and systematic change based on a deep understanding of issues in order to develop more effective organizations (Cheung-Judge and Holbeche, 2015). In such circumstances, there is a need to revitalize organizational development to address unprecedented changes as more difficult issues for organizational development professionals to address (Cummings and Worley, 2009). Organizational development professionals need to innovate and implement strategy quickly and efficiently regarding the subject of rough change. The key to this is agility — a set of capabilities that can help organizations to adapt to changing circumstances at a fast speed.

By aligning their work with larger projects such as total quality management, business process reengineering, and transformational change and leadership, OD practitioners can be more effective (McLean, 2007). Another important aspect of Schein et al.'s work (1988), is its focus on understanding the underlying problems involving human interactions and processes in organizations requires building relationships with clients in the organization by the consultant.

EXPERIENTIAL LEARNING AS A SYSTEMS CHANGE TOOL

According to the viewpoint of Senge (2006), systems thinking and organizational change are related to the importance of shared vision and team learning; also, in his view, organizational change requires the emotional change that comes from experimental learning. According to him, people are encouraged by collective motivation or a shared vision of the future to find leverage points to help bridge the gap between the existing and the conceptual situation. Little is known about the specific system levers other than the findings in the case studies. In Seng's work, for example, intimacy and authority are referred to as leverages of change. He also popularized in his idea the concept of organizational learning. The concept of a learning organization refers to an organization that purposely designs and builds its structure, culture, and strategies by building capacity for learning so that it can continually adapt and change as needed (Pierce and Gardiner, 2001).

The 6 to 12 month time frame for adopting organizational change processes in today's competitive world can be problematic. Some optimization and accelerating approaches to change have been modified to fit the today's business environment and organizations capabilities (Beer, 2001; Beer and Einsenstat, 2004). Organizational learning is also part of the process of optimal change, and is a continuous process that can facilitate organizational redesign. The learning-related stages of change according to Shani and Docherty (2003) are called learning dimensions that form a set of alternative solutions that can be selected to meet the needs of change.

The need for speed in affecting organizational change is emphasized by Blixt and James (2004) who identified the change drivers including increasing global competition, complex markets and the need for performance excellence in competing markets. They also refer to some of the elements of accelerating change such as shared strategy, leadership, critical mass and support systems; nevertheless, little attention has been paid to implement and overcome change and the application of systems thinking or systems methodology has not been addressed.

A SYSTEMS APPROACH TO CHANGE

A pluralistic perspective can provide a better understanding of the organizational behavioral environment in which change occurs. The mental models, beliefs and assumptions of managers that have been formed over the years inside and outside the organization can be shared or not. Managers may assume that people's shared assumptions about the business environment are self-evident, while different individuals may have a wide range of mental models and worldviews.

There are groups of people in most of the organizations that form social systems. Some groups are formed within the organization's formal structure whilst others within the system make up informal groups. The formal group has a specified boundary like the organization's boundary; however, the informal systems boundary may be ill-defined or invisible. There may be relationships, dependencies and beliefs in the informal group, or sub-system that differ or conflict with the formal group.

There may also be subcultures such as specialized subcultures, administrative subcultures, customer interface subcultures in different parts of the organization. People's behavior is explicitly in the form of culture that represents the prevailing beliefs and values, so a change in behavior reflects a change in culture. Therefore, the desirable change needs the acceptance and absorption of changes to the organization's culture.

Using SMS is raised as a new approach to applying change management to complex, turbulent and people-centered organizational challenges. Utilizing the open system view as well as an iterative and interactive process, this approach allows for the incorporation of subjective information and objective facts, and also unlimited thinking and problem solving for the development of a favorable future in a pluralistic environment.

The usefulness of SSM in diagnosing and addressing organizational problems and creating new systems in cultures, characterized by pluralist views and values, is stated in the research conducted by Molineaux and Haslett (2007). They noticed a significant increase in creativity through the implementation of SMS workshops in a large government organization. Although their research introduces opportunities to promote creativity, it does not speak about increasing and speeding up changes. Therefore, the literature gap on the use of SMS to accelerate change in the organization still remains.

People must be modeled as part of the change process and the model must explain the actual learning and change mechanism according to Lewin (1951). In his opinion, if change is not in line with one's beliefs and values, no amount of information can persuade them to create it. That is an attitudinal change is required to make behavioral change happened. As the human systems are a product of personality and experience, we cannot treat them objectively. It is needed that people apply their own method of reasoning to the process of learning and understanding. People face the threat of disconfirming data when dealing with change. According to Lewin, people need a level of psychological safety to deal with the anxiety of change. An appropriate environment such as SMS for exchanging views can provide such security so that concepts are accepted and motivated to change.

Churchman (1970), who was trying to access the complex and often irrational ideas constituting a person's world view, applied systems thinking to these ill-structured, messy and subjective mind sets based on a range of a priori assumptions that may differ from person to person. In his view, a system perspective is when you try to see the world from the perspective of others. For Churchman, change must work in the minds of the participants and in the outside world so that it can be accepted and approved. This indicates the need to collect and identify a range of people's perspectives and to develop a consensus between beliefs and values.

The individuals, organizations, socio-technical systems, and turbulent situations in an interdependent pluralistic environment are underlying factors to provide the skill and methodology needed for the organizational change. In this regard, SMS is a useful tool for finding insights into optimization of change that allows the development of assumptions, applying and discussing about the people's views, and thereby leading to the expression of opinions and contributions. People will be in the making of the future.

Schwab (2016) believe that the fourth industrial revolution has started that include combination of physical and virtual resources in new ways to produce a profound and systemic change to our world. Although there is uncertainty and constant change in jobs in such a world, problem solving and system skills are always required. Such a view is in line with the real organizational issues that OD specialists are facing in the current situation. This gets worse with budgetary and resource uncertainty and fundamentally a degree of tension in relation to OD's ability to offer a contribution of value and significance. Unless experts perceive the need to learn SMS to plan for action and deal with OD issues, it can be said that none have started their professional path yet.

CHALLENGES IN TRANSFORMATION

Various stimuli for transformation such as the need to integrate a new technology, the desire to substantially elevate performance or the requirement to adapt to changing needs of customers exist in a business environment. When a quantum leap is needed, whatever the reason, the following challenges can arise:

Identifying relevant change: The inability of leaders to understand the scope and depth of change required for transformation can lead to organizational stagnation. Often, managers spend time conducting routine operations; while this is a necessary task, informed managers are aware of the need for change. Of course, because of their focus on the current situation, their view may be inadvertently limited, this is not because they are not at the strategic position, but because their strategy base does not include the transformation element at all.

Managing different agendas: Individuals naturally have their own agenda in the socio-political environment, and the business environment is no exception. Depending on the level of influence a particular person has in the organization, these agendas can be a barrier to transformation. Such a distinction is accepted in the SMS as self-evident, and so the focus is on showing weaknesses and / or strengths in a rational way through modeling and structured discussion. Building a broader base of overlapping systems of meaning concerning what is important to transformation is common in SSM. In this regard, all participants are an integral part of the problematic situation and all are analysts. In order to move things forward, it seems necessary to have a greater degree of shared ownership in the solution as well as a greater awareness of actions.

Managing technological influences: Any adjustment within the business setting needed for a change in the way of doing work. SSM will draw out the key elements that are necessary to blend in the technological change when applied to a group of technical experts and other stakeholders, since it embodies systems thinking. For the particular organization, these elements will be organic not cookie cutter. Also as milestones in a project plan, they will be specified to achieve the transformation.

Managing different mental constructs: SSM imposes a shared vision (or new mental construct) among stakeholders concerning critical elements by adopting the systems thinking that constitutes the transformation effort. As a consequence of collaborating with stakeholders, this vision is formed to formulate root definitions and models of the problematic situation and then constructively debate how to compare these models with the real-world. Thus, a perception comes into view, by socialized inquiry that confines the most vital elements for transformation. The mentioned elements are then classified to structural, procedural (or process), and attitudinal change and based upon what is learned, the intervention is applied.

COMPANY CO-VALUE FOCUSED SYSTEMS THINKING

A major change in mindset, implying the need to embrace different management and decision-making approaches in the leadership style, is needed because Product-Service System (PSS) transformation needs recognition of value co-creation by supplier and client. In addition, the change in mindset must be pervasive in the organization; hence there is a need for a constructive approach towards full organization transformation. The appropriate methods and models should be selected by managers to effect the transformation. In such a situation, the use of SMS enables the understanding of existing problem situations and situation analysis using root definition techniques and conceptual models for identifying activities needed for transformation.

FACTORS AFFECTING SUCCESSFUL ORGANIZATIONAL CHANGE

The organizational change project is likened to group therapy by Atkinson, because in group therapy, individuals surrender themselves to the group, but they are born again. Atkinson shows that using the metaphor of participants' intense disagreements and their inconsistent behaviors in family therapy is effective in improving the influence of organizational change project. The range of motivation from rational to emotional and the impact of peer pressure, as well as interpersonal and individual issues in the group should be taken into account in such projects. For Atkinson, one of the most important ways for the organization to progress is through the evaluation process (Pattison, 1995).

Atkinson considers the task of a consultant or facilitator a structured thinking behind the project. In his view, the counselor should apply his or her counseling skills in the therapy process (e.g. pre-workshop interviews). He also believes that the power of the facilitator is similar to that of the therapist, but a more neutral and fair position is preferred in this case. However, for Atkinson, the facilitator cannot be a neutral observer, because political leverage is involved and inevitably, manipulations are done by the facilitator. It is important for the facilitator to communicate effectively and help people and utilize both empathy and rationalistic approaches within projects. Finally, Atkinson says that the relationship between the facilitator and the client group is vital to project success.

An example from healthcare projects is used by Checkland to show the way of creating changes in thinking (Pattison, 1995):

In project 1, questioning the C of CATWOE led to the perception that the buyer, not the patient, was the customer, and thought was crystallized in this way.

In project 2, based on an acceptance of a different conceptualization at director and manager level, a change in Weltanschauungen occurred from the needs identification to strategy making. The important point was the acceptance at director and manager level of this conceptualization.

In project 3 in a meeting with stakeholder where the facilitator is not present (i.e. not an SSM phase), organizational change is occurred.

Checkland lists some of the features for the organizations which embrace change that are as follows:

1. External funding available to carry out the project
2. Willingness to use SMS
3. Sponsor's personal agenda that must be reviewed in order to get started
4. Project approval by the Chief Executive, for example, a confirmation to start the project; ensuring key people are involved (CEO support is crucial if he or she has a specific position in the organization).

5. Continuously monitor the process and ensure meet deadlines by consultant (This way people in the workgroups realize that the project has a limited time).
6. Making projects fun.

How to use SMS is not technique in itself but also, depends on the consultant's and organization's style in terms of Checkland. The Brian Wilson's style (in which a consultant working to a client's project requirements) is named as "professional" by Atkinson. On the other hand, the Checkland's style, which Checkland described as "letting it emerge with the people themselves", is named as "liberal" (a guide and teacher) by Atkinson.

An example of a project with a media products group is used by Cole to present her understanding of the way of occurring organizational change (Pattison, 1995):

Most participants at the end of the first day still had no idea of the model position. At dinner, some high-level issues were discussed, and Cole developed a model for these high-level issues overnight. This was the project turning point - 'switched the light on'. The change in W was that the group, which first see themselves from the mechanical perspective as a flow system, now creatively shifted their view to what is being produced.

The characteristics of organizations, with the successful experience of organizational change, were also discussed by Cole. She believes that such a success relies on people, the quality of their thoughts and their positions. Also according to her, having the potential to successfully implement change, a learning organization has the capacity to evaluate what is being achieved in organizational change conditions.

Cole sees her style as more of a facilitator rather than leading, and she believes in empowering project participants in her role as catalysts. Noting that this style is not offensive, Cole expressed concern that it could be harmful if the role was not played well. She believes that people should see and believe their ideas without being ridiculed, and they should be encouraged and rewarded for their achievements in the process of rethinking. Cole considers the roles of transforming the driving force of change from herself to the organization, discovering talent in individuals, and identifying the barriers to change for herself. But she does not like to introduce herself as a change agent, since people may find it threatening.

A combination of factors is involved in successful organizational change in terms of Haynes. Although interpersonal and SMS facilitation skills are vital, communication is everything. Haynes also points to the vitality of the facilitator style and considers the following features (Pattison, 1995):

- Openness: encouraging people to be open by showing his openness
- Persuading people to tell stories (and knowing when to close the notebook).
- Empathizing with the needs of the people you work with
- Timely use of challenges, knowing when to be blunt and being streetwise

As last point, Haynes refers to the dramatic impact of a slide he and Checkland had used on one project that caused opening up a debate and territory which the participants had been avoiding. That was "the bad news", to convey anonymous statements of concern about the organization. Although it was a watershed, but challenging people to the point of making them uncomfortable rarely happens according to Haynes.

For him, change can either take the soft approach, for example through models or the blunt approach, and can also occur over a period of time with slight changes in values. Holistic changes are important for some, while some seek different perspectives (Weltanschauungen), and some seek models.

As a facilitator and depending on the client and project, Haynes says he plays the role of trusted consultant, message carrier, and personal adviser. As clients are looking for someone who is not a subject specialist in his view. Different roles from facilitator to decision maker can exist in different projects. Haynes knows the consultant as a very sensitive role who is responsible for managing conflicts. He also adds that the consultant should deal with the conflict as much as possible and understand that the conflict can be valuable to the learning situation because people present different perspectives in the conflict situation.

APPLICATION OF SSM FOR CHANGE MANAGEMENT

Duc to its rcputation for managing complex and ill-structured organizational problems through structuring rational thinking, SSM was used in Nakakawa et al. (2011) research to create enterprise architecture. Also, SSM techniques can be applied in complementing the collaborative process design in line with triggering discussions, creating a shared understanding and vision among stakeholders.

The challenge facing one of the US federal agencies was to establish an operations monitoring system to provide intelligence of regulatory and policy compliance, strategic initiatives, programs and performance. The budget of this system, which was to utilize data from a number of native independently developed unique-purpose applications, was extremely low compared to the budgets assigned to enterprise application. The complexity of the situation became clear when the agency sought to identify the desired benefits and methods of use with its limited understanding of the need. In other words, there is no understanding of usage, design and specifications of application. To solve this dilemma, by stakeholder satisfaction, SSM was applied to create an understanding of the way of interaction between various operating units to facilitate the agency's mission and how these interdependences where relevant to operational intelligence. A plan was developed and socialized based on these insights, that outlined the data sources, information structure and flow, as well as revealed the unique analytical capabilities the system would provide to each specific operating unit (Duggins, 2015). Consequently, task cycle times where reduced from over seven days to approximately 30 seconds by designing this new system. In other specific cases, the new system provides insights on key operation parameters that have never been available before, and the system can provide a set of other features.

SSM was also used in another case to facilitate benchmarking and strategic planning for a non-profit organization which is the local branch of a larger non-profit organization. Based on the understanding of the "model" institution in this application, the nonprofit wants to increase performance. Although the local entity has established its own set of criteria, there should be no general description of the "model" institution. Therefore, questioning the working definition of a model institution, orchestrating the benchmarking study and forming a strategic approach is the task of Thus SSM to integrate the findings from the benchmarking effort. Therefore, SMS moves the organization away from things like describing what is in the model institution, the new organizational structure focusing resources on goal-oriented activities, a pool of 60 management recommendations and a number of widely used recommendations (Duggins, 2015).

Dickinson (2009) has used SMS to examine its effectiveness in enabling systemic change in local government and the local National Health Service (NHS) environment as well as to examine the facilitator's role in this process. The variant Checkland's Mode 2 of SSM was tested in two environments, namely Herefordshire Health Authority and Sand well Health Authority. In

Herefordshire application, the SSM is used the design of an Integrated Care Pathway for stroke patients; while in Sandwell, SSM was implemented to help design of an Information Management and Technology (IM&T) Strategy for the boundary-spanning Sandwell Partnership. Both of these environments were experiencing considerable organizational change as the experiments unlocked.

The explicit goals of these studies are:

1. Examining the SSM evolution and development and contributing its further development,
2. Applying SSM in change processes within the NHS,
3. Evaluating the potential role of SSM in the broader change process.
4. Assessing the researcher role as a facilitator within the process
5. Developing a critical framework to understand and assess the impact of SSM on change.

CONCLUSION

Due to the gap in our knowledge of soft systems methodology (SSM) and organizational change management, this chapter seeks to develop new knowledge that explains the use of SSM as an intervention measure in optimizing change. In the collaborative learning process, where people's understanding of each other's perspectives is brought together, stakeholder engagement can lead to higher learning and the necessary levers needed to move forward with change without apparent or hidden resistance. The case studies presented here address issues related to stakeholder selection and management, communication assumptions in SSM, the ambiguous role of facilitator, and the effect of political problem environments on the effectiveness of the method in the change process.

The individuals, organizations, socio-technical systems, and turbulent situations in an interdependent pluralistic environment are underlying factors to provide the skill and methodology needed for the organizational change. Therefore, it is important to sclcct SSM as a suitable tool for finding insights in change optimization techniques. It is possible to make assumptions, explore individual points of view and discuss different points of view, and to express and interact with people in SSM, and that makes it possible to incorporate their views in shaping the future.

REFERENCES

Ackoff, R. L. (1974). *Redesigning the future: A systems approach to societal problems*. New York: John Wiley.

Argyris, C., & Schon, D. A. (1978). *Organizational learning: A theory of action perspective*. Addison-Wesley.

Beer, M. (2001). Embrace the drive for results capability development paradox. *Organizational Dynamics*, *29*(4), 233–247. doi:10.1016/S0090-2616(01)00030-4

Beer, M., & Einsenstat, R. A. (2004). How to have an honest conversation about your business strategy. *Harvard Business Review*, *82*, 82–89. PMID:14971272

Blixt, A. B., & James, S. (2004). Accelerating strategic change, application of the whole-scale approach to leading and managing change. *Learnende Organisation*, 1-16. Retrieved October 13, 2001, from: http://www.dannemillertyson.com/wp-content/uploads/2016/05/Accelerating-Strategic-Change-Article-pdf.pdf

Cavaleri, S., & Obloj, K. (1993). *Management systems: A global perspective*. Belmont, CA: Wadsworth.

Cheung-Judge, M., & Holbeche, L. (2015). *Organization development: A practitioner's guide for OD and HR*. Kogan Page.

Churchman, C. W. (1970). Operations Research as a Profession. *Management Science*, *17*(2), B37–B53. doi:10.1287/mnsc.17.2.B37

Cummings, T. G., & Worley, C. G. (2009). *Organization Development and Change* (8th ed.). Mason, OH: South-Western College Publishing.

Dickinson, S. (2009). *An analysis of the role of soft systems methodology in the change process and the contribution of the facilitator within this process* (Doctoral Thesis). Aston University.

Duggins, D. (2015). *Soft systems methodology as a catalyst for organizational transformation*. Retrieved July 03, 2019, from http://www.asq509.org/ht/a/GetDocumentAction/id/110488

Felton, G., & Earnshaw, A. (2017). Learning to think and act with systems: Improving OD with Soft Systems Methodology. *International Journal of HRD Practice, Policy and Research*, *2*(1), 51–66.

Handy, C. B. (1995). *Gods of management: The changing work of organizations.* Oxford University Press.

Hinterberger, F., Kranendonk, S., Welfens, M.J., & Schmidt-Bleek, F. (1994). *Increasing resource productivity through eco-efficient services.* Wuppertal Paper No. 13.

Hofstede, G. (1997). *Cultures and organizations: software of the mind.* London: McGraw-Hill.

Javidi, M. (2003). Collaborative change management: A systematic approach. *Intercultural Communication Studies.* https://web.uri.edu/iaics/files/08-Mitch-Javidi.pdf

Leifer, R. (1989). Understanding organizational transformation using a dissipative structure model. *Human Relations, 42*(10), 899–916. doi:10.1177/001872678904201003

Lewin, K. (1951). *Field theory in social science.* New York: Harper and Row.

McLean, G. N. (2007). *Organization development: Principles, processes and performance.* San Francisco, CA: Berrett-Koehler.

Miller, J. G. (1978). *Living Systems: The Basic Concepts.* Retrieved July 20, 2019, from: https://www.panarchy.org/miller/livingsystems.html

Molineaux, J., & Haslett, T. (2007). The use of soft systems methodology to enhance group creativity. *Systemic Practice and Action Research, 20*(6), 477–496. doi:10.100711213-007-9078 0

Mont, O. (1999). Clarifying the concept of Product-Service System. *Journal of Cleaner Production, 10*(3), 237–245. doi:10.1016/S0959-6526(01)00039-7

Morcos, M., & Henshaw, M. (2009). A soft systems methodology for transforming organizations to Product-Service Systems (application in defence and construction industry). In *Proceedings of the 7th Annual Conference on Systems Engineering Research.* Loughborough University.

Nakakawa, A., van Bommel, P., & Proper, H. A. (2011). Applying Soft Systems Methodology in Enterprise Architecture Creation Workshops, In M. Nttgens, O. Thomas, B. Weber (Eds.), *Proceedings of the 4th International Workshop on Enterprise Modeling and Information Systems Architectures (EMISA).* Hamburg, Germany: Academic Press.

Pattison, E. M. (1995). The contribution of soft systems methodology to the achievement of change in organizational Culture (PhD thesis). University of Warwick, Warwick Business School.

Peters, T. J., & Waterman, R. H. Jr. (1982). *In search of excellence: lessons from America's best run companies*. New York: Harper & Row.

Pierce, J. L., & Gardner, D. G. (2001). *Management organizational behavior: an integrated perspective*. South-Western College Publishing.

Robbins, S. P. (1990). *Organization Theory* (3rd ed.). Prentice Hall.

Rouse, W. B. (2005). A theory of enterprise transformation. *Systems Engineering*, *8*(4), 279–295. doi:10.1002ys.20035

Schein, E. H. (1988). Process consultation: Vol. 1. *Its role in organization development* (2nd ed.). Reading, MA: Addison Wesley.

Schein, E. H. (1999). *Process consultation revisited: Building the helping relationship*. Addison Wesley.

Schwab, K. (2016). *The fourth industrial revolution*. Geneva: World Economic Forum.

Senge, P. M. (2006). *The fifth discipline: The art and practice of the learning organization*. Random House Australia.

Shani, A.B.R., & Docherty, P. (2003). *Learning by design: Building sustainable organizations*. Bodmin: MPG Books/Blackwell.

Skyttner, L. (2001). *General Systems Theory: Problems, Perspectives, Practice*. World Scientific Pub Co Inc. doi:10.1142/4307

Sundarasaradula, D., & Hasan, H. M. (2004). A unified open systems model for explaining organizational change. In S. Gregor & D. Hart (Eds.), *Information Systems Foundations: Constructing and Criticizing* (pp. 125–142). Canberra, ACT, Australia: Australian National University Press.

Svyantek, D., & DeShon, R. (1993). Organizational attractors: A chaos theory explanation of why cultural change efforts often fail. *Public Administration Quarterly*, *17*(3), 339–355.

Tushman, M. L., & Romanelli, E. (1985). Organizational evolution: A metamorphosis model of convergence and reorientation. *Research in Organizational Behavior*, *7*, 171–222.

Von Bertalanffy, L. (1973). *General System theory: Foundations, Development, Applications*. Harmondsworth, UK: Penguin.

Young, J. T. (2009). *Developing a soft systems solution for enhancing and managing change in organizations* (PhD thesis). School of Aerospace, Mechanical and Manufacturing Engineering College of Science, Engineering and Health, RMIT University.

Chapter 4
Soft Systems Methodology for Organizational Culture Analysis

ABSTRACT

The main purpose of this chapter is to present the interlinkage of soft systems methodology (SSM) and organizational culture. Often, organizations find themselves within a problematic situation connected with cultural issues. Analysis of such issues is complex because of the numerous stakeholders involved and the multi-faceted and dynamic nature of the culture. This chapter focuses on organizational culture, which is among the most important assets on which an organization rely, particularly for the sake of change management. Here the authors begin with a review on the concept of organizational culture and proceed to discuss the factors affecting the organizational culture and then present a model of organizational culture, cultural aspects of SSM, and a real-world application of SSM in the form of a case study of corporate ethical culture analysis.

INTRODUCTION

The importance of ethical culture roots in not only the increased complexity of today's world, but also the recent dilemma indicating the decisive role of cultural aspects in the performance and life cycle of an organization. The future directions followed by an organization are affected by the changes

DOI: 10.4018/978-1-7998-4504-1.ch004

to which the organization is exposed by both internal and external factors. This is so significant that necessitates a change management system wherein cultural influences are well addressed. The problem is so complicated, calling for simultaneous contributions from the human minds, political-economic structures, and the environment – a goal that cannot be realized unless a system of change is established.

The above-mentioned issues highlight the need for a systems approach to cultural analysis, which is known to be a complex task to undertake. Such an approach provides the analyst with the ability to characterize the organizational culture at a larger scale, and hence formulate an action list to establish a widely participated culture when planning for the future. Despite the technical and strategic problems emerged upon founding the systems management on this systems approach, one will end up with bunch of useful systems solutions as well. The soft systems methodology (SSM) has been designed not to be implemented linearly (i.e. in a sequence of steps), but rather in the form of a holistic instrument dealing with the cultural in a wide scope. In combination with other theories and tools, it can address the change management comprehensively to achieve an organizational culture providing for extensive participation of all stakeholders when planning for the future.

Following the SSM, managers must acknowledge a relatively broad set of goals and prepare different solutions to approach the goals. The SSM further provides the managers with a body of understand about the elements of society: human beings. In this respect, managers should scrutinize perspectives, intentions, worldviews, and standard of judgments. In an organization, SSM deals with such issues as conflicts, arguments, mutual understanding, and the so-called change. For this purpose, it keeps focusing on not only the cultural issues (people's viewpoints, mutual values, and norms), but also the political issues (identifying the individuals' class and status according to their perspectives) (Goksoy, 2017).

Presenting a modification to the classic SSM, Kartowisastro *et al.* (1994) went for studying the problematic situations encountered more frequently with the eastern cultures. They came to focus on this topic with the initial aim of implementing the SSM to address a cultural conflict raised when an Indonesian institute of research and development (R&D) faced with modern technologies. Provided that the communicative competence represents a requirement for the SSM, the modification proposed by these authors (*i.e.*

replacement of the debate stage by indirect debate) could not be neglected as far as keeping the SSM kernel satisfied was concerned.

The focus of this chapter is on organizational culture, a very significant asset for any organization, especially in relation to the change management. Thus, beginning with a review on the concept of organizational culture and proceed to discuss the factors affecting the organizational culture and then to present a model of organizational culture, cultural aspects of SSM, and a real-world application of SSM in the form

ORGANIZATIONAL CULTURE

An organizational culture is brought up by the organization itself, and a knowledge of this process helps evaluate not only the essential role played by the culture, but also the effect it has on other organizational schedules run by the members of the organization. Dávila and Martínez (1999) highlight the difficulty of characterizing an organization culturally; for this purpose, one must scrutinize the actors' conscience where the processes are analyzed. The culture is an integrated and complex model of the general lives lived by various groups, their associations, interpersonal attitudes, values, norms, beliefs, traditions, and customs. According to Smirch (1963), the culture is defined as the set of beliefs, behaviors, knowledge, values, and objectives by/for/based on which people do live. Reichers (1969) referred to the culture as an assemblage of meanings presented symbolically to express a specific attitude toward life. Bradford and Harvey (1972) believed that any organization hosts a set of myths, rituals and organizational values that are even stronger than the official structure, rules and procedures of the organization: the culture. They saw the organizational culture as something beyond an abstract idea, fueling the sense of daily life and regulating the inter-personal interactions within a company. Every organization is supposed to have a preset perfect culture and an actual culture that is a mixed result of the spiritual values, habits, traditions, attitudes, symbols, etc. Significant functions receive large contributions from the organizational culture. It not only provides means to control people's behavior, but also captures the individuals' passions, attitudes and identities. The culture is developed through a long yet consistent process wherein beliefs are spread and actions are taken to have the people saw themselves belonging to the same tribe, rising a sense of similarity.

Based on a review on the literature, Reynolds (1986) distinguished between three inter-related concepts of organizational culture: (1) a cultural system on the basis of myths, values and ideology, (2) a socio-structural framework of the structure, strategies, policies and management processes across the organization, and (3) the organizational culture seen from the individual members' perspective considering their packages of experience and personality. Establishing a link between the behavior and the culture, Zanimuto and Krakower (1991) stipulated that the organizational culture refers to the set of values and ideas across an organization that together form the human behaviors and its implications.

CHANGE IN ORGANIZATIONAL CULTURE

A change in the organizational culture has been suggested by many authors. Edwards (1988) did not rule out the possibility for a change in the culture, but pointed out the difficult and lengthy process through which such a change can be implemented. In contrast, Frank (1987) argued that the culture is not changeable at all. In another work, Wilkins and Ouchi (1983) questioned the potential of culture being utilized as an efficient control instrument for managers as they thought that a change into the culture is not always an option. Wilkins and Ouchi (1983) identified two fundamental factors contributing to change acceptance: the type and extent of the change. They also suggested that a culture can be manipulated to a particular extent depending on the history depth, membership stability, lack of alternatives, inter-personal interactions, and common goals. Moreover, individuals were found to show more affinity toward new ideas if they become confident that the organization will treat them fairly and provide them with enough time to adopt with the new paradigms provided they are honest.

Other deliberate strategies have been proposed for changing the culture of an organization in an attempt to enhance the resultant efficiency. In this regard, Wilhelm (1992) believed in the possibility of behavioral modifications provided the corporate culture is strong enough and the top management delineates the values and strategy of the company clearly. Explaining the interactions between the roles and values, Davies and Ledington (1991) concluded that the values are much difficult to modify given the necessity of cultural analysis before such modifications can be implemented; this was while the roles could be altered following a relatively easy procedure. Another finding of this work was that the corporate culture is difficult to discover by an insider and rather impossible to understand by an outsider, unless the outsider turns into an insider. In consequence, they suggested a team of insiders and outsiders for exploring the culture. They further presented discussions on the authority (the power to make formal decisions), power (the ability to trigger things), and politics (the processes forming the power commodities) (Davies and Ledington, 1991).

Trying to define a procedure for culture change in an organization, Cummings and Worley (2005) formulated the following six-item guideline:

1) Define a clear strategic vision: The culture change can be fueled by a vision composed of a statement of purpose and a list of core organizational values; such a declaration motivates the members of the organization toward the culture change.
2) Demonstrate the commitment of the top management to the change: Subordinates are more likely to accept a culture change if they see the top management as being well prepared for and enthusiastic about the new values.
3) Apply the culture change at the highest levels: The clear support of the new values and behaviors from the top management increases the chances of the new culture being accepted. In the meantime, the current culture may not be terminated abruptly, but rather ruled out gradually through communicative change agents.
4) Undertake the required organizational changes to back the culture change: A new culture may not be appropriately implemented unless the required modifications are made to the structure, information and control systems, reward mechanism, recruitment system, and management procedures of the organization.
5) Build on newcomers and lay out the deviants: The new set of values must also be expressed in the employment, promotion, and firing mechanisms.
6) Promote the individuals' sensitivity to ethical and legal issues: Frequently, a change in the culture change leads to a conflict of interest between the organization and its members. This conflict is known to be associated with ethical and legal concerns related to job security, equitable treatment, control, etc. The culture change process shall be monitored periodically to see the extent to which the adaptation to the new culture has been realized.

FACTORS AFFECTING CULTURAL CHANGE

In an attempt to recognize the organizational structures admitting a culture change, Pettigrew *et al.* (1992) focused on the root causes of the difference in the rate of change among various National Health Service (NHS) localities, ending up with the following factors based on a literature review:

- Organization's environment (*i.e.* structure and culture): an integrative environment tends to admit the change while segmented organizations are less likely to accept that. By the term integrative, we refer to an environment dominated by team-orientation, holistic problem-solving, cooperation, strong idea generation and exchange, sense of purpose and direction, innovation, and stimulation.
- Flexibility: adaptability to internal and external factors affecting the organization rather than going through complicated bureaucracy. Other factors contributing to the flexibility include going from positions to persons, from efficiency to creativity, from rules to the ultimate results, from hierarchies to interactive teams, and from ownership and strict control to leverage and experimentation.
- Change sustainability: the ability to tolerate short-term disturbances to keep the change sustained,
- Human resource context: required context for the human force to accept and adapt to the change.

Cooperating with the NHS, Pettigrew *et al.* (1992) identified 8 factors contributing to a favorable context for accepting a change. These include:

- Qualitative level of the policies,
- Change leaders,
- The intensity and scale of the pressure imposed by the environment in long run,
- Organizational supports in the form of flexibility (instead of strict hierarchies), skill-orientation (instead of rank-orientation), risk-taking spirit, promotion of R&D activities, strict value acknowledgment, strong self-image and sense of achievement,
- Efficient managerial connections,
- Cooperative inter-organizational network, and
- Declaration of priorities and goals in a simple and clear fashion.

In 1992, Johnson elaborated on how the organizational culture affects and is affected by the adopted strategies and managerial practices, believing in the criticality of the role played by the cultural change when it comes to the formulation of effective strategies. He argued that the body of beliefs exhibited by the top management, i.e. the corporate culture, contributes to the current mechanisms across the organization and hence keeps the members from adapting to strategic changes. Moreover, the so-called strategic inertia and drift developed upon filtering the business environment regarding the cultural paradigm to react to external forces. According to Johnson, a culture audit can help managers explore the cultural paradigm and provides them with a foundation on which debates about the required cultural modifications can be made.

A number of researchers have referred to the organizational leadership as an important factor contributing to the declaration and change of corporate culture. Regarding the corporate culture, the leading management must develop and then clearly express a philosophy by which the goals and mission of the organization can be defined (Van de Ven, 1983). Based on the work by Edwards (1988), corporate culture beliefs are partly preserved by the behavior of the top management. Frank (1987) suggested that one can explore a corporate culture by exploring the things to which the corporate managers pay attention or reward.

When it comes to formulation of new strategies, researchers have placed an emphasis on the responsibility of leaders for cultural risk assessment with a focus on the gap between the current culture and the changes imposed to the culture by the newly adopted strategy (Schwartz and Davis, 1981). Schein (1983) and Gitlow (1992) focused on the resistance to change, defining the organizational culture as a ground on which people are trained to face the anxiety. With the cultural changes putting the maximum pressure on individuals, the top management plays a critical role in the success of such changes by getting deeply engaged with the changes. Such changes may also render effective if the current culture is significantly challenged.

The corporate culture receives large contributions from the power, politics, and segmentation. These variables are known to greatly affect the socio-technical approaches to the design of information systems where both technological requirements and human desires are targeted simultaneously (Waisham, 1991). An important characteristic of an organization in relation to the establishment of shared values and beliefs is the structure, to the extent that Jerome-Forget (1992) believed in occasional requirement of a critical structural reorganization before a change in the corporate culture can be realized.

Emphasizing on the gradual nature of a successful culture change plan, no single change program is likely to end up with a sustainable cultural change, but rather continuous actions shall be taken and consistent messages must be spread from the top management until a sustainable change is obtained (Krawczyk, 1992).

The SSM places emphases on the response and debate, making it in agreement with particular concepts in the context of corporate culture: shared understanding and sense-making. Checkland's (1981) Weltanschauung defined the culture as a default view to the world by which a specific system of human activities makes sense from a common point of view (with the minimum commonality being the shared Weltanschauung among a number of staff at the organization).

MODEL OF ORGANIZATIONAL CULTURE

A corporate culture model is not only linked to internal interactions, but also receives contributions from the external environment. By this model, the analyst is able to explore the mechanism and root causes of a culture change across the organization and its subdomains (e.g., strategy, structure) (Dauber *et al.*, 2012). The model equally treats the domains and processes (e.g., guidance, single-loop learning) to analyze the dynamicity of the culture, providing for better comprehension of the effectiveness of the change process across the corporate (Dauber *et al.*, 2012).

Gharajedaghi (2007) stipulated that a social system must engage with a collective process to adjust the deformed shared image and hence back the

Figure 1. Model of organizational culture (Adapted from Dauber et al, 2012)

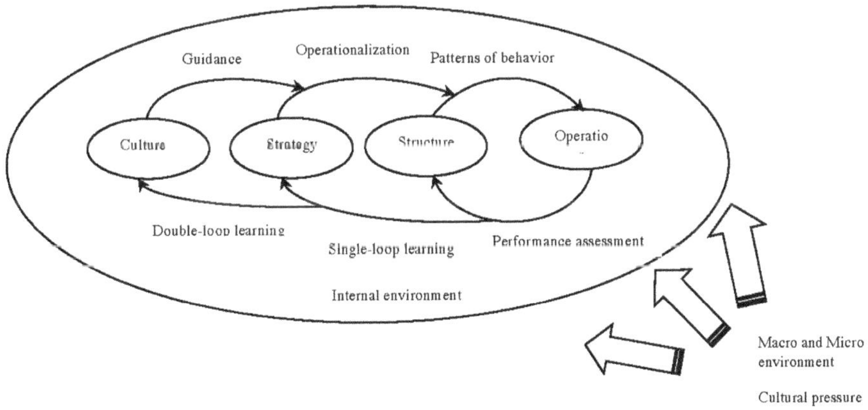

cultural change across the system, with the process being affected by the system background.

CULTURAL ASPECT OF SSM

Interpretation of the research on the culture is so complicated, as reflected in the literature demonstrating the differences in the way the work environment is perceived (*i.e.* the corporate culture) by people at various organizational positions, in different industrial segments, and/or from different nationalities (Reynolds 1986; Kelley, 1986). Add to that the multiple subcultures across a single organization, which makes it even more difficult to analyze the corporate culture (Smirch, 1983). The subculture divisions may be linked to professional grouping, social or ethnic grouping, and/or personal/organizational loyalties. There are cases where these divisions end up generating coalitions that bring up counter cultures (opposing the core values of the organization) and hence give rise to conflicts of control (Morgan, 1986).

The corporate culture and SSM are intimately associated with one another, to the extent that any change of Weltanschauung characterizes a cultural change, with the cultural stream of SSM analysis being at the center of attention for later versions of the methodology (Checkland and Scholes, 1990). Mingers (1992) kept the culture at the center of focus when elaborating on the Checkland's concept of Weltanschauung, suggesting that the culture is determined by the individual purpose and deals of knowledge, value, and expectation generated upon experiences and leading to differences (rather than invalidity) in worldviews among members of an organization. Organizations with more than one conflicting Weltanschauungs face difficulties in problem description and problem-solving at the organizational scale. In the meantime, Mingers referred to the problematic approach to a single shared Weltanschauung as individuals tend exhibit cohesion to their own perceptions.

Checkland (1985) referred to the conceptual models as an element of an organization-proportioned learning plan by which the individual members of the corporation learn to encounter different situations for enhancement. This process is clearly based on cultural values. The SSM includes not only this process, but also the logic behind the situation to improve managerial actions based on cultural processes (Checkland, 1985). A later version of SSM (Checkland and Scholes, 1990) was developed with an increased emphasis on the corporate culture, introducing the cultural stream of analysis. This analysis took into consideration not only the intervention itself, but also the surrounding social and political systems. Based on this methodology, the cultural learning occurred via a revised process other than the 7-step process that was proposed earlier (*e.g.* Checkland, 1981). The revised process set the cultural analysis limited to the first two steps of the previous approach.

Checkland and Scholes (1990) believed that one can capture the corporate culture by exploring relevant human activity systems; appropriate modifications to the culture was, however, impossible to determine unless a cultural feasibility study was performed. Finally, the researchers discussed possible adjustments to the Weltanschauung that could be practiced in the framework of an SSM project. The more important point to note is the long-term mechanism through which the individuals' perceptions are modified – a phenomenon that happens in the SSM users' minds upon implementing the methodology. Indeed, diverging the one's way of thinking toward a new and clearer perception goes through a cycle from perceptions to relevant systems, to models, and to new perceptions. The original perception seeks for the ultimate goal of taking appropriate actions to address a situation of problem rather than building models, and this is where all the debates on the feasibility of the change emerge. The core methodology is particularly important as it provides for a coherent and sharable thinking process (Checkland and Scholes, 1990).

A key component of the so-called organizational development is the modification of corporate culture (Yolles and Guo, 2003). Figure 2 demonstrates the three systems that must be analyzed to explore the cultural aspects in an SSM plan: (I) the plan itself, (II) the social system, and (III) the political system (Checkland, 2000). This process (i.e. stream of cultural analysis) gocs on until the interventional plan is accomplished (Checkland and Scholes, 1990) and hence spreads over all four main activities of the methodology. The four primary activities of SSM comprise the following logic-based stream of analysis:

1. Exploring the problem situation in terms of its cultural and political characteristics,
2. Modeling the relevant purposive activities,
3. Establishing structured debates about the changes in terms of their feasibility and reliability to make a balance among conflicting interests, and
4. Taking action to improve the situation (Checkland, 2000; Checkland and Poulter, 2010; Wastell, 2010; Yolles, 2006).

Evidently, the logic-driven stream does interact with the cultural stream, with each one keeping the other informed. The choice of related human activity systems has been found to be determined by the people involved in the problem situation (Checkland and Scholes, 1990).

The Analysis (I) assumes that the problematic situation is making troubles by itself. In this respect, one must investigate three roles: (1) the client (the root cause of the study), (2) the one(s) who seek to address the problematic situation in question, and (3) the owner of the problem. The client plays a critical role by triggering the study (rather than directly being triggered by the management). This makes the researcher taking part as not only the client, but also the would-be problem solver, and the problem owner, at the very starting point of the process (the required authority for treating the organization as a case study must of course be obtained from the top management). Later on, the participating staff and the corporate management serve as the problem solver and owner, respectively, with the required interventions determined based on their understanding, intention, body of knowledge, and accurate data (Checkland and Scholes, 1990; Rittel and Webber, 1973; Sykes and Treleaven, 2009; Yolles, 2006; Xia, 2011).

The Analysis (II) deals with ever-changing interactions among the values, norms, and roles (Checkland and Scholes, 1990; Sankaran *et al.*, 2009). In this respect, a role may refer to a social position that makes a difference for those engaged with the problem situation (*e.g.* leader(s) of the organization). The norm here means the leader(s)'s expected behavior and is evaluated based on the values or say local standards. This, in turn, leads to beliefs regarding the humanly rights and wrongs for the leader(s), for example. Magala (2010) believed that even more benefits for understanding human values and identities can be collected by investigating failures, rather than success stories, as the failures provide more useful information and pragmatic alerts.

Finally, the Analysis (III) investigates such factors as politics and power in terms of demonstration, allocation, and/or distribution (Checkland and Scholes, 1990). Magala (2009) concluded that the topics considered under the Analysis (III) (*e.g.* power and its generation, evolution, and sense-making across organizational settings) have been more extensively explored and analyzed in informal contexts (*e.g.* gossip) rather than formal research reports. The literature on organizational science with a focus on the problem of power, power struggles, individuals' passions, and conflicting interests (*i.e.* attempts for power acquisition despite the

Figure 2. Cultural and logic-based analysis of SSM (Checkland and Scholes, 1990)

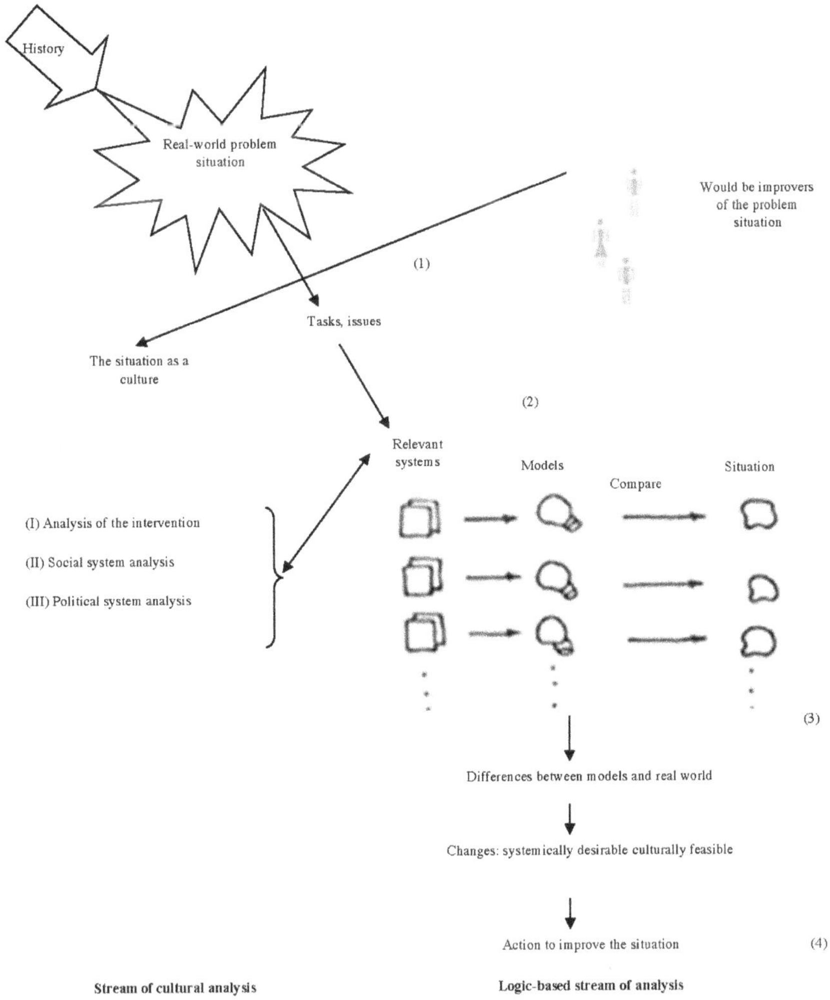

costs imposed to other members of the formal organization) is very much limited (Magala, 2009).

APPLICATION OF SSM IN CORPORATE ETHICAL CULTURE ANALYSIS

Scholars have referred to the corporate ethical culture (CEC) as an assemblage of the individual ethical values carried by directors as well as the formal and informal ethics-related policies adopted across the corporation. In fact, the CEC focuses on the leadership role of the directors in establishing the ethical culture across the corporation. Hunt *et al.* (1989) suggested that an organization is likely to be more successful if their top managers admit and implement ethical standards and norms, which are then extensively engaged by the members of the corporation. The CEC has been defined as an atmosphere in which the individuals have two main tasks: (1) to distinguish between right and wrong, and (2) to persuade ethical decisions in cases where all options are seemingly right. The CEC characterizes the profit-oriented companies wherein the staff are frequently working with internal/external stakeholders (Ardichvili *et al.*, 2009). The way the staff perceive the ethical and unethical dilemmas across the organization helps understand the mechanism through which they shape core values (*i.e.* corporate culture) for making ethical decisions.

Formulating the Problem (SSM: Steps 1 and 2)

The first step in this process is to identify the problem dimensions, structure, and main stakeholders. The ethical culture is a complex concept. First, both the ethics and the culture are multi-factorial in nature, meaning that no one factor alone (*e.g.* inheritance) may lead to the emergence of good ethics, but rather imposes various effects on different people. Put it differently, no single factor alone can determine the emergence of the ethical culture. It varies from one person to another based on many criteria including the inheritance, economic status, cultural maturity, social maturity, political maturity, and so on. In addition to the multi-factorial nature of the ethical culture, the emergence of this phenomenon is known to take more than ten years, *i.e.* there is a long gap between the time when one is exposed to relevant factors and the time when the resultant ethical culture implications are emerged, which makes the identification of the underlying factors and the traceability of one's exposure to relevant factors extremely uncertain and complicated. On the other hand, there are numerous stakeholders across an organization, each of whom can potentially contribute to the ethical culture significantly. Given the above, it can be argued that the ethical culture is inherently disordered. Characteristics of poorly structured problems about the ethical culture are summarized in Table 1.

Due to very high dynamic complexity (due to the multiplicity of and the interactions between the factors) and relatively high behavioral complexity (variations in desires, mental models and decision makers' values), this

Table 1. The poorly structured nature of the ethical culture, according to Dajkhosh (2018)

Problematic areas	Description
Multiple stakeholders	There are many stakeholders (*e.g.* banks, etc.) each with specific values, missions, and goals, with the goals conflicting with one another in some cases). The required data are spread across different information systems in different units and organizations.
Multifaceted nature	The ethical culture requires different subsystems, which are often sophisticated both technically and professionally, and given the real-world conditions, their implementation requires stable interactions between different sectors that may not be structurally related to each other.
Uncertainty	Different factors contribute to the ethical culture. There is a wide gap between the time when one is exposed to relevant factors and the time when the resultant implications emerge in the ethical culture.

situation is problematic and needs to be structured. To this end, one should draw a rich picture of the status-quo for the purpose of better describing the situation and presenting a framework of stakeholders agreement.

Drawing the Dimensions of the Problematic Situation

A rich picture of a system presents all the main actors and their relationships by means of graphical symbols and explanations. The rich picture of the ethical culture in the organization consists of two layers.

At the center of the rich picture (which represents the core of the organization) are the organizational hardware, human resources, organizational regulations and guidelines, and the board of directors. The second layer serves as a host for the environmental factors of the system including the customer, supply chain, environment, government, and financial institutions.

On this rich picture, there are various relationships, as detailed in Table 2.

Designing the Conceptual Model (SSM: Steps 4 and 5)

After defining the chaotic situation framework (status-quo) and once the stakeholders reached an agreement on the dimensions of the problem, one should draw on the desired status using the CATWOE analysis and the root definition, leading to the development of a conceptual model. The conceptual model presents a multi-layered or hierarchical system that includes the core system together with its subsystems. So, at the first level, as a way to improve

Table 2. Various relationships presented on the rich picture (Dajkhosh, 2018)

Type of relationship	Description
Horizontal communication	· Unhealthy competition for critical positions across the organization and job promotion has increased dramatically in the system. · There is no clear framework of expected behaviors for the staff. · There are conflicts between what is expected by managers and the board of directors (BOD), in one hand, and what is required by the human resource-related regulations. For example, the BOD is often seeking to cut costs by reducing the staff, while the body of management is looking to recruit and hence expand their organizational departments. · Lack of communication between departments. · Widespread unethical practices across the organization (*e.g.* non-productive use of organizational assets). · The organization provides solely negligible support for the personnel's ethical behavior. · The culture of discourse on organizational problems and deficiencies is by no means present, so that the slightest discussions are likely to cause discontent and conflict between departments.
Vertical communication	· Carrier promotions are based on relations rather than regulations. · Relationships between managers and personnel are disrupted.
Law enforcement	· Laws and regulations are frequently violated. · There are conflicts among different laws and regulations. · Some regulations and scientific procedures are missing. · The transparency of the rules has been dominated by the managers' tastes.
Two-sided unethical behavior between the system and the shareholders	· 80% of the submitted reports to the BOD are unrealistic and/or in one way or another concealing the reality. · The BOD members are members of multiple boards at the same time, keeping them from spending enough time to make appropriate macro decisions. · 80% of the declared dividend to shareholders is unrealistic. · Often, BOD members seek to impose particular staff or on the system or get the organization engaged with non-qualified contractors based on their personal relations rather than organizational procedures. · Most BOD members deal with minor financial problems of the system, neglecting the major issues that might play key roles in realizing the system's vision.
Destruction of environment	· Natural resources are used to produce non-renewable products.
Unethical relations with financial centers and banks	· Dissatisfaction with foreign exchange models (this model does not help support the national currency). · Reports submitted to financial centers are unrealistic and prepared solely for the purpose of receiving financial facilities. · Receiving financial facilities or financing from operating banks requires getting engaged with a bribery process in which many of the relevant authorities and stakeholders are involved.
Buyers	· The process of monitoring and controlling the quality of the products for export (especially to Europe) are stringent, but there is no such process for domestic destinations. · Most low-grade products are delivered to domestic customers. · Without some kind of lobby and direct contact with the business units at manufacturing companies, it is impossible to directly purchase from them. · Most customers have to purchase products through chains of dealers. · There is lack of trust in the market.
Supply chain	· Material prices are determined through lobbying. · High costs are incurred to the system due to reworks and lack of sensitivity to costs. · High-price consumables and accessories are purchased.
Government	· Unclear communication and control leverage between government and industry. · Tax evasion.

the turbulent state of the problem, the ethical culture model was designed and then the necessary subsystems were represented.

To define each of the elements P ("what" to do?), Q ("how" to do?), and R ("why" to do?), which are the elements of the root definition, as well as the elements C (customers), A (actors), T (transformation process), W (worldview), O (owner) and E (environmental constraints) of the CATWOE analysis, in-depth interviews were conducted with two groups of experts:

1. Academic experts who had a theoretical background in the ethical culture literature, and
2. Industry experts who had accurate information about the actual situation.

CATWOE Analysis

Transformation (T): After expressing the turbulent position of the problem in steps 1 and 2, it is necessary to take action to improve the status-quo. Since T represents the main process of the system that creates the desired (improved) condition of the system, and given that this element is used to define other elements of the CATWOE analysis, the start of this analysis with the element T was largely helpful for understanding and clarifying the root definition. In the literature on SSM, the element T has been acknowledged as the heart of the root definition, making it the starting point in most CATWOE analysis studies.

In other words, T is a process which receives, as input, the communication with the organization's stakeholders, ethical culture measurement documentation, and ethical culture evaluation, and then analyzes them based on the ethical knowledge to provide, as outputs, the stakeholders' rights, ethical culture risk assessment, ethical culture audit, and ethical culture factors prioritization.

Figure 3. Transformation in the root definition of ethical culture (Dajkhosh, 2018)

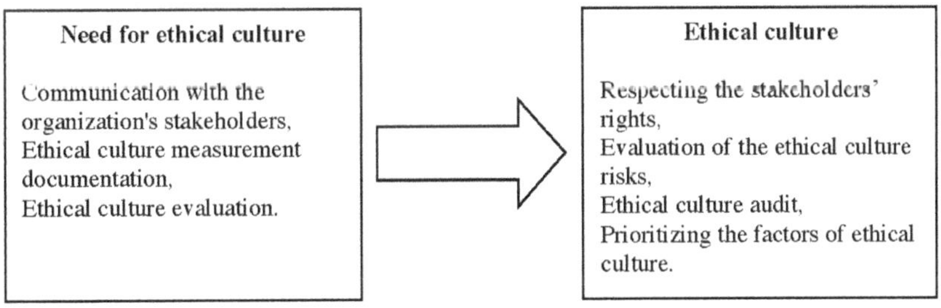

System Owner (O): Given the definition of T and the system structure, the owners of the ethical culture-based system include the client, semi-government investment companies, and private-sector investors. Due to lack of a structural link between these entities, ownership of the ethical culture-based system may become possible on the basis of a memorandum of understanding (MOU) among the entities mentioned above.

Worldview (W): W will be:

1. Importance of ethical culture: ultimate goal of the system is to develop an ethical culture across the system.
2. Potential of the existing system for reducing the system complexity: the presence of coded personnel and required job information, appropriate health insurance coverage, and the needed knowledge for the design and implementation of the system of ethical culture, facilitating the establishment of the ethical culture system, and reducing the complexities of the system.
3. Controlling high costs imposed to the existing system due to non-compliance with ethical culture by taking measures for prevention and early detection of such costs.

Customers (C): Application of the customer concept draws the analyst's attention to the positive aspects of T while ignoring its negative implications. However, considering the definition provided in the SSM, all stakeholders of the system should be taken into account. So, one should attempt to simultaneously address the negative and positive effects of T on customer definition. The customers include:

1. The official staff (both employed and retired).
2. The contract staff (based on temporary or fixed-term contracts).

Actors (A): The actors of the ethical culture system are employees.

Environment (E): Those that are outside the boundary of the system, including:

1. Transparent information on ethical issues in different subsystems requires organizational units to collaborate. Obviously, acknowledging the high sensitivity of this information, those should be in-house treated confidentially.
2. Common culture of society.

Root Definition

The root definition is the description of what the system does, how and why, known as the PQR formula: do P (what), by Q (how), in order to help achieve R (why). The components of this ethical culture system are rooted in:

1. **P:** Provide intervention strategies (including preventive and therapeutic interventions) for organizational culture.
2. **Q:** The key elements of ethical culture include communication with colleagues, boss-and-subordinate communication, customer relationship management, stakeholder communication, relationship with financial institutions and equity, relation with government, relation with the environment, and communication with the supply chain system.
3. **R:** Reduce the risk of unethical culture in the system.

So the root definition is:

"The ethical culture in a system provides the basis for the development and growth of ethics, and analyzes the ethics to develop interventions (preventive interventions and early detection provisions) for protecting the rights of all system stakeholders to reduce the risk of unethical behaviors."

Conceptual Model of Ethical Culture

CATWOE analysis provides for defining the T and other elements, while the root definition formulates interventions to improve the situation. The first step toward implementing the T and the root definition is to formulate the required activities for achieving the objective. These are logical steps that must be taken to realize what has been defined in the root definition.

Effective training of ethics has been identified as one of the most important components of the ethical culture system, according to experts' viewpoints.

Actions to Improve the Issue (steps 5 to 7 of SSM)

After identifying the activities needed to improve the system in terms of the conceptual model of the system and its subsystems, SSM, in the fifth step, compares the desirable situation (conceptual model) with the real-world conditions and proposes the necessary changes to achieve the conceptual

Figure 4. Conceptual model of corporate ethical culture (Dajkhosh, 2018)

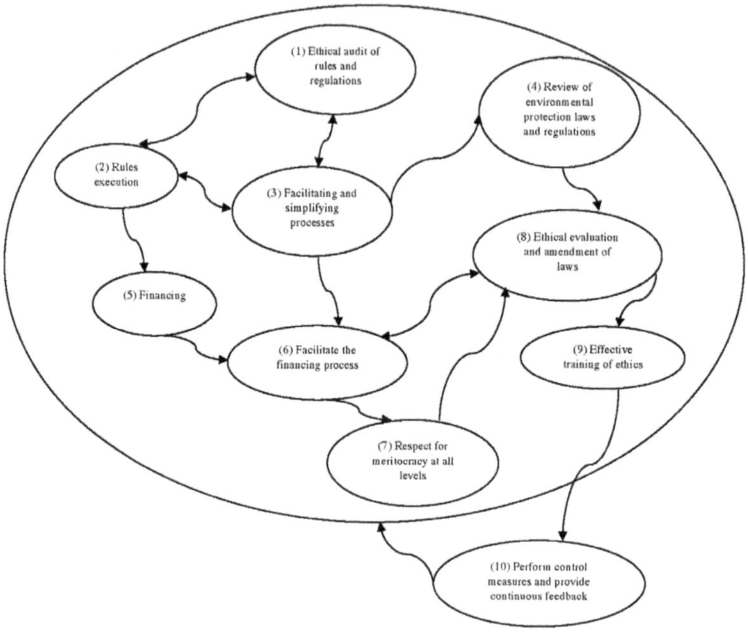

Figure 5. Conceptual model (L2) of effective training of ethics (Dajkhosh, 2018)

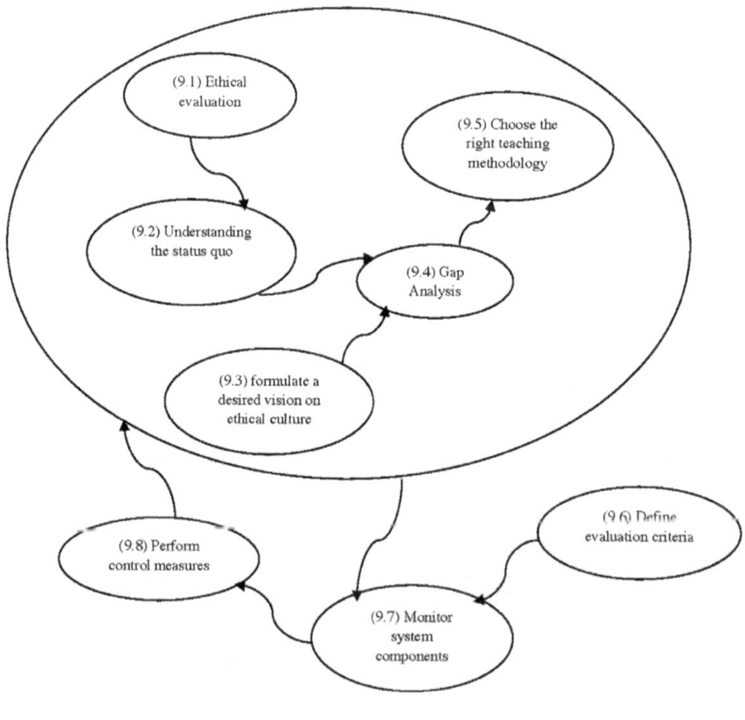

model. Then, in the sixth stage, from the pool of measures designed to make the changes, possible and desirable changes are selected. In the last step, the selected changes are implemented while monitoring the change process. In this regard, workshops on each of the subsystems were held for the owners, key players, and industry and academic experts. In these sessions, the conceptual model was confirmed (in some cases, the model was validated after minor modifications) and compared with real-world conditions to identify the necessary changes.

CONCLUSION

Culture analysis is a complicated task because of the large number of stakeholders encountered in an organization, each with specific values, missions, and goals, which are conflicting with one another in some cases. The culture is a multi-factorial concept with a long gap between the time when one is exposed to relevant factors and the time when the outputs are visible in the form of a culture. The fact that different organizations come with a number of subcultures adds to the complexity of analyzing the corporate culture. The soft systems methodology (SSM) is known to be intimately connected with various aspects of corporate culture. SSM should be a habit or norm for each and any member of the organization before the organization can be sustained upon changes to new cultures, structures, rules, procedures, political relations, controls, etc., thereby maximizing the organizational efficiency.

This chapter considered an essential resource to any organization, namely the organizational culture, placing a particular emphasis on the change management. Thus, after reviewing the concept of organizational culture and the factors affecting that and presenting a conceptual model of the organizational culture, cultural aspects of SSM and its application were investigated on a case study of corporate ethical culture analysis.

REFERENCES

Ardichvili, A., Mitchell, J. M., & Jondle, D. (2009). Characteristics of ethical business cultures. *Journal of Business Ethics*, *85*(4), 445–451. doi:10.100710551-008-9782-4

Bradford, L., & Harvey, J. (1972). Dealing with dysfunctional organizational myths. In W. W. Burke & H. A. Hornstein (Eds.), *The social technology of Organization development*. La Jolla, CA: University Associates.

Checkland, P. (2000). Soft systems methodology: A thirty year retrospective. *Systems Research and Behavioral Science*, *17*(1), 11–58. doi:10.1002/1099-1743(200011)17:1+<::AID-SRES374>3.0.CO;2-O

Checkland, P., & Poulter, J. (2010). Soft systems methodology. In M. Reynolds & S. Holwell (Eds.), *Systems approaches to managing change: A practical guide* (pp. 191–242). New York, NY: Springer. doi:10.1007/978-1-84882-809-4_5

Checkland, P., & Scholes, J. (1990). *Soft systems methodology in action*. Chichester, UK: Wiley.

Checkland, P. B. (1981). *Systems thinking, systems practice*. Chichester: Wiley.

Checkland, P. B. (1985). Achieving 'desirable and feasible' change: An application of Soft Systems Methodology. *The Journal of the Operational Research Society*, *36*(9), 821–831.

Cummings, T. G., & Worley, C. G. (2005). *Organization development and change* (8th ed.). Cincinnati, OH: South-Western College Publishing.

Dajkhosh, S. S. (2018). *Design a model of ethical culture* (PhD dissertation). Tarbiat Modares University, Tehran, Iran.

Dauber, D., Fink, G., & Yolles, M. (2012). A configuration model of organizational culture. *SAGE Open*, 1–16. doi:10.1177/2158244012441482

Davies, L., & Ledington, P. (1991). *Information in action: Soft Systems Methodology*. Houndmills: MacMillan.

Dávila, A., & Martínez, N. H. (1999). *Cultura en organizaciones latinas: elementos, ingerencia y evidencia en los procesos organizacionales*. Siglo XXI.

Edwards, E. (1988). Corporate culture. *Management Accounting*, *66*(5), 18–20.

Frank, E. (1987). Organizational culture: Some implications for managers and trainers. *Journal of European Industrial Training*, *11*(7), 29-3 2.

Gharajedaghi, J. (2007). Systems thinking: A case for second-order-learning. *The Learning Organization*, *14*(6), 473–479. doi:10.1108/09696470710825088

Gitlow, A. L. (1992). The chief executive and corporate culture. *National Productivity Review*, *11*(4), 479–490. doi:10.1002/npr.4040110406

Goksoy, A. (2017). *Organizational change management strategies in modern business*. IGI Global.

Hunt, S. D., Wood, V. R., & Chonko, L. B. (1989). Corporate ethical values and organizational commitment in marketing. *Journal of Marketing*, *53*(3), 79–90. doi:10.1177/002224298905300309

Jerome-Forget, M. (1992). Changing the corporate culture. *Business Quarterly*, *56*(3), 107–111.

Johnson, G. (1992). Managing strategic change - Strategy, culture and action. *Long Range Planning*, *25*(1), 28–36. doi:10.1016/0024-6301(92)90307-N PMID:10118379

Kartowisastro, H., & Kijima, K. (1994). An enriched soft systems methodology (SSM) and its application to cultural conflict under a paternalistic value system. *Systems Practice*, *7*(3), 241–253. doi:10.1007/BF02169173

Kelley, M. R. (1986). Programmable automation and the skill question: A reinterpretation of the cross-national evidence. *Human Systems Management*, *6*(3), 223-241.

Krawczyk, J. P. (1992). How video helped change a corporate culture. *Communication World*, *9*(11), 14–16.

LaMontagne, R. M. (2012). *Facing ethical dilemmas in the workplace: A qualitative study of HR managers' perceptions of the influences on their behavior and the implications for building an ethical culture in organizations*. PhD Dissertation.

López Garza, M. P., & Fernánde, A. D. (2003). Application of a systems methodology in the diagnosis of the organizational culture in a telecommunications company. *International Journal of Computers. Systems and Signals*, *4*(1), 22–32.

Magala, S. (2009). *The management of meaning in organizations*. Basingstoke, UK: Palgrave Macmillan. doi:10.1057/9780230236691

Magala, S. J. (2010). Perplexing images: Relational identities in cultural tempospaces. In S. Lowe (Ed.), *Managing in changing times: A guide for the perplexed manager* (pp. 241–259). Thousand Oaks, CA: SAGE. doi:10.4135/9788132108016.n7

Mingers, J. (1992). SSM and information systems: An overview. *Systemist, 14*(3), 82–88.

Morgan, G. (1986). *Images of organization*. Beverly Hills: Sage.

Ouch, W., & Price, R. (1978). Hierarchies, clans and theory Z: A new perspective on organization development. *Organizational Dynamics, 7*(2), 25–44. doi:10.1016/0090-2616(78)90036-0

Pattison, E. M. (1995). The contribution of soft systems methodology to the achievement of change in organizational culture (PhD thesis). Industrial & Business Studies, University of Warwick.

Pettigrew, A., Ferlie, E., & McKee, L. (1992). *Shaping strategic change*. London: Sage.

Reichers, A., & Schneider, B. (1969). Climate and culture: An evolution of constructs. In B. Schneider (Ed.), *organizational climate and culture*. San Francisco: Jossey-Bass.

Reynolds, P. D. (1986). Organizational culture as related to industry, position and performance: A preliminary report. *Journal of Management Studies, 23*(3), 333–345. doi:10.1111/j.1467-6486.1986.tb00958.x

Rittel, H. W. J., & Webber, M. M. (1973). Dilemmas in a general theory of planning. *Policy Sciences, 4*(2), 155–169. doi:10.1007/BF01405730

Sankaran, S., Tay, B. H., & Orr, M. (2009). Managing organizational change by using soft systems thinking in action research projects. *International Journal of Managing Projects in Business, 2*(2), 179–197. doi:10.1108/17538370910949257

Schein, E. (1983). The role of the founder in creating organizational culture. *Organizational Dynamics, 12*(1), 13–28. doi:10.1016/0090-2616(83)90023-2

Schwartz, H., & Davis, S. (1981). Matching corporate culture and business strategy. *Organizational Dynamics, 10*(1), 30–48. doi:10.1016/0090-2616(81)90010-3

Smirch, L. (1963). Concepts of culture and organizational analysis. *Administrative Science Quarterly, 28*(3), 339–398. doi:10.2307/2392246

Staadt, J. (2015). The cultural analysis of soft systems methodology and the configuration model of organizational culture. *SAGE Open, 5*(2), 1–10. doi:10.1177/2158244015589787

Sykes, C., & Treleaven, L. (2009). Critical action research and organizational ethnography. In S. Ybema, D. Yanow, H. Wels, & F. Kamsteeg (Eds.), *Organizational ethnography: Studying the complexities of everyday life* (pp. 215–230). London, UK: SAGE. doi:10.4135/9781446278925.n12

Van de Ven, A. H. (1983). *Creating and sustaining a corporate culture in fast changing organizations.* Paper presented at the Executive Seminar on Corporate Excellence, Santa Clara, CA.

Waisham, G. (1991). Organizational metaphors and information systems research. *European Journal of Information Systems*, *1*(2), 83–94. doi:10.1057/ejis.1991.16

Wastell, D. (2010). Managing as designing: "Opportunity knocks" for the IS field. *European Journal of Information Systems*, *19*(4), 422–431. doi:10.1057/ejis.2010.31

Wilhelm, W. (1992). Changing corporate culture - Or corporate behavior? How to change your company. *The Academy of Management Executive*, *6*(4), 72–77.

Wilkins, A. L., & Ouchi, W. G. (1983). Efficient cultures: Exploring the relationship between culture and organizational performance. *Administrative Science Quarterly*, *28*(3), 468–481. doi:10.2307/2392253

Xia, J. (2011). An anthropological emic-etic perspective on open access practices. *The Journal of Documentation*, *67*(1), 75–94. doi:10.1108/00220411111105461

Yolles, M. (2006). *Organizations as complex systems: An introduction to knowledge cybernetics*. Greenwich, CT: Information Age.

Yolles, M., & Guo, K. (2003). Paradigmatic metamorphosis and organizational development. *Systems Research and Behavioral Science*, *20*(2), 177–199. doi:10.1002res.533

Zanimuto, R. F., & Krakower, J. Y. (1991). Quantitative and qualitative studies or organizational culture. *Research in Organizational Change and Development*, *5*, 83–114.

Chapter 5
Multi-Methodology Approach:
Using Soft Systems Methodology and Simulation Modeling

ABSTRACT

The pluralistic approach in today's world needs combining multiple methods, whether hard or soft, into a multi-methodology intervention. The methodologies can be combined, sometimes from several different paradigms, including hard and soft, in the form of a multi-methodology so that the hard paradigms are positivistic and see the organizational environment as objective, while the nature of soft paradigms is interpretive. In this chapter, the combination of methodologies has been examined using soft systems methodologies (SSM) and simulation methodologies including discrete event simulation (DES), system dynamics (SD), and agent-based modeling (ABM). Also, using the ontological, epistemological, and methodological assumptions underlying the respective paradigms, the difference between SD, ABM, SSM; a synthesis of SSM and SD generally known as soft system dynamics methodology (SSDM); and a promising integration of SSM and ABM referred to as soft systems agent-based methodology (SSABM) have been proven.

INTRODUCTION

Multi-methodology can be considered as a challenging area of research because it combines methodologies from different paradigms which are disproportionate for some researchers (Holm et al., 2013). Mingers and Gill (1997) define multi-

DOI: 10.4018/978-1-7998-4504-1.ch005

methodology as the general or partial combination of more than one methodology, often belonging to different paradigms. It can also be considered a kind of mixed-methods research (Niglas, 2004), which is a more accurate word to refer to it.

In their research, Mingers and Gilles (1997) outlined five of the different approaches to combining methodologies. The first approach is whether more than one methodology should be used at all. The second approach determines whether the combined methodologies should be of different paradigms. The third approach determines whether these methods are used in a single intervention, and the fourth and fifth approach determines whether all or part of the methodology is used and whether a single methodology provides overall control, respectively. Mingers and Gill (1997) also give different names to different types of methodological combinations. If methodologies from different paradigms are used in an intervention while one methodology does not have full control but the two approaches are intertwined to form a single situation-specific methodology, this is called the multi-paradigm multi-methodology approach.

According to Behl and Ferreira (2014), engineers need holistic approaches to deal with today's workplace with complex challenges. Using holistic system perspectives, systems thinking provides ways to think about a problem and its solutions. Kotiadis (2007) believes that because of answering the questions such as what, why and how about modeling the system in question at this stage of problem structuring, conceptual modeling is a critical part of the simulation methodology.

The present chapter examines the methodologies combination using soft systems methodology (SSM) and simulation methodologies including discrete event simulation (DES), system dynamics (SD), and agent-based modeling (ABM). To this end, a multi-methodology is developed combining the SSM and DES, developed by Holm et al. (2013), soft system dynamics methodology (SSDM) as a synthesis of SSM and SD presented by Rodriguez-Ulloa and Paucar-Caceres (2005), and soft systems agent based methodology (SSABM) as a combination of SSM and ABM introduced by Novani and Mayangsari (2015). Using the ontological, epistemological and methodological assumptions underlying the respective paradigms, this chapter demonstrates the difference between SD, ABM, SSM, SSDM, and SSABM.

DISCRETE EVENT SIMULATION (DES)

Due to the dynamic, stochastic, discrete nature, DES simulation model accounts for randomness and time, as a discrete variable, has points where the system changes are displayed. DES models, which provide a more accurate representation of a system than other simulation techniques, are commonly used to analyze systems at the strategic level and are suitable for "what" scenarios in analysis to improve system capacity, using resources or queuing time.

Entities, events, activities, and attributes are key aspects of DES modeling that respectively represent objects flowing in the system, indigenous and exogenous events of the system responsible for changing the system that trigger the onset of activity, and attributes attributed to the entity. Event calendar contains status information of all entities and event-related information is another key concept of DES modeling. Also, tracking the simulation time and progress in discrete time steps of the next event in the calendar is done by the simulation clock as another component; when there are not enough resources in the model to process the activity, the entity queue emerges. Random draws of activities from a separate probability distribution is performed using a random generator that is responsible for the randomness of the model (Banks et al., 2010).

SSM AND DES

In complex numerical problems that are difficult to solve using analytical or numerical methods, DES is an efficient approach to model a system in the form of sets of mathematical equations and logical relations. However, because it does not provide any method for identifying system boundaries and system activities, simulation is not in itself a systematic approach. The present study uses SSM as an auxiliary tool for drawing system boundaries and identifying system activities (Lehaney and Paul, 1996).

A multi-methodology by combining SSM and DES is developed and tested in Holm et al. (2013) research at a Norwegian Hospital. In this study, basing DES-model on their narratives, the multi- methodology supported the project with the staff in its initial phases which also represents critical real-world mechanisms in the DES modeling. The DES-model was also used in other SSM steps to detect possible improvement areas.

Many articles have confirmed the usefulness of SSM in the study of simulation, and therefore, SSM is considered to be the most well-known problem structuring approach in DES. For example, to define the problematic situation in the form of precise questions and objectives, an SSM approach is used in Kotiadis (2006, 2007) and then, a simulation model is used to explore them. The advantages and constraints of combining SSM with DES within community-based intermediate care is investigated in the Kotiadis and Mingers (2006) case study research. In this study, they built models to answer questions that were more important to the stakeholders by adding the SSM process findings into the simulation models.

A theoretical discussion including SSM in simulation and discussion on the methodology's knowledge acquisition capabilities was presented in Montevechi and Friend (2012). Proposing a step-by-step SSM-Conceptual Modeling approach is the contribution of their study to simulation literature. SSM was also used by Lehaney and Paul (1994) to develop the simulation of out-patient services at Watford General Hospital. Because the simulation itself provides no methods in this regard, the methodology has been used by the authors to help identify relevant system activities. A review of using simulation models is conducted by Lehaney and Hlupic (1995) for resource planning in the health-care sector. In their research, they found that SSM could be used to improve these processes. Also, a discussion of the advantage of combining simulation and SSM through a mixed mode modeling approach is performed by Lehaney and Clarke (1997). A case intervention was also reported in an outpatient NHS dermatology clinic by Lehaney et al. (1999) in which, a soft systems approach combined with simulation was used to address the gaps between the customers' and service providers' expectations.

Figure 1. Multi- methodology SSM-DES (adapted from Holm, 2013)

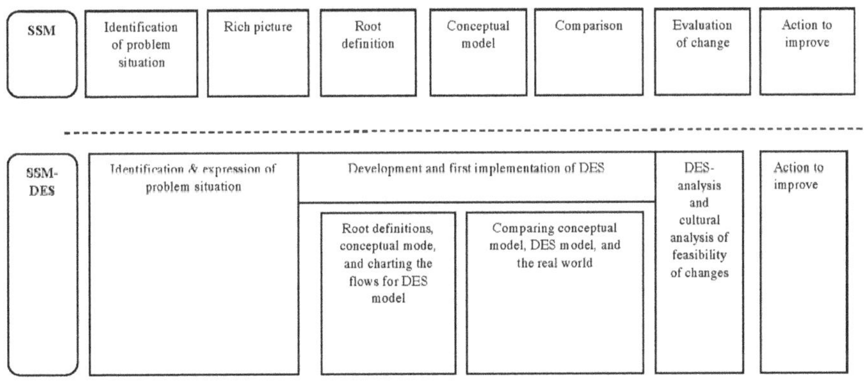

Lamé et al. (2018) used DES combined with SSM to support improved patient flow in an outpatient chemotherapy unit and a chemotherapy preparation pharmacy unit. Holm and Bjornenak (2017) applied SSM and DES in combination at the surgical unit at Radiumhospitalet in Norway to analyze the impact of different interventions on patient flow and resource utilization.

A Conceptual Combination of SSM and DES

The standard SSM approach, which is done in the first step of multi-methodology, involves identifying and expressing the problem situation. In the second phase, the root definitions and conceptual models as well as the flow draft for the simulation model is developed. The development and implementation of the DES model in the computer program, and drawing of existing information from step two is performed in step three. According to Figure 1, the design and development of the DES model is a continuous process throughout the stages 1 to 5. However, because the DES has not interacted with the SSM process prior to this third phase and it has been presented only abstractly, it can be as an independent phase as well. An initial implementation is performed in a programming tool during the third phase which is used in the later phases. The comparison between conceptual world and the real world is performed in the fourth phase of the multi-methodology. Finally, feasible and desirable improvements and possible actions to improve the situation are identified and discussed in phases five and six.

SYSTEM DYNAMICS (SD)

Basing on the theory of information feedback and control, SD is considered as a representation of hard systems thinking that is a relevant functional-structural systemic approach to complex-unitary problem situations. The structure and the dynamics of complex systems should be identified in order to understand the implications of feedback. It is not the interaction between system components, but the complexity of the components that determine the complex behavior of the systems. The fundamental assumption of SD is that the behavior of the system is influenced by its structure.

Levels and rates are the basic elements of the dynamic model which is critically importance for understanding SD. According to Forrester (1972), the present values of those variables resulted from accumulated difference between inflows and outflows constitute levels. On the contrary, rates are the present flows between the system levels. The system of equations (levels and rates equations) that control variable interactions of the given problem situation that change over time constitute the mathematical expression of the SD model.

Although different classifications of certain phases are provided, SD modeling process generally includes the following activities (Jackson, 2003): the phase of conceptualization to specify the problem and identify the variables affecting it. In the next phase, the feedback loop model is developed to show relations among variables, that is defining a certain feedback structure. Causal loop diagrams and stock/flow diagrams are the most commonly used diagrams applied to represent feedback structures. In the formulation phase, this model further develops into an appropriate mathematical model, i.e. develop into level and rate equations. Using the certain software, those equations provide relevant computer simulation of system behavior. At the test stage, the validity of the model is estimated, and at the implementation stage, possible ways to improve the results for the system performance, namely the design of the specific policy, are identified.

Using process-based models of feedback, SD attempts to objectively study social systems outside the system and counter the complexity of social reality, which is contrary to the function of the SSM. In this respect, SD simplifies some of the facts, because charts do not represent the cultural, ethical, and political factors and this lead to impede the rational decision-making that SD recommends (Jackson, 2003).

In the combined use of SSM and SD, there are some limitations associated with the process of problem definition and the underlying socio-political theory of intervention in SD. Defining the particular problem or issue to be considered is the first step in the SD modeling process. In this model, only the variables needed to study the aspects of interest are examined (to ensure that the models are of controllable size) (Lane and Oliva, 1998). Based on what has been said, it can be found that SSM can be useful in improving the first stage of the SD method, namely problem definition; because SSM essentially studies problem situations and does not focus solely on a particular problem (Rodriguez-Ulloa and Paucar-Caceres, 2005).

Thus, as an ontological description of the problem and objective representations of the pre-existing real world, models can be considered context-independent and viewed by a completely independent researcher. As such, models are the realistic and reductionist representation. Epistemological knowledge, generated through representation by modeling, can be used to form dynamic hypotheses about how the creation of a reference state (the situation under study) causes the observed behavior. In order to optimize the system under investigation, SD can be used as a quantitative method with observation, measurement and judgment of an analyst (Mingers, 2003) that according to Lane (1999), a realist, functionalistic, determinist and hard systems methodology match to the area of functionalist sociology should be used in this regard.

To enable the mathematical description of processes, human activities have been simplified to model systems using SD and other rigid approaches.

SD AND SSM

Different methodologies can be used to combine system methodology, including SSM and SD, soft system dynamics methodology (SSDM), and parts of them, including SSM and SD. In order to combine SSM and SD, the specific limitations of SSM and SD as well as their theoretical foundations must be identified. Also, systematically desirable and culturally feasible changes are an important measure of the dynamic cohesion identified by SSM.

The combination procedure, introduced by Lane and Oliva (1998) has the following characteristics: Firstly, a group of participants use SSM by explicitly generation of multiple worldviews (Weltanschauung) and analysis of norms, values, opinions of relevant stakeholders regarding the change that can be systemically desirable and culturally feasible (cultural analysis). Group members consider dynamic coherence desirable and important, while testing the dynamic coherence implies SD tools. By observing the changes identified as causal structures, which may reflect the impact of the proposed changes, the research continues. By this, the causal structure presented by diagrams and intuitive behavior of specified variables is represented. In order to produce the behavior representing logical conclusions on causal structure and effects caused by proposed changes, appropriate simulation is conducted and the behavior is then compared to intuitive behavior. Since team's intuition regarding the behavior of the whole that resulted in changes implementation is consistent with behavior resulting from causal structure, the iterative process of team learning results in identifying the final list of changes that are also dynamically coherent.

SSDM, contrary to synthesis, is a toolkit of 10 iterative stages so that stages 1, 2 and 3 are related to the problem-oriented systems thinking world, while stages 6, 7 and 8 are associated with the solving-oriented systems thinking world. According to Rodriguez-Ulloa and Paucar-Caceres (2005), SSDM is consisted of the following 10 stages: 1) unstructured problem situation; 2) structured problem situation; 3) problem-oriented root definitions; 4) building problem-oriented SD models; 5) comparison stage – comparing the stages 4 and/or 7 to the stage 2 (comparing problem-oriented SD models/ solving-oriented SD models to the rich picture); 6) determining culturally feasible and systemically desirable changes; 7) building a solving-oriented SD models of a problem situation; 9) implementation of culturally feasible and systemically desirable changes in real world; 10) producing lessons learned. Accordingly, it can be inferred that stages 1, 2, 3, 5, 6 and 8 are originated from SSM, while stages 4, 7 and 10 are related to SD. In order to show the usefulness of this approach in solving complex social problems, it is applied to case studies (Rodriguez-Ulloa and Paucar-Caceres, 2005).

Specified tools, i.e. methods and techniques of SSM, such as rich pictures, root definitions and conceptual models are used in the approach of use the parts of SSM and SD to examine different perceptions and perspectives of problem situation and also to identify and represent possible improvement solutions, i.e. to make the problem situation meaningful. By comparing to real world, it is possible to identify systemically desirable and culturally feasible changes. However, causal loop diagrams and/or stock/flow diagrams are used to specify interconnections and dynamic coherence of changes due to the fact that these changes should also be dynamically coherent; that is the effects of identified changes should be predicted. The diagramming presentation of identified changes aimed to communicate the key features of a SD model to describe the origin of different behavior of the models and the reason of effectiveness of certain policy levers (Lane, 2008). As representing causal assumptions through equations and also complex software's simulation of behavior are possible and understandable only for some, i.e. for experts, this provides greater users' access and understanding. In a case study referring to the combined use of SSM and SD in total quality management, this approach of combining SSM and SD is shown (Bennet and Kerr, 1996). In 2016, Ebrahimi applied these two systems approaches in a practical case; she used SSM in order to capture the essence of the problems in a research and development (R&D) company and SD for the policy making.

As a result, given the combined approaches of SSM and SD, the use of SSM and SD in combination allows for systematically desirable, culturally feasible, and dynamically coherent optimal changes that improve the specific situation of the problem, resulting in the elimination of some of the SD constraints on the conceptualization and identification stage of the problem are addressed. Also, SSM constraints are the subsequent effects of the proposed changes, meaning that future system behavior can be eliminated. In general, it is possible to have a comprehensive understanding of the specific problem situation using methodologies from different paradigms, as it leads to a different perception or insight of reality that makes it more complex than the various theoretical approaches.

Of course, there are some specific restrictions on the separate use of SSM and SD which is also true in their combined use. For example, in dealing with problem situations that use unequal distribution of power and information, the combined use of specific interpretive tools (SSMs) and structuralist functional systems (SDs) cannot be useful. In fact, it is necessary to use some of the tools of appropriate emancipatory systems approaches, namely critical systems heuristics, because the combined use of SSM and SD cannot help in coercive problem situations management.

Also, like any combination of different paradigms, the combined use of SSM and SD can lead to issues such as challenges, paradigm incompatibility, cultural, cognitive, and practical problems (Kotiadis and Mingers, 2006). Looking at one thing in one direction, but from a different paradigm perspective, leads to a different understanding among scientists. Organizational and academic culture is a cultural problem of combining systematic approaches. Problems in changing the paradigms and personality of the system methodology user are among cognitive problems. Longer time, inexperience in using multiple methodologies, inherent conservatism, pressure to not take risks by the organization/ client, etc. are also practical problems (Kotiadis & Mingers, 2006).

Rodriguez-Ulloa et al. (2011) introduced the problem of citizen insecurity in Argentina, particularly in the province of Mendoza, in which SSDM has been used to analyze the issue. Shahabi et al. (2019) in the analysis of formal science and technology collaborative networks used SSM to obtain a rich picture of the situation and SD to propose a dynamic model. Rodriguez-Ulloa (2018) applied SSM for the processes' modelling of the value chains in the energy and mining sectors, and SD for the explanation of the risks causalities in perilous events in the processes.

It should be noted that 10 stages of SSDM operates across the three worlds namely (1) the real world, (2) the Problem-Situation Oriented System Thinking World, and (3) the Solving-Situation Oriented System Thinking World.

The dialectical view of the real-world situation provided by SSDM becomes clear when applied to real-world intervention. Therefore, the SSDM is used

Figure 2. Soft System Dynamics Methodology (SSDM): A General View (adapted from Rodriguez-Ulloa and Paucar-Caceres, 2005)

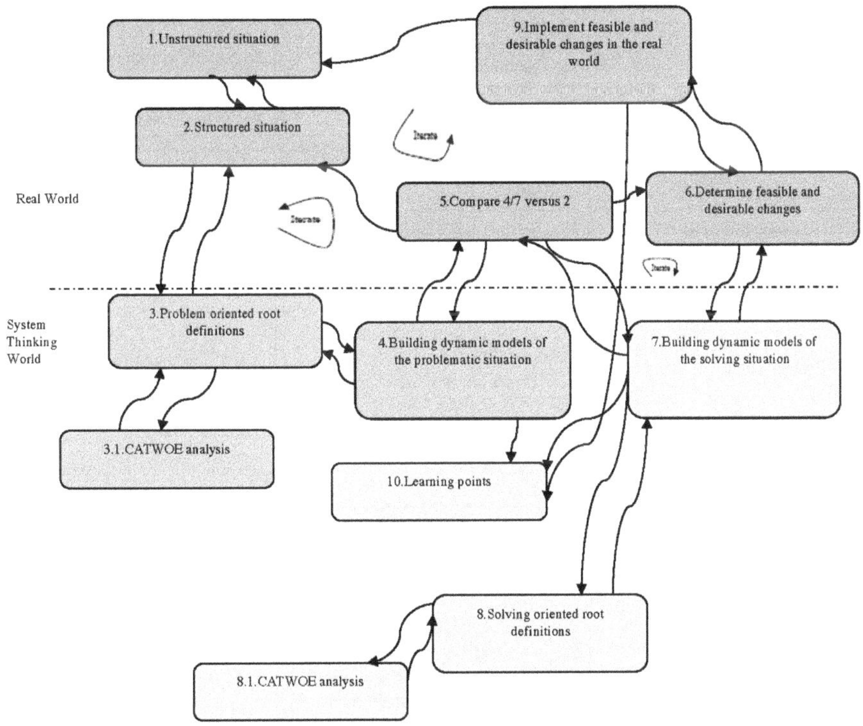

to appreciate the problem situation and understand its behavior in a holistic manner (called here World 2) when intervening the real world (World 1) in the first approach. On the other side (dialectical), systemic thinking of ways to 'solve', 'finish' or 'alleviate' the problem situation are studied and proposed in the Solving-Situation System Thinking World (called here World 3) after understanding the problem situation behavior.

REAL WORLD

Stage 1 (Un-Structured Problem Situation) and Stage 2 (Structured Situation)

As the first two SSM stages namely 1) (Looking at the Unstructured Problem – Situation); and 2) (Structured Problem – Situation or 'Rich Picture')

Table 1. Comparing SD, SSM and SSDM methods (Hawari, 2018)

<table>
<tr><th>System Dynamics (SD)</th><th>Soft System Dynamics Methodology (SSDM)</th><th>Soft Systems Methodology (SSM)</th></tr>
<tr><td rowspan="3">Stage 1: Problem Statement</td><td>Stage 1: The problem situation is unstructured.</td><td>Stage 1: Situation is unstructured.</td></tr>
<tr><td>Stage 2: The Structured Problematic Situation (Rich Picture)</td><td>Stage 2: The situation is structured.</td></tr>
<tr><td>Stage 3: Problem-Oriented Root Definitions</td><td>Stage 3: Root Definitions and CATWOE Analysis</td></tr>
<tr><td>Stage 2: Formulation of the Dynamic Hypothesis</td><td rowspan="2">Stage 4: Building SD Model of the "Problematic Situation"</td><td rowspan="2">Stage 4: Conceptual Models</td></tr>
<tr><td>Stage 3: Formal Simulation Model</td></tr>
<tr><td>Step 4: Testing Model</td><td>Stage 5: Validating Problem-Oriented Causal-Loop Diagram (CLD) and Stock-Flow Diagram (SFD) versus Real World</td><td>Stage 5: Comparing the Stage 4 and 2</td></tr>
<tr><td rowspan="5">Stage 5: Designing and Evaluating Policy</td><td>Stage 6: Creating Changes that are Systemically Desirable and Culturally Feasible</td><td rowspan="3">Stage 6: Culturally Feasible and Systematically Desirable Changes</td></tr>
<tr><td>Stage 7: Building SD Model of the "Solving Situation"</td></tr>
<tr><td>Stage 8: Solving-Oriented Consensual Root Definition</td></tr>
<tr><td>Stage 9: Implementation of Culturally Feasible and Systemically Desirable Changes in the Real World</td><td rowspan="2">Stage 7: Implementing Changes in the Real World</td></tr>
<tr><td>Stage 10: Lesson Learned</td></tr>
</table>

are considered as powerful steps to help understand and comprehend the phenomena and events occurring in a System of Reference, so they are used as Stages 1 and 2 of SSDM. A System of Reference is as a part of real world, defined and specified by the analyst for the systemic study purposes, where something is not working 'well' and something needs to be done to 'improve' the problem situation.

The problematic situation must be considered in an open manner and the situation should not be seen as a system itself (not to see the real-world as systems yet!) in order to study the problem situation in a holistic manner according to SSM; it is important to use a rich picture as an epistemological device to capture the real situation. Then, more or less similar to the method of establishing in the SSM seven-step mode of application, these two stages were incorporated as part of SSDM.

Any systemic study by constructing a 'systemic structure' known as the Context Diagram, including 'nouns' (i.e. an ontological way of describing the real world) which represent the 'sectors' of the system is the starting point of SD approach. As a basis for demonstrating and understanding the structure and behavior patterns of the problem-situation they face in the real world, these parts are linked together. The traditional system dynamics practitioner (analyst) uses this established structure as a specific way of interpreting what is happening in the real world. This is regardless of the various important aspects and events that are part of the real world (i.e. problem owners, customers, actors, world views, the level and type of power and the degree of influence on the situation, their relationships), the type of these relationships, etc.), that are exactly the factors that makes the situation problematic, messy and difficult to understand when someone tries to learn lessons for improvement.

Recently, many efforts have been made in the SD community to inform professionals of the benefits of group modeling and ways of incorporating different stakeholders using the SD approach and shifting the paradigmatic practitioner's view to the so called the learning paradigm.

In total, since it is felt that the early stages of SSM are based on the concepts and tools previously mentioned, and this allows you to consider all these aspects as part of SSDM, Stage 1 (Looking at the Unstructured Problem – Situation), and Stage 2) (Structured Problem – Situation or 'Rich Picture') of SSM are preferred to the first stages of SD.

FIRST SSDM SYSTEMIC LOOP: PROBLEM-SITUATION SYSTEMS THINKING WORLD

Stage 3: Problem-Oriented Root Definitions

Due to the importance for describing transformation processes and situational changes that are explicitly made in the real- world, Stage 3 of SSDM (root definitions) has also been adopted from SSM. Root definitions usually describe human activity systems that perform transformation processes oriented to 'improve' the problem situation in the real-world in most cases of using SSM.

The problematic transformation processes, that it is assumed to occur in the real-world, is described at this stage of SSDM which are 'problem oriented' transformation processes occurring in the real world and expressed in the 'rich picture' (Stage 2). Here root definitions are used for a different purpose namely to express ‘problematic’ transformation processes instead of expressing transformation processes oriented to provide ‘solutions’, ‘alleviations’ or ‘improvements’ to the problematic-situation encountered, as it is usually used in SSM. Furthermore, it is necessary for the analyst to know that in order to understand problematic-situation, so that the number of ‘problematic oriented’ root definitions can be abundant, there would be as many descriptions of ‘problematic situation’ transformation processes as problematic worldviews (i.e. Weltanschauungen).

Stage 4: Building System Dynamics Models of the "Problematic Situation"

At the end of step 3, the modeling process begins with any radical definition of “problematic status”. This modeling process begins with the usual terms in SD that express the phenomena that occur in the real world: through causal loops. Then, first of all, a problematic context diagram of the situation is built up at a first resolution level of complexity at the stage 4 of SSDM. Based on a particular weltanschauung (W) that the observer has emphasized in a particular problematic root definition at Stage 3, this context diagram is developed. In case of changing the W under which the real-world is observed by observer, the root definition will be changed that affects the structure of the problematic SD context diagram as well. Conversely, if the structure of the problem diagram changes, some adjustments and changes in the definition of the problematic root are necessary to establish a reciprocal correspondence between them. Observing the problematic situation to from a different W may be justifiable in other occasions which will cause a complete redefinition of the initial root definition, affecting the structure of the original problematic SD context diagram.

Problematic SD context diagrams after creation can be used as a basis for generating causal loop diagrams at the second resolution level of complexity, which illustrates the analyst’s specific interpretation of the exact structure and behavior of the problem situation. Thus, it is possible to explain the ‘logic’ and ‘rationality’ using the second resolution causal loop diagrams which is assumedly underneath in a particular ‘irrational’ behavior structure in the real world which is described by a particular problematic root definition (SSDM’s stage 3).

After considering the SD context diagram (that depend on the particular W of observing the real world situation by observer), the problematic status structure is modeled more precisely in SSDM step 4, which supports the SD approach for these purposes using ad-hoc software (i.e. Stella, Ithink, Dynamo, Powersim, Vensim, etc.).

This diagram goes on with its calibration and sensitivity analysis, after having a logically coherent causal loop computerized model of the problematic situation's behavior (observed under a particular W), to see the various results and consequences that the problematic situation, interpreted in a particular way, can produce in different situations of causal variables.

As a key aspect of the learning process, the study and understanding of the relationships between the causes and the consequences and sequels (i.e. the outcomes) while iterating among diverse W's, problematic root definitions, context diagrams and second resolution causal loops can be used by the group of analysts (i.e. the observers) in order to understand the patterns of behavior of the problematic situation.

As a result, given the number of primary definitions that the observer described in stage 3 of SSDM, this process can be repeated n times based on the purpose, to obtain different problematic system dynamics computerized models, just to understand the types of interpretations that underlie the behavior of a problematic situation with respect to each interpretation and its consequences.

REAL WORLD

Stage 5: Compare Stage 4 (Stage 7) Against 2

In the first SSDM systemic loop, Stage 5 addresses comparing the problematic-oriented system dynamics models against the rich picture developed at Stage 2. If possible, the comparison in observing and validating consists all the nouns, verbs, adverbs and relationships established in the problematic system dynamics models (problematic context diagram and detailed causal-loop models, originated by each problematic root definition) the rich picture description, observing at the same time if the outcomes of the sensitivity analysis reproduce the problematic situation behavior; in other word, it can express sufficiently what is happening in the real-world) if it expresses sufficiently the real-world situation (or part of it) shown in the rich picture (i.e. problematic context diagram and system dynamics models based on particular Ws).

In the second SSDM systemic loop, Stage 5 also consists of the solving-oriented system dynamics models, against the rich picture developed at Stage 2. Observing and validating all the nouns, verbs, adverbs and causal relationships in the solving system dynamics models (solving context diagram and detailed causal – loop models done at Stage 7) are emphasized in the comparison in this case to compare with the rich picture achieved when outcomes of the sensitivity analysis reproduce the behavior of a solving situation for the problem-situation under studied and if the proposed changes can be culturally feasible and systemically desirable.

SECOND SSDM SYSTEMIC LOOP: SOLVING-SITUATION SYSTEMS THINKING WORLD

Stage 6: Determine Culturally Feasible and Systemically Desirable Changes

In order to improve the problematic situation presented through the model (s) in Step 4, the culturally feasible and systemically desirable changes (Step 6 of SSDM) should be specified after validating the mode (s) presented in Step 4. In other words, in order to 'improve' (or change) the problematic behavior of the situation encountered at SSDM's stages 3 and 4, stage 6 looks for making culturally feasible and systemically desirable changes, in terms of variables (at the context as well as in detailed levels of the models done at Stage 4) and it is needed to remove, vary and/or add links (if possible all of this). PERT and CPM techniques and also Project Dynamics can be utilized here to manage this Stage.

Since it is impossible to analyze feasibility and utility without seeing the effects over time, it is necessary to move to Step 7 of SSDM to simulate future prospective solution options that analysts can predict for the problematic situation.

Stage 7: Building System Dynamics Models of the 'Solving Situation'

Possible courses of action to 'improve' the problematic situation, proposed at Stage 6 by different feasible and desirable changes obtained, can be drawn and predicted using the computerized systemic modeling tool (i.e. SD), and in this way, support the SD approach to SSM. According to our experience in using SSM, often what was thought to be a good change was not the case in the real world.

A detailed understanding of whether the proposed changes are able to "improve" the problematic structure of the problem can be achieved in step 7 using the simulation process. It will be necessary to return to SSDM's stage 5 and iterate among Stages 5, 6 and 7 in case that some of them do not help, until developing a culturally feasible and systemically desirable problem-solving diagram context and system dynamics model.

Therefore, a context diagram on solving-oriented approach that can be implemented in the real world is done in stage 7; that is, we can go forward to next modeling details (next resolution levels of the SD models), doing sensitivity analysis to observe the outcomes according to the variations of the causes and/or their relationships (desirable and feasible changes); that provides observer with the important insights about the diverse results and outcomes of the 'solutions'.

Stage 8: Solving Situation- Oriented Root Definitions

Stage 8, in the second SSDM systems world namely the 'Solving Situation Oriented Systems Thinking World' (World 3), is performed when the problem-solving model has been achieved. In SSDM terms, 'Solving Situation Root Definition' aims to express the transformation process needed to make 'improvements' of the problematic situation. Doing CATWOE analysis is necessary after doing all the linguistic corrections, in order to clearly define what is the 'solving-oriented' transformation process proposed by the computerized model as the basis to build up this solving-oriented root definition in stage 7 to implement in the real-world.

A comparison between the 'solving' oriented root definition and the real-world problematic situation is made (i.e. a comparison between stages 8 and 2 must be performed) after performing all the adjustment. In case that despite the literally interesting 'solving' oriented root definition, due to systemically undesirable or culturally unfeasible factors there are difficulties in the transformation process proposed by the comparison with the implementation in real-world problem situation, then in order to make the change proposals culturally feasible and systemically desirable, it is necessary to make some adjustments among stages 2, 8 and 7, as well as in the loop composed by stages 5, 6 and 7, until some 'good' transformation processes are find among them, .

Stage 9: Implementation of Feasible and Desirable Changes in the Real-World

After finding a good balance among stages 2, 8 and 7, it is necessary to return to Stage 6 to make the ultimate culturally feasible and systemically desirable changes happened. Changes created in previous stage can be implemented in Stage 9 namely the implementation phase.

Stage 10: Learning Points

Collecting and compiling all learning points for study and reflection from time to time and future interventions are done in Stage 10 as the last activity of SSDM. The learning points are resulted from the modeling sensitivity analysis of 'problematic situation' (Stage 4), the 'solving situation' (Stage 7), and the proper implementation in the real world (Stage 9). This is done with the purpose of directing people involved in the analysis and design of social systems (i.e. Problem Solving System) to the learning paradigm, in order to create real world concrete interventions by self-analysis, synthesis and reflection.

ABM

An alternative approach is provided by ABM so that a non-exhaustive list of situations, where ABMs can be useful for capturing emergent behavior are provided by Bonabeau (2002):

1. When there are complex, non-linear, discontinuous, or discrete interaction between agents (i.e. the agent behavior can be changed dramatically, even discontinuously, by other agents) which can be particularly useful when describing discontinuity of individual behavior.
2. There is a significant ability to design a heterogeneous population of agents with an agent-based model in which, agents can show any type of unit.

According to Axelrod (1997), there is more attention to 'reality' in the agent-based approach compared to other modeling approaches. Social theory which cannot easily be described using mathematical formula, can be represented and tested by Agent-based simulations. By determining simple behavioral and transition rules related to well-defined entities, the models often map more naturally to the structure of the problem than equation-based models (Parunak et al., 1998). In particular, as Bonabeau (2002) states, when it is more natural to describe the constituent units of a system under some of the following conditions, the agent-based approach can be useful:

1) The individuals' behavior cannot clearly be defined by aggregate transition rates (e.g. the decision to move);
2) Individual behavior is complex and the complexity of differential equations increases exponentially by increasing the behavior complexity, although any process can be hypothetically explained by an equation. Describing complex individual behavior with equations can therefore become intractable;
3) a more natural way of describing a system compared to processes in based on activities; and,
4) Since the agent's behavior is random rather than arbitrarily within aggregate equations, the randomness can be applied strategically within agent-based models.

LIMITATIONS OF ABM

Despite all the benefits, the ABM approach has some limitations to use in modeling. The first limitation relates to the purpose of the model, which, of course, is limited to common modeling techniques and that the model applies only to the specific purpose for which it was developed. Couclelis (2002) believes that for every phenomenon, the model should be built at the right level of abstraction, and with the right amount of detail for the model to serve its purpose. Excessive simplicity of the abstraction level may override the main variables, while too much detail leads to limitations and complexity of the model.

Another limitation is related to the nature of the modeling system. For example, a human-based system is associated with irrational behavioral factors, subjective selections, and complex psychology, leading to difficulty in measuring, grading and sometimes justifying the model and also, makes it difficult to implement, develop, and interpret the simulation outputs of the model.

Seeing systems at a non-integrated level, which is specific to agent-based models, involves describing multiple agent characteristics and behaviors and their interaction with the environment. Only through multiple implementations and systematically changing initial conditions or parameters to evaluate the power of the results can the complexity of these systems be addressed (Axtell, 2000).

SSM AND ABM

Soft Systems Agent-based Methodology (SSABM), which is based on the combination of SSM and agent-based modeling, due to emerging SSDM limitations is discussed in this section. Handayati et al. (2014) proposed a problem conceptualization of soft agent-based coordination model for value co-creation that can be implemented in agricultural supply chain.

Figure 3. Steps in Soft Systems Agent – based methodology (Novani and Mayangsari, 2015)

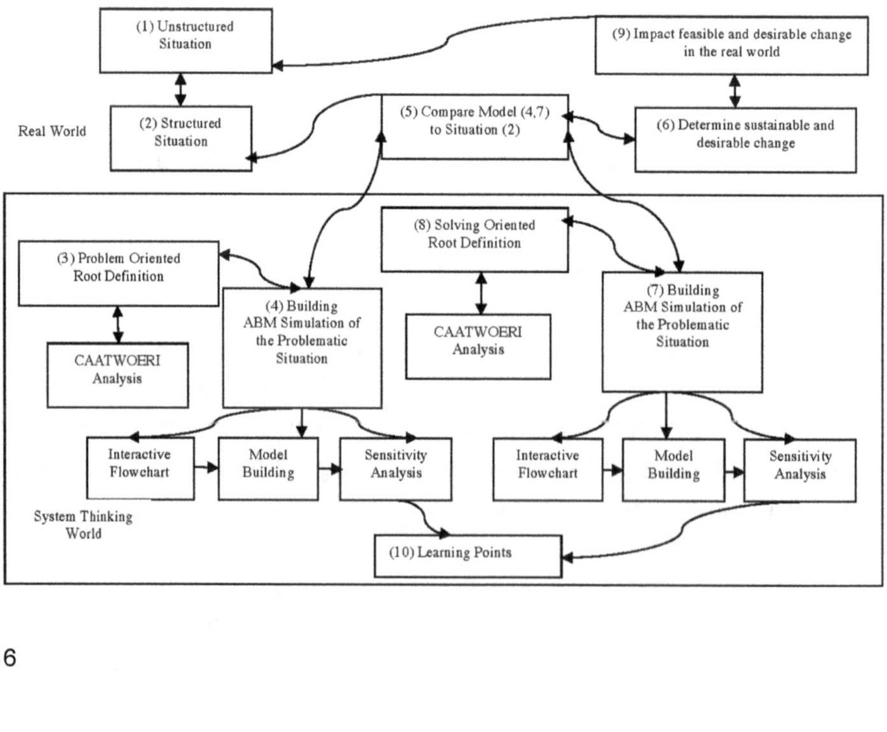

STAGES IN SSABM

Rodriguez-Ulloa and Paucar-Caceres (2005) first developed SSABM stages which are basically adopted from SSDM stages. Ten stages of SSDM methodology are grouped in three different worlds:

- The real world which briefly describe the whole situation in the reality the problem;
- Situation-oriented systems thinking world, which is related to problem situation appreciation and holistic behavior recognition
- Solving situation-oriented systems thinking world that happens to be dialectical side.

Subsequently, after getting to know what the reality is, it should be addressed how systems thinking can solve, finish, or mitigate the problem situation and proposed it in the solving-situation world. The SSABM methodology includes ten stages organized in three worlds and of course, stages 4 and 7 are somehow different in focusing on model building which is shown in Figure 3.

Stage 1: Unstructured Problem Situation

The purpose of this stage, which is borrowed from the SSM is to acknowledge, explore, and define the situation in some way. When SSM researchers start a real world problem, they examine the situation in a highly unstructured way and then, develop some models to show that situation. Any situation where a mismatch can be perceived between two people or more can be referred to as an unstructured problem. Although doesn't define the problem, but this stage assesses the general area of interest. It is possible to open a situation boundary to include more aspects, but it is not possible to define the problem or its environment precisely and in each event, different people will be involved with different opinions.

Stage 2: Structured Situation

Again originated from SSM, this situation should be stated so that researchers easily understand the problem using a rich picture. Including all relevant elements and stakeholders of a system, this approach can help to organize complex situations and identify underlying problems. The use

Table 2. CAATWOERI definitions (Novani and Mayangsari, 2015)

Clients	People who are affected by T as victims or stakeholders
Agents	People who perform T
Attributes	Information such as the properties of an object (person, thing, etc.) owned by an agent.
Transformation	Turning input to output
Weltangschauung	Worldview of creating T meaningful in context
Owners	Having the power to stop T
Emergent properties	The behavior of whole system caused by the interactions
Rule of interaction	Algorithms of decision-making or probabilities of behavior

of rich pictures is due to the fact that thoughts can be organized by drawing detailed representations of problematic situations, better understand can be achieved of what is going on in the system, and the root problems are identified. The relationships and connections can be seen through this holistic thinking that otherwise, might be missed. In order to draw a rich picture any technique and in any situation can be used. However, structure, process, and concerns are elements that should be considered in building a rich picture.

Stage 3: Problem – Oriented Root Definitions (CAATWOERI Analysis)

As one of the parts of SMS, CATWOE analysis includes client, agents, transformation, Weltanschauung, owners and emerging features. Two fundamental elements of ABM to SSM, namely are attributes and rules of interactions are added by combining SSM and ABM so that CATWOE analysis becomes CAATWOERI analysis which is presented in Table 2.

Actors in the SSM are the people involved in the changes implementation phase in the system. However, agents are a feature of agent-based modeling including people, companies, projects, assets, animals, products, and so on. Attributes of agents that are often described by simple rules and interactions with other agents, influence their behaviors. It is also needed to change the input and the nature of inputs to outputs in CAATWOERI analysis. The system should be analyzed to deal with the positive or negative impact of the real world as the big picture and the impact of the transformed system. It is needed to define how our model can cover the problem in agent-based modeling. The authority to make the changes, stop the program, set the goal of simulation of the model, and so on can be existed in some decision makers. It is possible to observe the full effects of the diversity of their attributes and behaviors by modeling agents individually, to emerge the behavior of the whole system. It is needed for researchers to make an algorithm as a rule interaction among agents involved in the system because agent-based modeling usually runs in computer simulation.

Stage 4: Agent –Based Model Building in the "Problematic Situation"

A model is developed by researchers build at this stage, based on the real situation. Three elements can be considered for an agent model including a set of agents (attributes and behaviors), a set of agent relationships, and the agent environment as the interacting agents. Researchers develop a model based on the real situation at this stage. These elements must be identified, modeled, and programed by the model developer to create an agent-based model without any intervention. A model is a specific problem that should be solved by researcher. There should also be clear agents, decision makers, and entities involved. Several approaches are proposed to designing and implementing agent-based models. For example, both design methodologies and selected implementation environments are discussed in depth by North and Macal (2007). Highly iterative design methodologies might be most suitable and effective for practical development in bottom-up methodology like agent-based models.

Stage 5: Comparison Between Stages 4 and 2

The model, developed in a process of modeling based on the system abstraction for a specific purpose, should be compared to the real situation after developing by the researcher. We cannot use the model term about an abstraction that does not represent its modeling target. Therefore, the researcher should ensure that the model represents the reality. We cannot model everything but an abstraction of the target should be modeled. Indeed, the way of constructing the abstraction from the observed system is precisely what distinguishes one modeling paradigm from another. About the errors and artifacts that constitute a model, we can know the error as a mismatch between what the modeler thinks a model is and what it actually is. Artifacts, contrary to errors, refer to situation of no mismatch between what the modeler thinks a model is and what it actually is. In this case, there is a kind of inconsistency between the set of model assumptions that producing a certain phenomenon in terms of the modeler and the assumptions that are real cause of the phenomenon.

Stage 6: Culturally Feasible and Systematically Desirable Changes Determination

Referring to SSM paradigm at this stage, the changes should cover all aspects of the system under analysis and all agents' viewpoints in the model in the ideal situation. The real-world projects are of course always subject to schedule and resource constraints. Consequently, decisions should be made by researchers to prioritize different requirements. Change need to be systematically desirable and then culturally desirable contrary to hard systems approaches that emphasize that change should be systematically feasible and actually desirable.

Stage 7: Agent- Based Model Building in the Solving Situation

The researchers develop a model to solve situation at this stage. A model is a specific problem that researcher should solve it. We develop an improvement model in order to solve the situation based on the real-world model already developed in stage 4, and also apply desirable change from stage 5 and 6.

Stage 8: Solving Situation-Oriented Root Definitions (ACCTWOERI Analysis)

It is also needed to turn the input and the nature of change inputs to outputs in CAATWOERI analysis. As the big picture and the impact of the transformed system is important in worldview, to match with the positive or negative impact of the real world, the system should be analyzed. How our model can cover the problem should be defined in ABM. Sometimes decision makers have the power of making changes, stopping the program, setting the goal of model simulation and so on. The full effects of the diversity of their attributes and behaviors can be observed to emerge the behavior of the whole system through modeling agents, separately. The researcher should construct an algorithm as a rule interaction among agents involved in the system because the ABM usually runs in computer simulation.

Stage 9: Feasible and Desirable Changes Implementation in the Real World

The 'feasible and desirable' developments or/and changes should be implemented in the real word. Specification and implementation of them can be easy by changing the structure the procedure and attitude, although it is difficult in the real word.

Stage 10: Learning Points

By reflecting the whole stages involved in the process of situation problem solving, the learning point is the final and essential stage of the SSABM process. The wrong and right based on the attributes implanted in the agents along the process are accumulated by it. Finally, the direction of the decision solution is weighted by it. Process conditions provide many learning tips and lessons learned.

COMPARISON OF SSM, ABM, SD, SSDM, SSABM

SSDM and SSABM are different in their ontological, epistemological, and methodological assumptions based on SD and ABM principles set according to the table 3.

CONCLUSION

Engineers need holistic approaches to deal with the complex challenges in today's workplace. In this regard, they can utilize the ways provided by systems thinking to think about a problem and its solutions using whole system perspectives. Nowadays it is possible to combine multiple methods developed in the form of multi-methodologies. In this regard, the present chapter is prepared with the approach that it is possible to further collaborate between these methods because of their strengths and weaknesses.

Table 3. SSM, ABM, SD, SSDM and SSABM Principles (Novani and Mayangsari, 2015; Rodriguez-Ulloa and Paucar-Caceres, 2005)

	SSM	ABM	SD	SSDM	SSABM
Ontological principle	It is assumed that systems do not exist in the real world. The social world of meaning attribution	Existence of real-world systems, emphasis on the meanings based on changing links between heterogeneous autonomous social factors	Existence of real-world systems, defining the real world in ontological terms (use of nouns).	It is assumed that systems do not exist in the real world. The meaningful social world for observer	It is assumed that systems do not exist in the real world. The meaningful social world interaction and behavior for observer.
Epistemological principle	The claims are interpretive, phenomenological and (possibly) hermeneutical.	Post-positivistic; model-centered with logic algorithm and simple probabilities	Assumptions are mainly positivistic.	Assumptions that are interpretive, rationalistic, phenomenological and hermeneutical.	Assumptions that are interpretivist, rationalistic, socio-psychological, phenomenological, and hermeneutical; Including bounded rationality and KISS logic algorithm.
	The real world is described in epistemological terms (verbs)	The world is described in terms of emerging attributes, behavior and interactions (verbs, noun, and adverbs)	The structure underlying the real world is described in terms of flows and rates (verbs, nouns and adverbs)	The real world is described in epistemological and ontological terms (verbs, nouns, and adverb)	The real world is described ontologically from the individual interactions and epistemologically from the model built by the governed behavior (verbs, nouns, and adverb)
	The real world and systems thinking world are separated; the process systemiticity.	The real and system world is not very clearly separated.	The real world and systems world is not very clearly separated.	The real world and system thinking world is clearly separated; SSDM systems thinking world is divided into two: 1) problem situation oriented systems thinking world; and 2) problem solving situation oriented systems thinking world	The real world and system thinking world is clearly separated; 1) problem situation oriented systems thinking world; and 2) problem solving situation oriented systems thinking world
Methodological stages	Systemic approach based on human activity systems that are 'logically' linked	Systemic approach based on interrelations among controlled-behavior individuals in a specified area and time	Systemic approach based on 'rational' cause-effect relationships,	Systemic approach based on human activity systems that are 'logically' linked and 'rational' cause-effect relationship	Systemic approach based on human activity systems that are 'logically' linked and interrelations among with controlled-behavior individuals in a given area and time

continued on following page

Table 3. Continued

	SSM	ABM	SD	SSDM	SSABM
Methodological stages	It looks for creating real-world changes which are culturally feasible and systematically desirable.	It earns insight from cultural feasible as an input for agent behavior rules	It does not explicitly note the culturally feasible changes in the real world	It looks for creating real-world changes which are culturally feasible and systematically desirable.	It looks for creating real-world changes which are culturally feasible and systematically desirable.
	A problem-solving oriented methodology	A problem-solving oriented approach	A problem-solving oriented approach	A problem-solving oriented methodology	A problem-solving oriented methodology
	Lack of the ability to measure and evaluate the possible changes over time	Having the ability to predict, measure, and evaluate the changes by itself though controlled behavior in a period of time	Having the ability to measure and evaluate the changes by itself through time	Having the ability to measure and evaluate the problematic and improved situation by itself over time	Having the ability to predict, measure, and evaluate the changes by itself though controlled behavior in a period of time
	Explicitly setting the "what" and "how" transformation process to improve it in the real world	An explicit 'what' and 'how' transformation process implemented in the real world	Non-explicit 'what' and 'how' transformation process implemented or to be implemented in the real world	Two transformation processes are explicitly established to (1) explain 'what' is the problem situation and 'how' it behaves and (2) explain 'what' and 'how' should be the transformation process to 'improve' or 'alleviate' that problem and 'how' the improved situation should behave	Two transformation processes are explicitly established to (1) explain 'what' is the problem situation and 'how' it behaves and (2) explain 'what' and 'how' should be the transformation process to 'improve' or 'alleviate' that problem and 'how' the improved situation should behave
	Not a dialectic approach	Not a dialectic approach	Not a dialectic approach	A dialectic approach	A dialectical approach
	It officially ends with the learning process resulting from the application of the whole methodology.	It officially ends with the informal process of learning process of the model building	It officially ends with the informal process (Interactive Dynamics, Holon Dynamics, Group Model – Building, Modeling for Radical Learning) of learning process of the model building.	It officially ends with the formal learning process from three positions: (a) from the problematic view of the problematic sit (SSDM's World 2); (b) from the solucionatic view of the problematic sit (SSDM's World 3); (c) from the implementation process in the real world (SSDM's World 1)	It officially ends with the formal learning process from three positions: (a) from the problematic view of the problematic sit (SSABM's World 2); (b) from the solucionatic view of the problematic sit (SSABM's World 3); (c) from the implementation process in the real world (SSABM's World 1)

Therefore, the present study investigates the methodologies combination using SSM and simulation methodologies including discrete event simulation (DES), system dynamics (SD), and agent-based modeling (ABM). To this end, a multi-methodology combining soft systems methodology (SSM) and DES developed and tested by Holm et al. (2013), soft system dynamics methodology (SSDM) presented by Rodriguez-Ulloa and Paucar-Caceres (2005), and soft systems agent-based methodology (SSABM) introduced by Novani and Mayangsari (2015) were discussed. Using the ontological, epistemological and methodological assumptions underlying the respective paradigms, this chapter demonstrates the difference between SD, ABM, SSM, and SSABM. SSM is considered as the most popular problem structuring approach in DES. Furthermore, the identification of systemically desirable, culturally affordable and dynamically coherent changes to improve the particular problem situation is possible through using SSM and SD, in combination. By SSM illustrating human activity model and ABM simulation seeing the micro interaction among the entities, SSABM can operate in a real world problematic situation consisted of interaction between entities.

REFERENCES

Axelrod, R. (1997). *The complexity of cooperation: Agent-based models of competition and collaboration*. Princeton: Princeton University Press. doi:10.1515/9781400822300

Axtell, R. (2000). *Why agents? On the varied motivations for agent computing in the social sciences*, Working paper 17. Washington, DC: Center on Social and Economic Dynamics (The Brookings Institute).

Banks, J., Carson, J. S., Nelson, B. L., & Nicol, D. M. (2010). *Discrete-Event System Simulation*. Pearson.

Behl, D. V., & Ferreira, S. (2014). Systems thinking: An analysis of key factors and relationships. *Procedia Computer Science*, *36*, 104–109. doi:10.1016/j.procs.2014.09.045

Bennet, L. M., & Kerr, M. A. (1996). A systems approach to the implementation of total quality management. *Total Quality Management*, *7*(6), 631–665. doi:10.1080/09544129610531

Bonabeau, E. (2002). Agent-based modeling: Methods and techniques for simulating human systems. *Proceedings of the National Academy of Sciences of the United States of America*, *99*(Supplement 3), 7280–7287. doi:10.1073/pnas.082080899 PMID:12011407

Couclelis, H. (2002). Modelling frameworks, paradigms, and approaches. In K. C. Clarke, B. E. Parks, & M. P. Crane (Eds.), *Geographic information systems and environmental modeling* (pp. 36–50). London: Prentice Hall.

Ebrahimi, M. (2016). Technology scenario planning with system multi methodology: In the Petrochemical Research and Technology Company. *The 34th International Conference of the System Dynamics Society*.

Forrester, J. (1972). *Industrial dynamics*. Massachusetts Institute of Technology.

Forrester, J. (1994). System dynamics, systems thinking and soft OR. *System Dynamics Review*, *10*(2–3), 245–256.

Handayati, Y., Simatupang, T. M., & Perdana, T. (2014). Soft agent-based modeling for Agri-food supply chain coordination. *The 6th International Conference on Operations and Supply Chain Management*.

Hawari, N. N. (2018). Integration of soft systems methodology and system dynamics modelling for supply and demand analysis of the rising cost in higher education. *International Journal of Supply Chain Management*, *7*(4), 234–241.

Holm, L. B., & Bjornenak, T. (2017). Using discrete event simulation and soft systems methodology for optimizing patient flow and resource utilization at the surgical unit of radiumhospitalet in Oslo, Norway. In W. K. V. Chan, A.D'Ambrogio, G. Zacharewicz, N. Mustafee, G. Wainer, & E. Page (Eds.), *Proceedings of the 2017Winter Simulation Conference* (PP. 1646-1657). Academic Press.

Holm, L. B., Dahl, F. A., & Barra, M. (2013). Towards a multimethodology in healthcare – synergies between Soft Systems Methodology and Discrete Event Simulation. *Journal of Health Systems*, *2*(1), 11–23. doi:10.1057/hs.2012.21

Jackson, M. C. (2003). *Systems thinking: Creative holism for managers*. New York: John Wiley and Sons.

Kotiadis, K. (2006). Extracting a conceptual model for a complex integrated system in healthcare, In *Proceedings of the Third Operational Research Society Simulation Workshop* (pp. 235-245). Birmingham: The Operational Research Society.

Kotiadis, K. (2007). Using soft systems methodology to determine the simulation study objectives. *Journal of Simulation*, *1*(3), 215–222. doi:10.1057/palgrave.jos.4250025

Kotiadis, K., & Mingers, J. (2006). Combining PSMs with hard OR methods: The philosophical and practical challenges. *The Journal of the Operational Research Society*, *57*(7), 856–867. doi:10.1057/palgrave.jors.2602147

Lamé, G., Jouini, Q., & Cardinal, J. S. (2019). Combining soft systems methodology, ethnographic observation, and discrete-event simulation: A case study in cancer care. *The Journal of the Operational Research Society*, 1–18. doi:10.1080/01605682.2019.1610339

Lane, D. (2008). The emergence and use of diagramming in system dynamics: A critical account. *Systems Research and Behavioral Science*, *25*(1), 3–23. doi:10.1002res.826

Lane, D., & Oliva, R. (1998). The greater whole: Towards a synthesis of system dynamics and soft systems methodology. *European Journal of Operational Research*, *107*(1), 214–235. doi:10.1016/S0377-2217(97)00205-1

Lane, D. C. (1999). Social theory and systems dynamics practice. *European Journal of Operational Research*, *113*(3), 501–527. doi:10.1016/S0377-2217(98)00192-1

Lehaney, B., & Clarke, S. A. (1997). Soft systems methodology (and simulation) for mixed modeling. In Operational Research Keynote Papers (pp. 16-33). Operational Research Society.

Lehaney, B., Clarke, S. A., & Paul, R. J. (1999). A case of an intervention in an outpatients department. *The Journal of the Operational Research Society*, *50*(9), 877–891. doi:10.1057/palgrave.jors.2600796

Lehaney, B., & Hlupic, V. (1995). Simulation modeling for resource allocation and planning in the health sector. *Journal of the Royal Society of Health*, *115*(6), 382–385. doi:10.1177/146642409511500611 PMID:8568788

Lehaney, B., & Paul, R. (1996). Soft systems methodology and simulation modeling. In *Proceedings of the 1996 Winter Simulation Conference* (pp. 695-700). Coronado, CA: Academic Press.

Lehaney, B., & Paul, R. J. (1994). Using soft systems methodology to develop a simulation of outpatient services. *Journal of the Royal Society of Health*, *114*(5), 248–251. doi:10.1177/146642409411400507 PMID:7844787

Mingers, J. (2003). A classification of the philosophical assumptions of management science methods. *The Journal of the Operational Research Society*, *54*(6), 559–570. doi:10.1057/palgrave.jors.2601436

Mingers, J., & Gill, A. (1997). *Multi-methodology: The theory and practice of combining management science methodologies*. Chichester: Wiley.

Montevechi, J. A. B., & Friend, J. D. (2012). Using a Soft Systems Methodology framework to guide the conceptual modeling process in discrete event simulation. *Proceedings of the 2012 Winter Simulation Conference (WSC)*. 10.1109/WSC.2012.6465179

Niglas, K. (2004). *The combined use of qualitative and quantitative methods in educational research* (Doctoral dissertation). Tallin Pedagogical University.

North, M. J., & Macal, C. M. (2007). *Managing business complexity: discovering strategic solutions with agent-based modeling and simulation*. Oxford, UK: Oxford University Press. doi:10.1093/acprof:oso/9780195172119.001.0001

Novani, S., & Mayangsari, L. (2015). Soft Systems Agent-Based Methodology: Multi-methods Approach Between Soft Systems Methodology and Agent-Based Modeling. In Agent-Based Approaches in Economics and Social Complex Systems IX (pp. 165-176). Springer.

Parunak, H. V. D., Savit, R., & Riolo, R. L. (1998). Agent-based modeling vs. equation-based modelling: A case study and users' guide. Proceedings of Multi-Agent Systems and Agent-Based Simulation (MABS'98), 10–25.

Rodriguez-Ulloa, R. (2018). Systemic methodology for risks evaluation and management in the energy and mining sectors (SYSMEREM-EMS) using bayesian networks. *Journal of Decision Systems*, *27*(1), 191–200. doi:10.1080/12460125.2018.1468157

Rodriguez-Ulloa, R., Montbrun, A., & Martínez-Vicente, S. (2011). Soft system dynamics methodology in action: A study of the problem of citizen insecurity in an Argentinean province. *Systemic Practice and Action Research*, *24*(4), 275–323. doi:10.100711213-010-9187-z

Rodriguez-Ulloa, R. L., & Paucar-Caceres, A. (2005). Soft System Dynamics Methodology (SSDM): A Combination of Soft Systems Methodology and System Dynamics. *Systemic Practice and Action Research*, *18*(3), 303–334. doi:10.100711213-005-4816-7

Shahabi, A., Azar, A., Radfar, R., & Asadifard, R. A. (2019). Combining soft systems methodology with interpretive structural modeling and system dynamics for network orchestration: Case study of the formal science and technology collaborative networks in Iran. *Systemic Practice and Action Research*, 1–26. doi:10.100711213-019-09490-z

Chapter 6
Soft Systems Methodology in Technology Management Practices

ABSTRACT

Technology management (TM) is a series of management disciplines designed to manage the technological fundamentals of the organizations for creation of competitive benefits. A successful technological development and commercialization can be rarely accomplished through diffused and undirected efforts. In such a complex situation, modeling can play a decisive role in the analysis of complexities and management of the dynamics of technology-based companies. In this context, the chapter describes five processes of TM, namely identification, selection, acquisition, protection, and exploitation. Soft systems methodology (SSM) is one of the soft operations research (OR) tools and techniques that can be implemented in TM phases as a hard OR. Furthermore, two case studies that addressed the use of SSM in policymaking to commercialize the new technologies and technology scenario planning in a research and development (R&D) organization will be also reviewed.

INTRODUCTION

Technology refers to the ways of doing something. In this context, it implies the means of accomplishing our objectives. Technology includes all the knowledge, tools, products, processes, methods, systems, and procedures used

DOI: 10.4018/978-1-7998-4504-1.ch006

to achieve the desired goals. In another way, technology can be defined as the implementation of knowledge for creating products and services in response to human needs and ambitions. In this definition, technology can include various areas: hardware, software, brain-ware, and know-how (Khalil, 2000). Technology management (TM) deals with planning, design, optimization, operation, and control of the technology-based products. Technology management is intended to maximize the cost-effectiveness of investment; which can further contribute to enhancing the organization value. TM refers to a series of management disciplines designed to manage the technological fundamentals of the organizations for creation of competitive benefits. The major reason for focusing on the technological part is wealth creation. In this content, TM requires in-depth comprehension of the technology, product, process, and technology life cycles (LCs). TM can be regarded as an R&D catalyzer (Namdeo et al., 2016).

TM has been considered as both a problem structuring and management framework, which could be combined through soft systems methodology (SSM) for extra development of the multi-methodology. Subjective and social constructionist principles are now implemented and translated to the real world systems on the basis of the more objective reality. Based on Checkland and Holwell (2004), TM can be regarded as a hard operations research (OR) method in which: it is the positivistic, functionalist, talks of systems and solutions, that ontologically supposes the functional and data models as a part of the real world, assuming that the system can be efficiently engineered to become goal seeking-orientated.

TM was defined as a multifunctional and multidisciplinary field by Phaal et al. (2004a); in their opinion, TM requires both commercial and technical functions combined with the academic perspectives (e.g. engineering, economics, business studies, social science, and psychology). Although not many practical methods were developed to undertake TM, they continued by a few TM-supporting conceptual models.

Chanaron and Jolly (1999) defined the task force on TM, which was also supported by the National Research Council as: "the management of technology links engineering, science and management disciplines to plan, develop and implement technological capabilities to shape and accomplish the strategic and operational objectives of the organization". They justified the TM as a means to link the organizations' technology profile to their objectives and goals.

In this chapter, TM process model will be explained; the SSM will be also reviewed as a Soft OR tool which can be incorporated in each phase. 2 case studies will be reviewed which addressed the use of SSM in policymaking for commercializing new technologies (Azar et al., 2017) as well as a technology scenario planning for a research and development (R&D) organization (Ebrahimi, 2016).

TM AND SSM

According to Gregory (1995), Phaal et al. (2001) state that the TM process framework encompasses five procedures. These five processes are illustrated in Figure 1.

As Figure 1 suggests, the TM process model involves 5 stages: identification, selection, acquisition, protection, and exploitation (ISAPE) which were presented by Phaal et al. (2001) as:

- Identifying the technologies, which is (or may be) crucial for the business.
- Selecting technologies that must be supported by the organization.
- Acquisition and assimilation of the selected technologies.
- Exploiting technologies to create profit or other advantages.
- Protecting the knowledge and expertise used in products and manufacturing systems.

Similar to SSM which can be employed as an overarching framework in any stage of ISAEP, 'Soft OR' tools and techniques can be also implemented into each phase as well as other models, for instance, in the rich picture, flow charts or conceptual models, or the SSM itself. The communication aspect seems to be more emphasized, as it plays a key role in the development of a common dialogue between the stakeholders, of the framework. The assumption is that if the participants use a definite format, within a known process, as long as

Figure 1. Technology management process model (Venus, 1999)

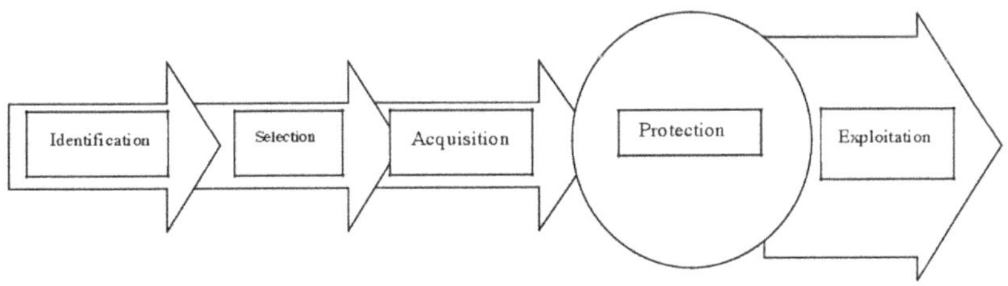

what is occurring or seems to occur could be uniformly communicated, the format should remain valid for those individuals. Thus, the communication seems to be a significant issue; since TM programs through frameworks, language development can affect the system performance (Zehner, 2000; Ortega et al., 2012).

Rather than a mechanical methodology, TM is a process facilitating the flexible learning experiences which can be adapted to special situations (Phaal et al., 2004a) as well as each process using the feedback and learning (Phaal et al., 2004b). The theories of the learning organization can also help in the establishment of the method, enabling the participants to exploit single and double-loop learning schemes. Senge (1990) claimed that all mental models of the stakeholders and learning organization are challenged. Regarding the emphasis on the learning experiences, TM process model using SSM has been considered suitable for the development of a learning framework to plan, implement and manage a technology.

In Table 1, the details of each TM stage breakdown are presented when SSM was used.

POLICY MAKING FOR THE COMMERCIALIZATION OF NEW TECHNOLOGIES

The technology development inevitably requires identification of the market demand, investigation, and commercialization. Various definitions have been mentioned concerning the issue of technology commercialization. According to one of these definitions, technology commercialization refers to producing an appropriate product at a reasonable price to fulfill the market demand. In another definition, commercialization is a procedure to strengthen the science-economy link through technology transfer. In a different expression, technology commercialization is a stage during which the knowledge and technology could be transferred from academic centers to industries and new businesses (Dehghani, 2015). Commercialization by definition of Jolly (2009) refers to a process in which a pre-idea creation evolves into an idea, a technology, and finally a new product.

The simplest commercialization policy includes all the actions, programs, and plans implemented in the countries around the world to increase the tendency for commercialization, including formulation, implementation, and evaluation of policies. The public policy of each government is based on its

Table 1. Technology management process model using SSM (Small and Wainwright, 2014)

TM Stage	Description	Techniques	Tools
Identification	Technology identification is carried out based on a more unstructured ad-hoc. The identification phase is aimed to resolve this problem and gather a wide diversity of data, and the appropriate stakeholders. The data can be then discussed. This phase, as well as the others, is intended to examine the participants' mental models and determine whether it is crucial to identify a technology. If necessary, how. Furthermore, development of the personal mastery, creation of a shared vision, and conducting team learning are also among the objectives. Upon identification of all appropriate technologies, the most suitable requirements should be selected.	• Identifying the proper technologies by internal and external access to the information. • Considering the technology vendors, experts or off the shelf solutions. • Communicating this information with all the stakeholders.	• Pre-selection framework • Scanning the Technology/Market • Information management • SSM
Selection	Technology Selection involves decision making by all the stakeholders. To this end, the entire implications of the technology should be derived. Decision criteria could be also employed in this phase considering the benefits and restrictions of a specific technology. Explicit consideration of these issues will help the team to establish a more effective 'dialogue' giving rise to selecting the most appropriate technology.	• Development of the procedures which facilitate the decision making on selecting the best technologies obtained from the identification phase. • The decision making should be explicit and consider all the stakeholders. It is possible to compare the organization with its competitors or other organizations that develop similar technologies.	• Benchmarking • Decision criteria and monitoring the process improvement SSM
Acquisition	After selecting the best technology, it can be acquired through different channels. Regardless of the chosen path, the process has to be officially managed for optimal use of time and budget. This could be a demanding phase; hence, the team should be sure about the availability of supports, in particular, upon the technology implementation. All the involved departments should work on close collaboration. The training issues and implementation approaches should be also addressed in this phase. The 'human' aspect of the technological development should be well noted.	• Acquiring the selected technology through the development of technology in an organization. • Purchasing a technology from 'off the shelf', or the experts out of the specialist developer.	• Licensing and joint ventures • Project management • Technology insertion • SSM

continued on following page

Table 1. Continued

TM Stage	Description	Techniques	Tools
Exploitation	Technology exploitation refers to the optimal approach by which the organization can be benefited from the advantages and resolve a problem. By technology exploitation, the technology should not be only applied to attain the perceived benefits, but it should also highlight the other possible issues of an organization that are not yet officially documented. This objective is achievable through the correct function of the technology. This can explain the close interaction of the exploitation and protection phases.	• Helping the stakeholders in exploiting the acquired technologies by assuring them that the technology will perform according to the standards. • Construction of the short, medium, and long term programs for investigating the technology suitability. • Conducting the required updates. • Maintaining the communication with the stakeholders for prompt resolving of the problems.	• Incremental development Product management • Complementary assets • SSM
Protection and Evaluation	More effective exploitation of technology requires technology protection. Protection should minimize the chances of data delete or destruction. The access of the competitors to the data should be also cut. To overcome the problems of data loss, some strategies have to be considered to run the technology and update it, if necessary. The participants have to put their to-do list into action. Furthermore, all the stakeholders should be in communication.	• The technology protection and evaluation by determining possible further exploitation of the technology. • Considering the requirements for substituting the already available technologies. • Finding suitable resources (e.g., internal expertise, support contracts, and regular maintenance) to continue the run of technology, while supporting the data requirement of a technology (i.e. customer information, sales). • Exploitation could be also be associated with more training issues. • Fully trained participants can better exploit the technology.	• Establish a strategy • Monitor effectiveness

political philosophy and doctrine and is aimed at governing (Anderson, 1994). "Policy" generally refers to a series of attitudes of an actor or the actors (e.g. officials, governmental agencies, or the legislatures), in a field of activity (i.e. consumer protection).

Public policy could be also regarded as the governments' decision to act or not. In definition, the policy refers to a relatively stable and targeted course of action performed by an actor or set of actors to deal with a problem or resolve a concern. This definition associates the policy to a targeted or goal-oriented action rather than a random behavior or chance-based occurrences. Second, the policies involve courses or patterns of action carried in a course of time by the governmental officials; in this definition, they differ from the separate and discrete decisions by these individuals. Third, the public policies arise as a response to the policy demands, or the calls for action or inaction regarding a public issue caused by other actors (e.g. private citizens, group representatives, or legislators and other public officials) by the governmental officials and agencies. Fourth, the policy implies the actual acts of the governments rather than their intentions or words. Fifth, public policy could be positive or negative (Anderson, 2003; Smith and Larimer, 2009). Public policies can be related to various fields such as population, environment, energy, housing, medicine, agriculture, and technology.

From the perspective of governments, universities, and research institutes, as important sources of intellectual property and new technologies, the sources of income and employment are ultimately recognized as an important force in the economic development (Klofsten and Evans, 2000). Acknowledging the increasing importance of science and technology in economic development has a logical consequence which is extraordinarily important in the production capacity of a science-based innovation in society (Etzkowitz, 2006). New and pristine ideas are created by firms, and economic change is driven by the success of technologies and solutions that abolish the previous methods (Krugman, 1994).

Kollmer and Dowling (2004) examined the established companies in terms of the new technologies; they concluded that lack of funding is one of the biggest challenges as these companies' need for the fund is one of the effective factors in the technology commercialization. Spilling (2004), in a study entitled knowledge commercialization, provided a conceptual framework and concluded that the intermediary entities such as science and technology parks play a significant role in the commercialization process and can resolve or reduce the barriers of its implementation, hence, enhancing the capacity of converting knowledge into a sustainable capital.

Styles and Genua (2008) conducted a research to examine the companies that were formed within the universities, they found that the creation of these companies and their internationalization help the researchers to seize opportunities. Rasmussen and Gulbrandsen (2006) highlighted the importance of several factors such as universities reformations, growth of centers, and supportive laws to promote the science commercialization in the universities. Markman et al. (2009) also emphasized the significance of the technology transfer offices to support and protect the ideas by various types of intellectual property, growth of the income stream of the universities and researchers, and reduction of the time interval between the knowledge transfer and its commercialization. Siegel and Phan (2006) reviewed the role of technology transfer and concluded that these offices could facilitate the knowledge commercialization and evolve it from the university to application

The purpose of this section is to delineate an application of SSM approach in policymaking to commercialize new technology.

Step One: Exposure to a Problematic Situation

The SSM approach is a collaborative process because it goes through the discussions. Unlike many other approaches, this approach is not solely based on the study of professional experts, regardless of the attitudes of the involved parties. Firstly, a real-world problem is discovered. At this point, the problem is not defined; but the researcher's goal is exactly determined. The general view of the issue is also plotted. At this stage, the issue is brought to the forefront and the relevant information is gathered through various interviews and meetings with the experts in the field of technology commercialization policy at the national level. The interviews are semi-structured. The problem situation is as follows:

Despite the differences in the goals and approaches of the governments regarding the national technology plans, there are also some similarities. For example, most countries' technology plans include all or parts of the innovation value chain that may include: increase of the public awareness, human resource development and training courses, dissemination of scientific findings, development of laboratory infrastructure, patent and intellectual property rights, standardization, technology transfer, research and development, industry support, private sector investment development and new technology dissemination in the existing industries. In this study, a new technology policy-making began with institutionalizing and legalizing, mainly through government and continued by the government as it influences the research and innovation and provides and allocates the resources for knowledge formation, creation, development, and dissemination. Then emerging market functions and entrepreneurial activities will emerge.

Step Two: Draw a Rich Picture

In the second stage, the situation, the people involved in the situation, and the structure of the problem are plotted in a rich picture. A rich picture is a textual representation such as caricatures of people involved, issues, processes, and interactions between the components of a situation which can help in a better understanding of the problem. At this stage, according to the data collected through interviews with experts, the rich picture is drawn by the consensus of all the experts. To draw a rich picture, the actors and involved people should be identified. The actors' relationships can be also determined during meetings with experts.

Step Three: Extract the Root Definition

At this point, we depart from the real world to a conceptual and systemic world to present the root definition of the problem. The root definition is a statement describing the ideal system, its goals, and the involved people in the situation and the participants as well as the affected people and systems. The CATWOE method is used to formulate a definition by problem owners. On this basis, a set of root definitions may be created that will help in reaching an agreement on a root definition by the group discussions.

Identification of the CATWOE elements can highly contribute to a root definition, but before that, the PQR formula was used, as it can provide a perfect template for a proper root definition. In other words, the PQR formula allows the root definition to be written as a descriptive sentence; hence it could be very useful in enriching the root definition. Its function in SSM is as follows: Run P through Q to help achieve R. In fact, PQR refers to what?, how?, and why? Before defining the CATWOE elements from the root definitions, the PQR formula was applied for better understanding on the purpose of the root definition.

- P refers to what we want to do: providing a model for policy making to commercialize the new technologies.
- Q means how to get to P in these circumstances (How): Experts of Vice Presidency of Science and Technology, as the executives in this field, understand the state of policymaking for the commercialization of the new technologies in the past and determine the contribution of each factor and design a new model. The policy-making is based on the national macro goals.

- R is our ultimately intended achievement (Why): entering the technological breakthroughs into the market, wealth creation, improvement of peoples' quality of life, scientific development of the new technologies at the national level, building the capacity to develop new technologies, facilitating the university-industry relationship, improving the existing products and processes, enhancing the competitiveness of the industrial enterprises, employing technologists and graduates in the field of new technologies, improving the commercialization process of the new technologies, reducing the costs and increasing the revenues gained from the commercialization of the new technologies in national level.

Three criteria must be considered in defining the components of CATWOE: efficacy, efficiency, and effectiveness. The efficacy refers to the proper transformation. It evaluates whether the transformation works properly in producing the expected output. In other words, this criterion examines the implications of the system (medium-term goals related to national macro goals). Consequences (such as job creation and productivity growth) are the direct effects of the projects. The measure of efficacy of this system is to improve the commercialization of new technology-based products.

The efficiency of the system indicates whether the transformation was achieved by the minimum use of the resources. In other words, this criterion examines the system outputs (short-term goals related to national macro goals). By outputs, we mean the technical results of projects, such as papers and products. This criterion is aimed to develop a new model of policymaking to commercialize the new technologies through optimal utilization of materials and non-material resources during an appropriate time, identifying all the components and actors involved in the process of policymaking, defining their roles, and performing their tasks correctly.

The measure of effectiveness determines whether the transformation helped in achieving some of the top or long-term goals. In other words, this criterion examines the impacts of the system (national macro goals in the area of new technology development). The impact refers to the wider effects of the plan implementation on society, such as improved technology diffusion and improved competitiveness. According to this criterion, the model of policymaking for the commercialization of new technologies should be designed in such a way that the commercialization of new technologies is an important intermediary for enhancing the community health, improving people's lifestyles, enhancing society's satisfaction, increasing turnover,

Table 2. CATWOE components of policymaking for commercialization of new technologies (Azar et al., 2017)

CATWOE	Policymaking for commercialization of new technologies
Customer	Government, industry, and people
Actor	Institute of Technology Development to Market Services (Commercial Corridor), Vice Presidency of Science and Technology, Society of Technologists including academic graduates, university professors, knowledge-based companies, Science and Technology Parks, Growth Centers; industries including pharmacy, laboratory equipment, textile, agriculture, automotive, petrochemicals, National Research and Technology Support Fund Organization, ministries, National Standards Organization, new technologies dedicated research institutes, new technology laboratories, Planning and Budget Organization
Transformation	Putting the ideas into innovation, conversion of the applied research into applicable products, conversion of the applied processes into the economic added-value
World view	The overall insight is that the risk of commercializing new technologies can improve the society's health, people's lifestyles, and productivity increase the public satisfaction and turnover, create jobs, save energy and reduce consumption, as well as producing technology-based products which can improve the efficiency and features, as well as organizing and managing the country's capacities under a coherent system which will lead to a high level of technological achievements.
Owner	Vice Presidency of Science and Technology, Society of Technologists, knowledge-based companies
Environment	Business rankings, economic transparency, government rules, industry competitiveness status, technology development capability, the infrastructure needed to industrialize new technologies, R&D infrastructure, business infrastructure, and the status of international relations

improving productivity, creating employment, saving energy, reducing consumption as well as producing more efficient new technology-based products, enhancing the scientific and technical empowerment of the private sector in the country, providing the infrastructure needed to conduct R&D internationally, interconnection of major agencies of research, technology and innovation in the country, promoting the implementation of macro and strategic plans rather than small projects, and the development of capability in macro management and promotion.

Taking into account the elements and concepts of CATWOE, a root definition of policymaking for commercialization of new technologies can be:

"A system of new technology commercialization policymaking governed by the of Vice Presidency of Science and Technology, Society of Technologists, and knowledge-based companies that converts the results of innovative applied research relevant to new technologies into the commercial achievements with the help of multiple stakeholders, provides the necessary support for development, paves the way for the continued development of innovation, commercializes the achievements, and takes measures to develop the market which can ultimately improve society's health, people's lifestyle, and productivity increase the public satisfaction and turnover, create job, save energy, and reduce consumption as well as producing more efficient new technology-based products that with improved features to reach a high level of technological achievements."

Step Four: Build a Conceptual Model

The conceptual model in SSM is a graph of the activities or their corresponding relationships that determines the process of problem-solving or achievement of goals. The conceptual model is built on the concepts formed in the development of root definitions. The model typically has five to nine activities that are logically dependent on each other. A conceptual model can contribute to better visualization and understanding of the activities. Every problematic situation in the real world involves people who take action purposefully. This means that purposeful activity models are constructed as system models to express a particular view and can be used as a tool to discover the qualities and characteristics of any problematic human situation. The representation of causal relationships between the system concepts is important because it can help in identifying the unrelated concepts as well as factors influencing the decision-making process.

At this stage, according to the root definition, a conceptual model is formed as shown in Figure 2.

Step 5: Compare the Conceptual Model With the Real World

This step is designed to structure the discussion of improving the current situation and compare the developed model with the real world. The following questions can be asked to compare the conceptual model with the real world situations:

- Does this activity also occur in the real world? How?
- How does it behave?
- How is it evaluated?
- Is this process appropriate in its current state?

These questions are posed for each activity in the conceptual model. For example, after the review, it was concluded that there was insufficient effort to involve the stakeholders in the decision making regarding the new technology commercialization policy. This can be then suggested to be changed.

Figure 2. Conceptual model of policymaking for commercialization of new technologies (Azar et al., 2017)

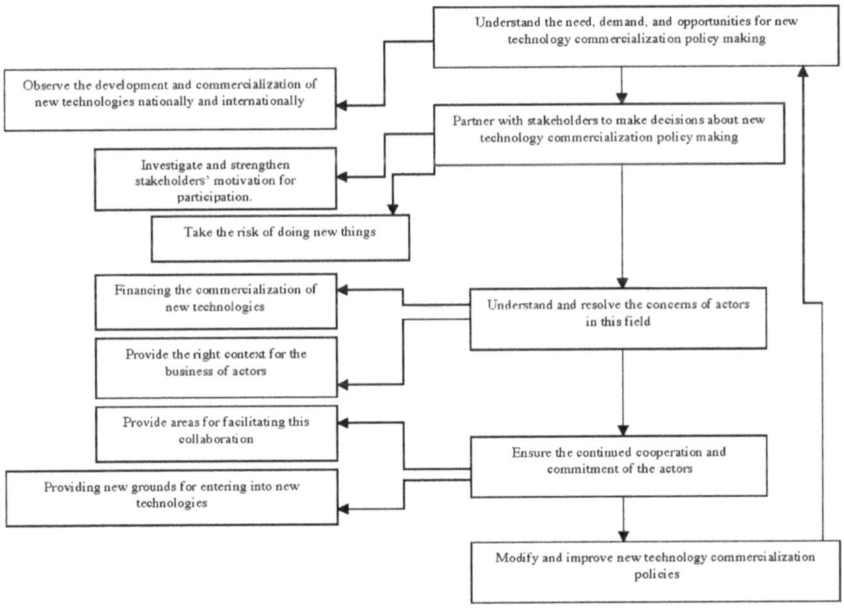

Step Six: Define Changes for Improvement

This stage involves the systematic identification of the desired and feasible changes that are consistent with the values and cultures of the society. At this point, the changes that need to be made to the actual system are identified. For example, it was assumed under Stage 5 that there was an insufficient effort in the dimension of stakeholder involvement in the decisions regarding new technologies commercialization policymaking. Therefore, as a change, it is suggested to explore and strengthen the motivations which may encourage the stakeholders to participate in decision-making on the new technology commercialization policy.

Step Seven: Work Plan for Making Changes

This step involves putting the changes identified in the previous step into action and is usually accomplished by the creation and approval of an operational plan. In other words, the identified changes will be implemented to improve the system. For the proposed change at the previous step, a practical plan is set up a cooperation committee in the related ministries and organizations.

TECHNOLOGY SCENARIO PLANNING IN AN R&D ORGANIZATION

The R&D organizations are the major actors in the technology development, and the public research institutions and research policies can conduct major transformations. The technological development and commercialization are hardly achievable through scattered and untargeted efforts. In other words, for such a complex activity requires something more than hard-working and high spirits. For this purpose, the companies should possess a well-defined and specific plan to clarify the path to technological development and commercialization (Ebrahimi, 2016).

To determine the direction of the business and its future shape, business strategies could lead to improved performance. About two-thirds of the researches have reported a significant correlation between strategic planning and performance. Therefore, the determination of the path of technological development and its commercialization can improve the performance of both sections. Meanwhile, technology development and commercialization are highly demanding with high levels of uncertainty, in particular in the case of new technology. In this regard, modeling approaches can considerably help in analyzing the complexities and managing the dynamics of research and technology organizations (Ebrahimi, 2016).

The system under study is an R&D organization as a public company under the supervision of a parent company in an industry. The company is focused on research, targeting innovation in any research field. Regarding the project-based nature of the company, all its activities are carried out through the teams' communication. To improve the revenue and supply the industrial needs, the company also considers the technology development and commercialization. The system's issues are complex with no structure; moreover different stakeholders define the problems based on their points of view.

Rich Picture

The preliminary information on the problems was first obtained by interviewing with the experts. Then the stakeholders (i.e. individuals, groups, and companies) with a significant role in the decision-making process were identified and analyzed. Depending on the system's rich picture, the manager could be highly concerned with the following issues:

- Which objectives and strategies: technological competencies, investment level, source of technology and competition should be handled according to a strategic viewpoint; the company should also provide the annual plans on the basis of the industry demands and available knowledge.
- Means to enhance international cooperation: in the cases with insufficient of technological knowledge and expertise and financial resources, development of the international interaction can efficiently facilitate the technology development.
- Means to augment the revenue: the company must try to increase its revenue through privatization and restricting the budget allocation.
- Means to improve technology: the development of better technologies is a prerequisite in providing the industry demands, reducing the import-induced expenditures, and declining the effect of budget insufficiencies.
- Means to alleviate the structure and process: regarding the research-based structure of the company, management of the new processes (i.e. technology development and technology commercialization) could be difficult for the company. Moreover, these issues may be limited due to the need for new staff.
- Means to improve the regulation infrastructure: improvement of the regulatory infrastructure is required to support the technology developers and hold contracts and agreements with the customers.
- Means of performance evaluation and improvement: the process of decision making can be easier if the current status and future expectations are comprehensively reviewed by evaluating the system performance.
- Personnel motivation tools: promotion of the incentive mechanisms is a must in retaining and absorbing the experienced employees.

Root Definition

After identification of the different concerns, the root definition technique was employed by CATWOE analysis. In another expression, the ideal system was described according to the CATWOE definition.

From the customer's point of view, the ideal system can supply their raw materials and technological demands with no operation disturbance. Based on the industrial experts' definition, an ideal system should facilitate the

Table 3. CATWOE components of technology scenario planning (Ebrahimi, 2016)

CATWOE	Technology scenario planning in an R&D organization
Customer	Stakeholders; for whom the systems exist. For instance a producer in an industry
Actor	Stakeholders whose duty is to implement the modifications, they often include the professional employees of an industry
Transformation	The changes offered by the system (e.g. creation of technical knowledge, development of required technologies, and solutions to the industrial problems)
World view	The reasons justifying the systems or processes transformation are the improvement of the market position of the company and its revenue increment
Owner	The entrepreneurs or the investors as well as the company's manager and parent company who are authorized to make the modifications, stop the project or decide on continuing with these changes.
Environment	The external constraint (e.g. political, legal, economic, and cultural) of the system operation media, which may hinder or limit the changes to the system.

creation of technical knowledge and technology development. Based on the manager's perspective, an ideal system can increase the company revenue, and its position in the industry, while preparing it for privatization.

Conceptual Model

After the definition of an ideal system, its conceptual model (including the major functions and their relations) was proposed. All the mentioned functions are interrelated.

The company should establish a steering committee consisting of the other firms and individuals (e.g. technology, marketing, management, law, and international relation experts from industry, universities, research centers, and engineering companies, the manager of the parent company and company managers as well as the government representatives) to determine the plans and strategies. This steering committee is responsible for tracking the new technologies, identifying and forecasting the market needs, effective decision making, and designing long-term plans.

To establish and enhance the processes and modifications of the organizational structure in accordance with the proposed process, the company should design a process management system based on the definition of organizational process, as well as benchmarking the best practices leading to the desired processes and structures, and define an action plan to progress from the current condition to a favorable status. Furthermore, the performance criteria should be determined in terms of the objectives, evaluating the company's performance, and obstacles and problems (as well as their solution) to assess and enhance the performance.

Regarding the basic need of the company to improve the regulation infrastructure, a regulation system was proposed to recognize the problems due to the lack of regulation, find the solutions, and resolve them. Moreover, the international interactions and cooperation should be reformed by identifying the international opportunities and negotiation for the bilateral or multilateral agreements or contracts for cooperative development and commercialization of the technologies.

For research promotion and acceleration, the projects could be delegated to the universities and R&D centers in which the company's research staffs serve as the supervisors. Such a regulatory research system involves the following functions: universities and R&D centers categorization according to their expertise, supervision definition, generation ideas and their revision based on the market demands and plans, proposal approval, library and laboratory studies, and bench scale.

The technology development requires the implementation of a technology development system involving pilot plant, demonstration, and industrial scales. Regarding the significance of revenue enhancement, technology commercialization is a vital aspect. Thanks to the patent system in the company, three functions should be implemented: efficient pricing and marketing approaches, identification of the potential clients, and application of the client retention strategies.

A communication system can facilitate the interactions among the researchers, developers, marketers, and producers in the industries, universities, research centers, engineering companies, and the company's supporters. A communication system needs 3 major functions: information and knowledge definition, effective application and infrastructure development, and system users training. Additionally, the application of a documentation and knowledge management system can help the companies in managing (creation, overview, saving, and sharing) the reports and experiences.

The organizations should to motivate their employees to retain them and increase their productivity. Thus the employees' needs should be identified; moreover, some mechanisms should be defined and implemented to satisfy their needs.

CONCLUSION

The majority of the countries are now aware of the potential benefits of intellectual property commercialization. Recently, many governments have developed an infrastructure for supporting technology commercialization; some even have searched for external resources. The governments are now highly concerned about the development of higher technologies, as it can dramatically contribute to their industrial development. Technological development and commercialization are rarely achievable through scattered and non-targeted efforts. For this purpose, the companies should possess a well-defined and specific plan to clarify the path to technological development and commercialization. In this regard, modeling approaches can considerably help in analyzing the complexities and managing the dynamics of research and technology organizations.

This chapter described the technology management (TM) process framework and its five constituting processes including identification, selection, acquisition, protection, and exploitation. Soft systems methodology (SSM) is a Soft OR tool that could be implemented in each phase as well as other models. 2 case studies were also reviewed in terms of SSM application in policy-making to commercialize new technologies (Azar et al., 2017) and a technological scenario planning in an R&D institute (Ebrahimi, 2016).

REFERENCES

Anderson, J. E. (1994). *Public policy making: An introduction*. Boston: Houghton. Mifflin Company.

Anderson, J. E. (2003). *Public policymaking: An introduction*. Boston: Houghton Mifflin Company. Retrieved July 20, 2019, from: http://www.kropfpolisci.com/public.policy.anderson.pdf

Azar, A., Vaezi, R., & Mohammadpour Saraiy, V. (2017). Designing a model of policy making of commercialization of nanotechnology using soft systems methodology. *Quarterly Journal of Public Organzations Management*, *5*(2), 89–106.

Chanaron, J. J., & Jolly, D. (1999). Technological management: Expanding the perspective of management of technology. *Management Decision*, *37*(8), 613–620. doi:10.1108/00251749910291578

Checkland, P., & Holwell, S. (2004). Chapter three 'classic OR' and 'soft OR' - An asymmetric complementarity. In M. Pidd (Ed.), *Systems modeling: Theory and practice* (pp. 45–60). Chichester: John Wiley & Sons Ltd.

Dehghani, T. (2015). Technology commercialization: From generating ideas to creating economic value. *International Journal of Organizational Leadership*, *4*(2), 192–199. doi:10.33844/ijol.2015.60449

Ebrahimi, M. (2016). Technology scenario planning with system multi methodology: In the Petrochemical Research and Technology Company. *The 34th International Conference of the System Dynamics Society*.

Etzkowitz, H. (2006). The entrepreneurial university and the triple helix as a development paradigm. *Conference on Launching a Program to Transform University-Industry-Government Relation in Ethiopia*, 29-31.

Gregory, M. J. (1995). Technology management - A process approach. *Proceedings - Institution of Mechanical Engineers*, *209*(5), 347–356. doi:10.1243/PIME_PROC_1995_209_094_02

Jolly, V. K. (2009). *Commercializing new technologies: getting from mind to market*. Boston: Harvard Business school press.

Khalil, T. (2000). *Management of technology: The key to competitiveness and wealth creation*. New York: McGraw Hill.

Klofsten, M., & Evans, D. J. (2000). Comparing academic entrepreneurship in Europe - The case of Sweden and Ireland. *Small Business Economics*, *14*(4), 299–309. doi:10.1023/A:1008184601282

Kollmer, H., & Dowling, M. (2004). Licensing as a commercialization strategy for new technology-based firms. *Research Policy*, *33*(8), 1141–1151. doi:10.1016/j.respol.2004.04.005

Komkov, N. I., & Bondareva, N. N. (2007). Problems in the commercialization of scientific research and ways of addressing them. *Economic Policy*, *18*(1), 2–18.

Krugman, P. (1994). The myth of Asia's miracle. *Foreign Affairs*, *73*(6), 62–78. doi:10.2307/20046929

Markman, G. D., Gianiodis, P. T., & Phan, P. H. (2009). Supply-side innovation and technology commercialization. *Journal of Management Studies*, *46*(4), 625–649. doi:10.1111/j.1467-6486.2009.00835.x

Namdeo, P., Ansarie, M. A., & Bhatnagar, A. (2016). Introduction to technology management. *Industrial Engineering and Management*, *5*(2), 195. doi:10.4172/2169-0316.1000195

Ortega, C. H., Garrido-Vega, P., & Machuca, J. A. D. (2012). Analysis of interaction fit between manufacturing strategy and technology management and its impact on performance. *International Journal of Operations & Production Management*, *32*(8), 958–981. doi:10.1108/01443571211253146

Phaal, R., Farrukh, C. J. P., & Probert, D. R. (2001). Technology management process assessment: A case study. *International Journal of Operations & Production Management*, *21*(8), 1116–1132. doi:10.1108/EUM0000000005588

Phaal, R., Farrukh, C. J. P., & Probert, D. R. (2004a). A framework for supporting the management of technological knowledge. *International Journal of Technology Management*, *27*(1), 1–15. doi:10.1504/IJTM.2004.003878

Phaal, R., Farrukh, C. J. P., & Probert, D. R. (2004b). Technology roadmapping - A planning framework for evolution and revolution. *Technological Forecasting and Social Change*, *71*(1-2), 5–26. doi:10.1016/S0040-1625(03)00072-6

Rasmussen, E., & Gulbrandsen, M. (2006). Initiatives to promote commercialization of university knowledge. *Technovation*, *26*(4), 518–533. doi:10.1016/j.technovation.2004.11.005

Senge, P. M. (1990). *The fifth discipline: The art and practice of the learning organization* (1st ed.). New York: Doubleday/Currency.

Siegel, D. S., & Phan, P. H. (2006). *Analyzing the effectiveness of university technology transfer: Implications for entrepreneurship education*. Retrieved July 13, 2019, from: http://www. economics.rpi.edu

Small, A., & Wainwright, D. (2014). SSM and technology management: Developing multimethodology through practice. *European Journal of Operational Research*, *233*(3), 660–673. doi:10.1016/j.ejor.2013.08.049

Smith, K. B., & Larimer, C. W. (2009). *The public policy theory primer* (2nd ed.). Boulder, CO: Westview Press.

Spilling, O. R. (2004). Commercialization of knowledge-conceptual framework. *The 13th Nordic Conference on Small Business (NCSB) Research.*

Styles, C., & Genua, T. (2008). The rapid internationalization of high technology firms created through the commercialization of academic research. *World Business*, *43*(2), 146–148. doi:10.1016/j.jwb.2007.11.011

Venus, T. (1999). *Getting value from technology a guide to technology management*. Cambridge: University of Cambridge Centre for Technology Management.

Zehner, W. B. (2000). The management of technology (MOT) degree: A bridge between technology and strategic management. *Technology Analysis and Strategic Management*, *12*(2), 283–291. doi:10.1080/713698470

Chapter 7
Soft Systems Methodology as an Approach to the Management of Education

ABSTRACT

Soft systems methodology (SSM) as an action research process has been applied to education systems and, according to the main objective of this chapter to design an improved education system, the applications of SSM in the process of teaching and learning, educational planning, analysis of the examinations department, an educational context for enhancing students' perception and understanding, the cheating problem in the national examination in Indonesia, and personalized learning environment are reviewed. The SSM can be used to analyze the system through providing a deeper understanding as well as the possibility of more clearly capturing the change, which is necessary to prepare the ideal education system that will satisfy the concerned people, specifically students and lecturers.

INTRODUCTION

Secondary schooling has been the target of soft systems approach, hypothesizing headmasters as managers of resources rather than head teachers (Wilson, 1992). Moreover, high education lecturers can use soft systems methodology (SSM) to analyze their teaching and learning methods. It provides the chance for them to conduct a self-audit of teaching and learning strategies. Therefore,

DOI: 10.4018/978-1-7998-4504-1.ch007

SSM is considered as a particularly good tool for self-analysis since it involves the intellectual activity of conceptual modeling. Patel (1995) conducted a study at the level of undergraduate education in order to obtain a deeper understanding of teaching and learning process in this level, providing an appropriate action to improve the process.

Hawkesbury Agricultural College, as Macadam and Packham (1989) reported, was the first place where reforming the educational programs began in 1978. The new programs, mainly departed from the previous methods, i.e. didactic and discipline-based curricula, are relied on experiential learning and systems thinking and practice. As a result of considering the needs of the new curricula and failures to overcome them, the projects improved in 1983-4, leading to a radical restructuring of the School of Agriculture in 1985. The way was indicated by SSM.

Implementing technology at universities has two sides; one side is the university using technologies for virtual learning that is outdated since the needs of the students are more digital now, and the other side the focus is primarily on technology rather than the learning process. According to Nair (2015) SSM may contribute to bring the two sides together through working with different stakeholders at the university as well as considering the needs and requirements to satisfy the learning needs and styles of learners in a personalized learning environment; hence, the institution/tutor-centric approach would shift to a learner-centric one in the educational paradigm.

SSM was the method by which Yadin (2013) could identify the students' difficulties, particularly on unstructured and poorly defined problems. This study aimed at identifying the cause for the low grades in the assignments on computing issues in order to plan corrective actions. Widely used in messy situations to provide a better and deeper understanding of the system while incorporating a variety of viewpoints, SSM was selected to be under investigation in this study. The students' specific difficulties were identified by using SSM to analyze their perceived learning system and a real life example, on the other hand, could be provided as well. Then, the changes were applied to the course structure to address them in a more appropriate way. In addition, SSM as an action research process is performed in several analysis cycles. In case of arising new problems or insufficient improvements after applying the change suggestions, a new cycle of analysis is performed.

Designing an improved education system by using SSM is the main objective of this chapter. In this context, the application of SSM to the teaching and learning process (Patel, 1995), the educational planning (Mehregan and Hosseinsadeh, 2008), analysis of the examination department (Memon, 2011), an educational context for enhancing the students' perception and understanding (Yadin, 2013), the cheating problem in the national examination in Indonesia (Iriani and Manongga, 2018), and personalized learning environment (Nair, 2015) will be reviewed.

PROCESS OF TEACHING AND LEARNING

SSM is of great importance for a reflective practitioner. While requiring only a pen and paper to be used, this methodology is considered as a comprehensive and perceptive to identify the problematic issues (for example, lack of information flows) and to provide recommendations for improving the specified problems. Reasonably, students attempt to achieve the highest possible degree classification in a desirable learning process. Hence, many of the university activities are planned to satisfy the students' learning needs and it remains, however, as a constantly unanswered question for lecturers how this might be best achieved. .

The practitioner could not formulate this issue as a definite hard problem resulting in a feasible solid solution. There are variable matters influencing the process of teaching and learning, such as the topic being taught, students' attitudes or the lecturers' mood as well as teaching method. The real world scenario is preferred to be considered, in SSM, as an area of concern requiring the reflective analysts' attention. Moreover, it seems appropriate to regard the process of teaching as an area of concern, so that it continually focuses the attentions to improve it.

Therefore, the philosophy and thinking of SSM can be applied to this area of concern, aiming at determining any impact of the practitioners' unrecognized activities to satisfy students' learning needs, and any improvement of the new activities and the existing ones to provide an efficient and effective teaching and learning process.

Two components of a rich picture for the main area of concern in this study include the structure; that is, the elements of structure in the real world, which would be the type of activities, the physical layout of the lecture, and seminar rooms and boundaries. The second component is the processes. The elements of this component are the answers to this question "what is going on?" and can include teaching and learning. The climate of situation can be represented by the relationship between the structure and process. A root definition of a particular system could be suggested by the rich picture

Root definition-1 (RD1): A lecturer-owned system is defined as a system operated by both lecturer and students with the available teaching and learning resources to provide the required opportunities and facilities for the students to pass or achieve higher marks in assignments and examinations in a realistic setting while being subject to the requirements and constraints of the University.

In RD1, passing or achieving higher marks in assignments and examinations in a realistic setting is the major transformation. A transformation requires precise input(s) and the accurate output(s) derived from the input(s). In the area of concern under study, the inputs include the students who are not yet passed, and the passed students or those with higher marks are the outputs. The students, here, are considered as customers and the lecturer and students are the actors. The lecturer is the owner of the system, with no restriction to have a single owner of the system. The environmental constraints imposed by the University are considered to be the constraints in this area, too. Lecturer and students in RD1 have a single aim, i.e. weltanschauung. Weltanschauung is the major characteristic through which one root definition can be distinguished from another.

Root definition-2 (RD2): A jointly owned system is operated by lecturer and students using available teaching and learning process to provide the required opportunities and facilities for students to learn relevant knowledge, for their vocational and educational benefit, through delivering lectures while being subject to the various constraints of time, learning and absorption rates of students, limitations of the room and other teaching and learning resources, under the required quality standards by the University and the performance measurement criteria posed by the lecturer.

Learning relevant knowledge is the main transformation in RD2. The input and output for this transformation is relevant knowledge; the first one is to be learned and the other is the learned one. The knowledge beneficial for the students' vocational and educational life and enjoyable to be learned is the weltanschauung in RD2. While the weltanschauung in RD1 focuses on the students' level of achievement, the weltanschauung in RD2 aims at providing worthwhile knowledge for the students to benefit them in both education and vocation. Enjoyment of teaching and learning process is of great importance in the weltanschauung in RD2 as well. Here, the customers are considered to be students and the actors and owners of the system are lecturer and students. The constraints include time for delivering lectures, the learning and absorption rates of students, the physical environment of education, the limitations of the available teaching and learning resources, meeting the quality standards required by the University and performance criteria imposed by the lecturer.

The following 13 activities are the components of a conceptual model of the process of teaching and learning derived from RD2:

1) Know the available teaching and learning resources,
2) Specify available time,
3) Assess the relevant knowledge,
4) Assess beneficial knowledge for vocational and educational life,
5) Set assignments and examinations,
6) Define learning and absorption rates of students,
7) Clarify limitations of the room,
8) Present the lecture,
9) Assess the students' enjoyment of learning,
10) Monitor and control the enjoyment and benefit of the learning process for students,
11) Assess students' achievements in being passed or getting higher marks,
12) Monitor and take control of action to ensure meeting the quality standards of the University,
13) Monitor and control the lecturer's performance.

EDUCATIONAL PLANNING

Educational planning refers to the allocation of educational resources such as teachers, courses, time and educational facilities (classroom, laboratory, and etc.). Educational planning is one of the most important issues repeated every semester for universities. These issues are administrative tasks that must be done each semester in education groups1 or departments. Most universities have a set of organizational goals besides the individual goals and desires influencing this planning. The goals of planners are usually determined by changing students' demands for courses or the willingness of those involved in the planning process to provide some of the necessary courses.

Other factors affecting educational planning are resource constraints such as time and the number of classes available over a given period of time. One of the most important factors to be considered in the process of curriculum development is the teachers' preference for teaching their favorite subjects. There are also preferences for training at a specific time. These issues exist in all academic education systems. Educational planning must be designed and addressed to meet the following objectives:

1) The objectives of the various courses,
2) System policies and resource constraints,
3) Obtaining the approval of professors for their courses and available time,
4) Students' satisfaction with the offered curriculum.

Assigning classes of students to appropriate faculty members, suitable classrooms, and available timeslots can be considered as typical course timetabling problems in a system, requiring students, teachers, and institutional administrators to be involved. A variety of hard operational research technique addressed such problems over the years. Since the universities grow and the teaching programs become more complicated, the heightened complexity and enormous size nature of the course timetabling make it as a problem which is continuously becoming more complex as well. In this context, dealing with the real world situations may contribute to develop new strategies to overcome such complexity in real instances (Mehregan et al., 2012).

One of the strategies applied to overcome such difficulty of complexity is the soft operational research (Soft OR). While Hard OR seeks to solve a problem, Soft OR structures it. The target in SSM is organizational business and process modeling; it reveals the unstructured problems and non-obvious problem solutions. This approach particularly contributes to capturing the required change in order to prepare the ideal university course timetable, leading to the satisfaction of the concerned ones. (Mehregan et al., 2012).

SSM IN EDUCATIONAL PLANNING

Steps 1 and 2: Dealing With Problematic Conditions

The main issue in this study is how to appropriately allocate academic resources in the educational system with regard to the views of the stakeholders involved in the system, and the limitations relevant to the educational regulations and policies in the system as well as the limited physical resources of the faculty, and the time constraints for educational planning. In any educational system, the satisfaction of teachers, students, and other stakeholders with the type of course and its time schedule has a direct impact on the quality of education. Therefore, the quality of education will improve through increasing this

Figure 1. Rich picture of an educational planning system (Mehregan and Hosseinzadeh, 2008)

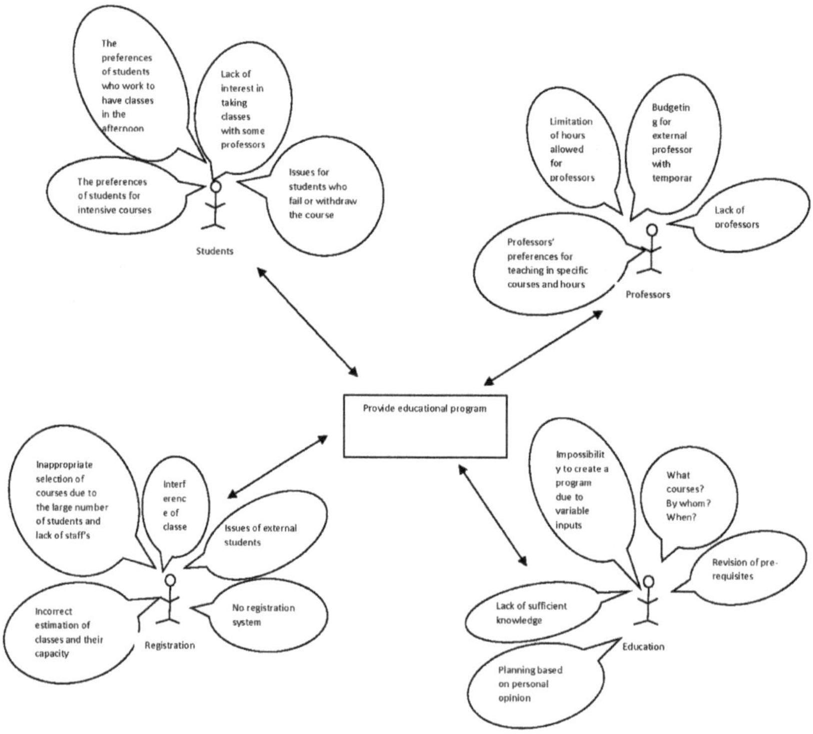

satisfaction. Obviously, in an educational system, the quality of education is very important. On the other hand, appropriate educational planning can be very effective in saving time.

At this stage, using the results from interviews and questionnaires, the rich picture (figure 1) illustrates all the processes, relationships, problems and constraints that exist in the current educational planning of this educational system.

Step 3: Developing Root Definition

Main Root Definition: Educational planning is a system administered by the school authorities, which allows for the provision of a fixed curriculum for the entire course of study for students. This program is developed by the staff of the education department, with the cooperation of the professors and the deputy of education. The final program is designed to maximize

Table 1. CATWOE components of educational planning system (Mehregan and Hosseinzadeh, 2008)

CATWOE	Educational planning system
Customer	Students, professors
Actor	Staff in education department, professors, students, and university in terms of educational rules and regulations
Transformation	Courses are devoted to professors and time.
World view	Providing a curriculum that is sufficiently satisfying for students, professors, education staff, and faculty, thereby raising the level of educational quality.
Owner	Department of Education, Deputy of Education, Professors, University, School officials
Environment	Various restrictions due to academic laws and regulations

the satisfaction of students, professors, and faculty as much as possible and to enhance the overall quality of education. This system is limited by all restrictions imposed on professors, students, courses, etc.

Root definition based on the perspective of students: It is a system operated by the staff of education department, deputy of education, and the group. This program is developed by the staff of education department, with the collaboration of professors and deputy of education for students and professors. Students' preferences are based on pre-enrollment evaluation forms in the preparation of the program and are ultimately submitted to students to enroll. In the prepared curriculum, the courses are delivered in the most compact time, with the least interference and the desired professors, aiming at enhancing the quality of education. This system is limited by student-related restrictions such as students' preference for afternoon classes.

Root Definition based on the perspective of professors: It is a system operated by the staff of education department, deputy of education, the group, and the university. This program is developed by the staff of education department, with the collaboration of professors and deputy of education for students and professors. In this system, professors select the courses they are able to teach and declare their time to education department and then the prepared program is referred to them to make changes based on their preferences. The program is prepared in the most compact time and in accordance with the professors' preferences, resulting in increased quality of teaching. This system works well with restrictions related to professors, students, courses, deputy of education, and classes.

Root definition based on the perspective of the staff of education department: It is a system operated by university, deputy of education, and

Table 2. CATWOE components from perspectives of stakeholders of educational planning system (Mehregan and Hosseinzadeh, 2008)

CATWOE	Students	Deputy of Education	Professors	Staff of education department
Customer	Students, Professors	Students, Professors, Faculty	Students, Professors	Students, Professors
Actor	Staff of education department, Students, Professors, University	Staff of education department, Students, Professors, University	Staff of education department, Students, Professors, University	Staff of education department, Students, Professors, University, Other relevant faculties in curriculum development
Transformation	Takes the curriculum out of the education department and enrolls in classes.	It receives the curriculum developed by the department of education and makes changes to it according to its own authority.	Announces their preference of time scheduling of the courses they are able to teach. The program is then referred to them to make changes based on their preferences.	The educational program is determined according to the educational rules, and syllabus. The prerequisites, teachers' preferences, the number of classes per week, class limitations, and programs offered from other relevant colleges are provided and then referred to the group and the deputy of education for approval. After making their comments, they prepare the final program and present it to the students. Students are provided with the necessary guidance at the time of enrollment.
World view	Deliver the curriculum in the most compact time, with the least interference and with the desired teachers in order to ultimately enhance the quality of education.	The curriculum is designed to increase the satisfaction of students, professors, and groups, reduce complains after enrollment, and ultimately enhance the quality of education.	The program is prepared in a compact and timely manner in accordance with their preferences and enhances the quality of education.	The prepared curriculum will increase the satisfaction of students, professors, groups and the deputy of education, and provide registration with the least difficulty and interference with the program.
Owner	Staff of education department, Deputy of education, Group	University	Staff of education department, Deputy of education, Group, University	University, Deputy of education, Group
Environment	Laws and regulations and restrictions of students	Restrictions on professors, students, courses, deputy of education, and classes	Other rules and regulations regarding professors, students, courses, deputy of education, and classes	Restrictions on professors, students, groups, classes, time scheduling, and educational regulations

the group. This program is developed by the staff of education department, with the collaboration of professors and deputy of education. The educational program is determined according to the educational rules, determined syllabus, the prerequisites, professors' preferences, pre-registration forms and student survey forms, the number of classes per week, class limitations, and programs offered from other relevant colleges and then referred to the group and the deputy of education for approval. After making their comments, they prepare the final program and present it to the students and professors. Students are provided with the necessary guidance by the staff of education department at the time of registration. This system is restricted by all laws and regulations and other restrictions related to professors, students, courses, deputy of education, and classes.

Root definition based on the perspective of the deputy of education: The system is owned by the university and is operated by the staff of education department with the collaboration of professors and deputy of education. In this system, the deputy of education receives the curriculum developed by the department of education and makes changes to it according to its own authority. The curriculum is designed to increase the satisfaction of students, professors, and groups, to reduce complains after enrollment, and ultimately to enhance the quality of education. It operates on restrictions related to professors, students, groups, classes, time scheduling, and educational regulations.

Step 4: Making Conceptual Models

At this point, the root definition is presented in the context of conceptual models whose primary emphasis is on the process of converting data to output in CATWOE components. In other words, the emphasis is on the activities that must be taken to achieve the final output of the system. This model contains the verbs used in the root definitions. Finally, they are linked by a logical definition. In this section, a conceptual model for each of the root definitions is presented. The important point is that these models are not the only models that can be drawn according to the root definitions; but, they are possible models derived from the general agreement of the participants in the study.

The conceptual model for students (Figure 2)

The conceptual model for professors (Figure 3)

The conceptual model for the deputy of education (Figure 4)

Figure 2. The conceptual model for students (Mehregan and Hosseinzadeh, 2008)

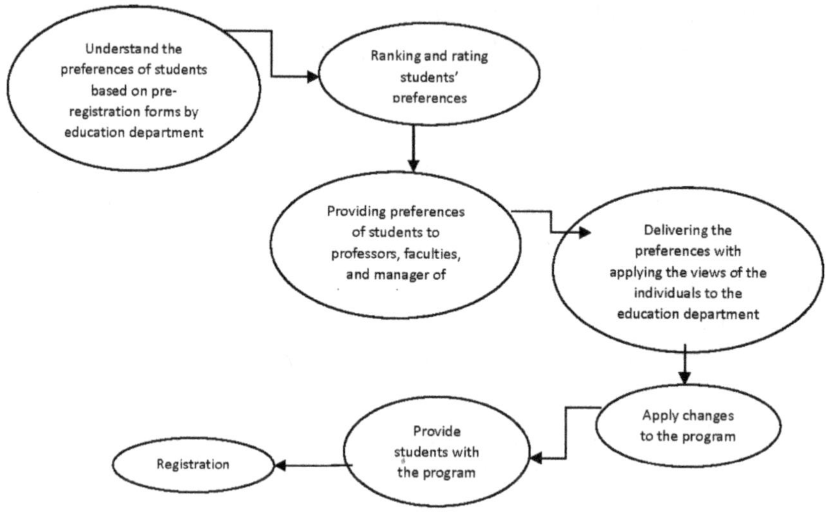

Figure 3. The conceptual model for professors (Mehregan and Hosseinzadeh, 2008)

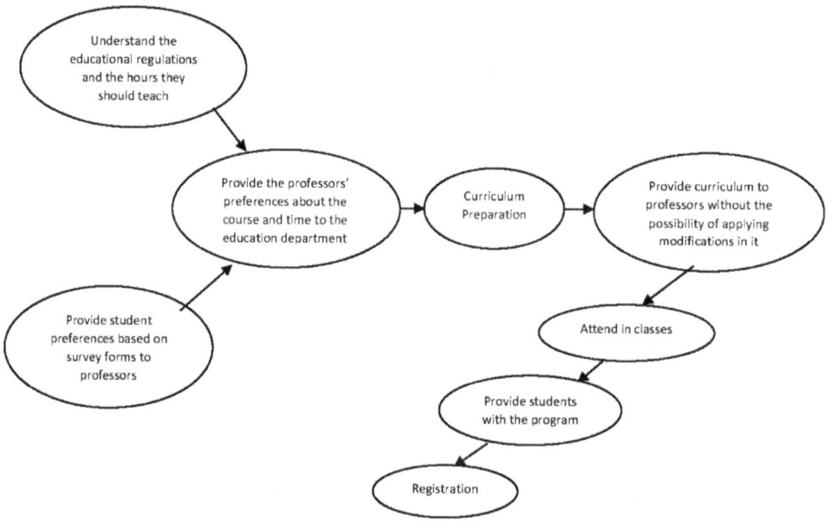

Step 5: Comparison With The Real World

The model reflecting the overall views of all participants is a fully subjective model and must be compared with reality to identify changes that will improve the current situation toward the proposed model. In fact, this step is used

Figure 4. The conceptual model for the deputy of education (Mehregan and Hosseinzadeh, 2008)

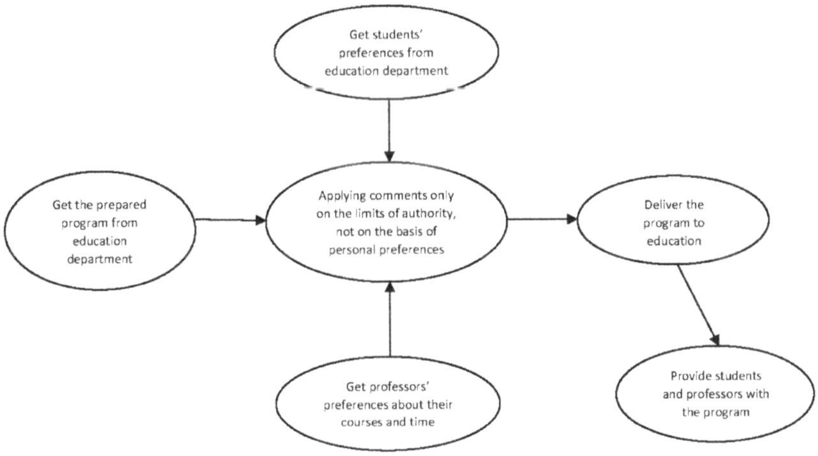

to test the validity of the model. At this point, the models are compared to the real world, using a series of regular questions about each activity and every relationship in the model. For example, the following questions may be asked:

1) Does this happen in real life?
2) How does it happen?
3) By what criteria is it evaluated?
4) And is it considered a problem in the current situation?

Step 6: Identify Required Changes

This step involves systematically identifying the desired changes that are culturally possible. At this stage, two questions are asked to ensure the desirability and possibility of the changes:

1) Are potential changes logically desirable?
2) Is it culturally possible?

Desirability is important because the success of an idea requires a commitment behind it or, in other words, the motivation to make change is critical and must be culturally possible to ensure that these potential changes are worth pursuing. These changes include:

1) Preparing a full course program for students,
2) Initial coordination between groups on the common curriculum,
3) Pre-registration of students in each semester,
4) Providing student with feedback forms to improve the schedule of each semester,
5) On-the-job training of current staff of education department to make appropriate program modifications and assist students at the time of enrollment as well as to hire qualified staff with academic background and experience in educational planning,
6) Understanding the full-time presence of faculty and students,
7) Improved software system for course selection,
8) Establishing a discipline in course selection.

Step 7: Implementation

At this stage, the necessary changes specified in the previous step are implemented in action.

A DIAGRAMMATIC REPRESENTATION OF THE PROBLEMATIC SITUATION IN AN EXAMINATIONS DEPARTMENT

Regarding the increasing number of admissions in the University, affiliated colleges and institutes and considering the examinations around a year, the data of the students is considered to be a critical issue to be managed and retrieved at the right time. The examinations department of the University is not equipped with a fully computerized information system. The vast amount of student information and examination records at the end of every examination faces the existing infrastructure of the examinations department with a lot of problems in processing the results. Hence, all examinations activities have to be manual, paper-based and repetitive from processing of the results to developing the ledgers for the results. This, naturally, takes a lot of time and labor and is subject to human errors and delay in work and frustration for the employees.

Table 3. CATWOE Analysis for the examinations system (Memon, 2011)

CATWOE	examinations system
Customer	Students, Faculty, Staff, Management, Government/Autonomous bodies
Actor	University Staff
Transformation	Students' examinations record error-free, prompt certificates, and reports to the end-users
World view	A secure, reliable and transparent digital examination information system ensures the effective, error-free and prompt service to the end users.
Owner	The university governing body
Environment	Higher education and assessment standards

In addition, delay in results makes problems for the students, including errors in certificates, delay in verification and getting a response for their queries. Sometimes, it indirectly harm students or graduates' career by loss of job opportunities when other stakeholders such as government, autonomous bodies, higher education commission, engineering council and other recruitment agencies cannot get immediate response for their queries and data verifications for them.

Considering the objectives and problems of the new system, the root definition is defined as: an examinations system that is secure, reliable and transparent, and stores, retrieves, manages, monitors, and controls the examinations records through developing and implementing integrated examinations information system that ensures providing the stakeholders with effective, error-free and prompt service.

The main purpose of the system is revealed: controlling the examinations records through developing and implementing integrated examinations information system that ensures providing the stakeholders with effective, error-free and prompt service.

The students in a system are considered as the main customers. Unavailability of the automated integrated information system of the examinations department may lead to a lot of problems for students, including delay in getting results, frustration to know their academic status and errors in certificates. Furthermore, faculty members who can send student results online and check their academic records, and other Government/ autonomous bodies for degree verification are part of the system. Dealing with students' record and playing roles in transforming the examinations records into meaningful error-free reports and certificates, the staff are important stakeholders and actors. Providing a secure, reliable and transparent management of the examinations record as well as error-free and prompt service to the stakeholders can be guaranteed by using a centralized integrated examinations information system. Such a system is helpful for the staff to get relief from intensive repetitive manual activities that may cause frustration. On the other hand, the governing body of the university can impose certain changes or decisions to stop or apply the system, based on the environmental constraints led by higher education and assessment standards.

THE CAUSE FOR THE LOW GRADES IN THE ASSIGNMENTS

This study was basically aimed at identifying the cause for the low grades in the assignments on computing issues in order to plan corrective actions. Here, the course and the problematic situation regarding the assignments in the first group can be defined as the system. The students, in this case, play the role of clients and use the system and the conceptual models developed by the analysts who suggest feasible changes, too. The decreased difference between the average grades of the two groups of assignments can be regarded as success. Regarding using SSM and as an action research, this exercise will repeat itself until the anticipated results will be achieved.

Engaging in a class exercise to develop a definition of the conceptual model for the course was the next step for students after learning the SSM. Slightly different approaches and definitions were suggested after a short moderated class discussion. Finally, the following CATWOE definition was agreed.

Table 4. CATWOE Analysis to the course as a system (Yadin, 2013)

CATWOE	For the course as a system
Customer	Students
Actor	Lecturers, students (in teamwork and in class discussions)
Transformation	Extending knowledge related to organizational consulting using various methodologies. Specifically "new knowledge" from unfamiliar disciplines like SSAD.
World view	With the degree graduates will be able to find better, more interesting jobs and increase their salaries. The potential employer is looking for a specific degree and since this is a mandatory course, it is required for obtaining the degree.
Owner	Department head, college management
Environment	The higher education counsel (that monitors all academic studies), academic excellence, college regulations, other courses, work and family

Based on this CATWOE, the root definition was presented as: "This course is a system by which the students are provided with the required knowledge to fulfill the requirements to obtain the degree. Future potential employers are looking for such degrees to hire new employees. Special emphasis should be given, in providing this knowledge, to new disciplines, such as SSAD2, that were not previously learned or required during enrollment to the program. Performing the transformations within constrains imposed by laws and regulations, and providing a flexible study format to help students meet their time requirements in other courses, their works, as well as social and family commitments are considered to be the main abilities of the system."

Using the SSM, the next step was defining a set of activities required for achieving the root definition by drawing the conceptual model.

- Identifying lecturer
- Defining content
- Defining constraints
- Making the course
- Defining prerequisites
- Teaching
- Working with new stuff

Table 5. CATWOE Analysis for the honest national exam (Iriani and Manongga, 2018)

CATWOE	For the honest national exam
Customer	Students and parents
Actor	Teachers, principals as policy makers for school and teachers, local government who make educational policies in their local region and provide education facilities, central government who defines the policies of the national examination.
Transformation	Establishment of a national examination with a higher level of honesty or integrity, low rates of cheating, and without anxiety on students and schools.
World view	All stakeholders involved are responsible to provide an honest national exam.
Owner	Parents, teachers, principals, local government, and central government can stop the transformation if they do not follow ethics, standards, and their duties.
Environment	Success meaning in the society, agencies who recruit graduates with high score of the national exam, and limitation of budget

Table 6. CATWOE Analysis for supporting online assessment by a PLE at universities (Nair, 2015)

CATWOE	For supporting online assessment at universities by a PLE
Customer	Students
Actor	Teachers, IT team, examination committee
Transformation	Teachers create an online assessment for students
World view	Students do exams/assessments to get credits
Owner	examination committee
Environment	Computer lab/ home

CHEATING IN THE NATIONAL EXAMINATION

Iriani and Manongga (2018) applied SSM to understand the reasons why the cheating happened continuously in the national examination in Indonesia. The honesty or integrity of parties who are involved in the national exam is one of the key issues. In this regard, several problems were presented in rich picture: 1) risk level of passing encourages some parties to cheat, 2) lack of governmental policies in defining passing standards throughout the country, 3) success meaning in the society identical with high score in the national exam, 4) the fear of graduation for students and schools, and 5) known patterns and keys. To describe the honest national exam and formulate the root definition, CATWOE analysis was used.

Referring to the root definition, a conceptual model has been created to identify the activities needed to develop a system for an honest national exam. Some activities and their interactions in the conceptual model are defined as follows:

1) The national exam should be converted to computer based test (CBT) by allocating more budgets for improving IT infrastructure,
2) Improving teachers competencies by allocating more budgets,
3) Changing the meaning of success in the society,
4) Changing the standards of recruitment and universities,
5) The result of the national exam should be accompanied by the results of schools for the graduation.

PERSONALIZED LEARNING ENVIRONMENT (PLE)

In the study of Nair (2015) about shifting to a learner-centric approach, some concerns during identifying problem situation and rich picture are specified: 1) policy implications of creating a PLE at universities, 2) teachers' beliefs about a PLE-enabled classroom such as workloads of teachers, 3) students acceptance of a PLE such as the ability to create learning community, 4) online assessment support at universities by a PLE, 5) the necessity to update a PLE, and 6) cyber security of the PLE. Afterwards, some of the important perspectives are explained by the CATWOE analysis. For instance, CATWOE analysis for supporting online assessment by a PLE are presented in Table 6.

After finalizing root definitions, the relevant conceptual models have been developed by the following steps:

- Define activities to be carried out according to the Transformation in the CATWOE,
- Define dependencies or independencies of activities,
- Check whether the model for having systems properties such as:

Figure 5. The conceptual model for the online assessment (Nair, 2015)

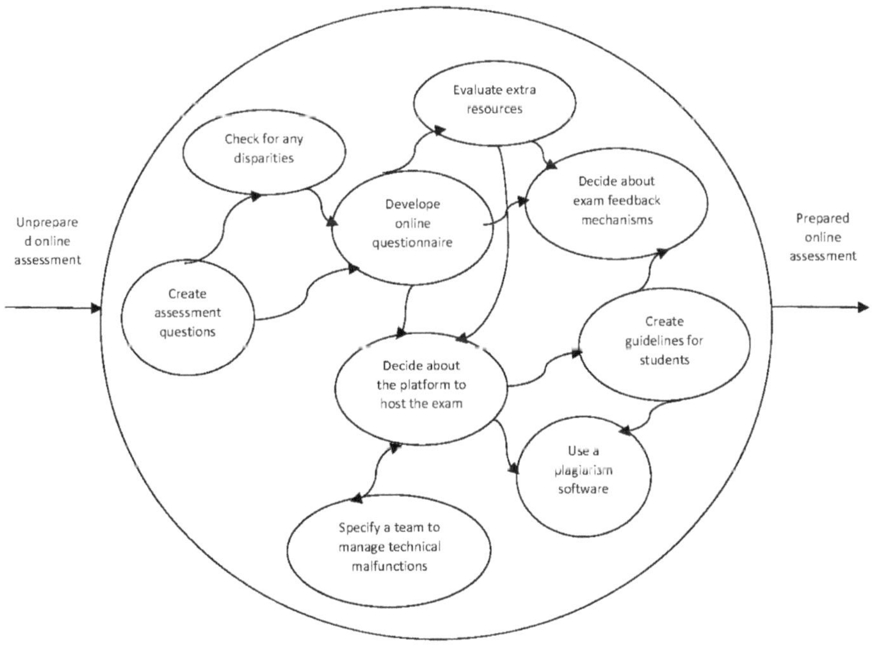

1) input and output for the accepted input,
2) transformation that is taking place,
3) boundary that separates the system from its environment,
4) integrated elements including control, power, decision making, and resources,
5) the purpose of the system,
6) performance measurement of the system,
7) clients as beneficiaries or victims of the system,
8) decision makers who affect the operations of the system,
9) constraints that cannot be changed,
10) unexpected outcomes in the system in case of a change,
11) system hierarchy, and
12) mechanical nature of the system.

After developing conceptual models, they have been compared to what actually happens in the real world. What is present? What is missing? What is the stakeholders' viewpoints about the system? Then, based on the analysis and insights created, a change should happen in the situation.

CONCLUSION

The target in SSM is organizational business and process modeling; it reveals the unstructured problems and non-obvious problem solutions. This approach particularly contributes to capturing the required change in order to prepare the ideal university course timetable, leading to the satisfaction of the concerned ones.

Two components of a rich picture for the main area of concern include the structure; that is, the elements of structure in the real world, such as class rooms. The second component is the processes such as teaching and learning and examination. The climate of situation can be represented by the relationship between the structure and process. A root definition of a particular system could be suggested by the rich picture. Designing an improved education system by using SSM was the main objective of this chapter. In this context, the application of SSM to the teaching and learning process, the educational planning, analysis of the examination department, an educational context for enhancing the students' perception and understanding, the cheating issue in the national examination in Indonesia, and personalized learning environment at universities were reviewed.

REFERENCES

Iriani, A., & Manongga, D. (2018). Using soft systems methodology as an approach to evaluate cheating in the national examination. *Journal of Theoretical and Applied Information Technology*, *96*(11), 3344–3355.

Macadam, R. D., & Packham, R. G. (1989). A case study in the use of soft systems methodology: Restructuring an academic organization to facilitate the education of systems agriculturalists. *Agricultural Systems*, *30*(4), 351–367. doi:10.1016/0308-521X(89)90004-8

Mehregan, M. R., & Hosseinzadeh, M. (2008). An application of Soft System Methodology in educational planning of a university. *Basirat Journal*, *15*(40), 51–84.

Mehregan, M. R., Hosseinzadeh, M., & Kazemi, A. (2012). An application of soft system methodology. *Procedia: Social and Behavioral Sciences*, *41*, 426–433. doi:10.1016/j.sbspro.2012.04.051

Memon, S. (2011). *Designing Examinations Information System Management: a comparative case study application of Soft Systems Methodology* (Master thesis). Aalborg University.

Nair, U. (2015). Soft systems methodology for personalized learning environment. *E-Learning and Digital Media*, *12*(1), 34–56. doi:10.1177/2042753014558375

Patel, N. V. (1995). Application of soft systems methodology to the real world process of teaching and learning. *International Journal of Educational Management*, *9*(1), 13–23. doi:10.1108/09513549510075998

Wilson, B. (1992). *Systems: Concepts, Methodologies and Applications* (2nd ed.). London: Wiley.

Yadin, A. (2013). Soft systems methodology in an educational context—Enhancing students perception and understanding. *International Journal of e-Education, e-Business, e-. Management Learning*, *3*(5), 351–356.

ENDNOTES

1 Each group refers to a subject area in a faculty.

2 Structured Systems Analysis and Design (SSAD) methodologies used in software-based projects.

Chapter 8
Application of Soft Systems Methodology to the Real-World Processes of Human Resource Management

ABSTRACT

Systems approach to human resource management (HRM) regards it as a unified and purposeful system containing interrelated parts. In order to develop HR decisions and practices, the soft systems methodology (SSM), as an approach, causes a better understanding of the system and more meaningful decision making. Various applications of SSM in HRM were reviewed in this chapter, including employee participation, group creativity, HR development, HR maintenance, and knowledge worker productivity. The main discussion of this chapter is that SSM can strongly improve the intersubjective understanding necessary for effective group development and progress. It is especially helpful to challenge paradigms, leading to enhanced group creativity. The issue of current HR development resulting from the lack of any argument on the central role of SSM in this development was another topic. Finally, low knowledge worker productivity through SSM was explained.

DOI: 10.4018/978-1-7998-4504-1.ch008

INTRODUCTION

Management is primarily aimed at finding solutions to human problems. Human Resource Management (HRM) is a central sub-system that interacts closely and continuously with other sub-systems in an organization. The policies, programs and practices of the HRM sub-system determine the quality of people in all sub-systems. In the modern era of automation and computerization, HRM is considered to be very significant since competent people are needed to work with machine; otherwise, it seems useless. The factors making HRM seems significant include increased size and complexity of organizations, trained professional and knowledge workers, rapid developments in technology, increased number of women in the workforce, increased expectations from employers, revolution in technology of information, and rapid changes in jobs and skills requiring long-term planning of manpower.

The organization is viewed, by the systems approach to management, as a unified, purposeful system containing interrelated parts. The manager, through this approach, regards the organization as a whole and as a part of the larger external environment. Being abstracted from the broader social context, much of the data providing the basis for many HRM decisions is meaningless. Soft Systems Methodology (SSM) identifies the importance of the organizational culture and considers the organizational problems as the result of people's different viewpoints about the same situation. Dealing with the practical human interest, SSM uses the interpretative paradigm assumptions about social context to develop mutual understanding. In fact, SSM is the response to the complexity of everyday problems hardly possible to fit into mathematically expressed general theory of systems (Checkland, 1993). According to Checkland (1993), stakeholders' different views towards the problems and therefore the components of the system caused them more complex. Hence, the SSM identifies the problem owners who play roles in giving the points of view in the system. In this context, it can be said that SSM is useful for HRM.

In order to identify competence requirements in HRM, Brocklesby (1995) used SSM. Utomo and Yulia (2018) also used SSM to formulate human resource development (HRD) strategy/ method. The formulation of HRD strategy for medium and small industries in Laweyan, Surakarta, was the finding after using the method of SSM. This chapter reviews various applications of

SSM in HRM such as employee participation, group creativity, HRD, HR maintenance, and knowledge worker productivity.

SSM IN PARTICIPATION

One of the applications of SSM, which is politically intricate, multifaceted and technically indeterminate category is employee participation (or workers' participation). It contains multiple meanings, various concepts and aims and is an important component of the HRM package (Leonardi, 2015). Participation is a process through which the employees can be involved and provided with the opportunity to influence and, where appropriate, take part in decision making of the related matters (Au, 2016).

The practical human interest and the assumptions of the interpretative paradigm can be considered as concerns of goals agreement, performance feedback, and the participation of staff. SSM can play an important and effective role in improving inter-subjective understanding indispensable for effective group development and progress.

A major condition to achieve freedom in organizations is participation. According to Mumford (1996), there are two conditions for choice and decision to manifest group desires. First, all interested users of a system or their representatives must be included in the group, i.e. the meaning of participation. Second, effective communication referring to free and open discussion of needs, accepting challenges and negotiating agreed outcomes.

SSM can be used to increase mutual understanding in groups by providing full participation through identifying problems and learning to make improvements. The following cases can be achieved by using SSM: agreement on goals, explaining the expectations and actions of management, providing feedback on performance of individuals and the group, and most importantly, achieving mutual understanding in all the above subjects.

SSM AND GROUP CREATIVITY

In order to survive and grow in a new competitive environment, organizations will not have a way beyond the acquisition of sustainable competitive advantage. Regarding the fact that the competitive advantage based on creativity is one of the key factors in the survival of organizations in the present age, it is necessary to consider the factors affecting the formation of the organizational creativity process in organizational decision-making. Many people and factors are involved in the process of organizational creativity, and hence, the decision in this regard is one of the real and complex issues of the real world. SSM is one of the operations of research methods that represents, structures and solves complex problems.

Creativity is inherently a complex concept. According to some views, creativity is the use of mental abilities to create a new thought or concept (Morgan, 1953). In all definitions presented for creativity, there is a common element: development of something unique (Mackinnon, 1962). From an organizational point of view, creativity is the concept of new thinking and design to improve and enhance the quality or quantity of organization activities such as productivity, service and product development, cost reduction, and new and better services and products (Oldham and Cummings, 1996). Therefore, creativity does not happen by itself, but the organization's staff cause it to occur (Sternberg et al., 1997). Many organizations try to recruit people with more creative ideas (Amabile, 1996). Some studies have shown that the only recruitment of creative people cannot be effective in enhancing organizational creativity; rather, environmental conditions must be adjusted in a way to stimulate inner motivation (Amabile, 1996), and increase the agility of the creativity of the staff and consequently organizational creativity (Cummings and Oldham, 1997). Accordingly, organizations must work to eliminate the barriers to creativity and increase the factors making the creativity possible (Connell, 2001).

Creativity can arise by SSM through appropriate context and circumstances. SSM is particularly useful in complex situations of problem-solving and where a human activity system is of major concern. It is regarded as an ideal tool in designing systems. Other methodologies have been frequently used with SSM, aiming at enhancing its flexibility and usefulness (Molineux and Haslett, 2007).

According to Molineux and Haslett (2007), the three categories of creativity techniques include: paradigm preserving techniques, paradigm stretching techniques, and paradigm breaking techniques. It is stated that brainstorming as a paradigm preserving technique encourages the participants to build on others' ideas, resulting in developing the ideas but not significantly changes and hence, the paradigm boundaries are maintained. However, the paradigm breaking techniques can depict the rich pictures through using unrelated stimuli and forced association to stimulate creativity. Using these techniques to apply all their senses and express themselves, the participants can use other modes of communication including drawing, dreaming, and role playing. SSM contains the technique of rich pictures, and hence, is more useful to breaking paradigms and can cause enhanced group creativity. Only once trust has been developed between the participants as well as between the participants and the facilitator, paradigm breaking techniques can be used. Groups can undertake these techniques only where team feelings are concerned and the facilitator supports the participants' emotions, identity, and self-awareness.

Steps 1 and 2: Dealing With Problem

Step 1: The fundamental issue here is the representing and structuring of organizational creativity to create creative output, resulting in sustainable competitive advantage. In the new organizations, the competitive advantage is considered to be the survival factor of the organization. One of the most fundamental factors in creating the competitive advantage is innovation in products, services, ideas, processes, and business models. In order to achieve organizational innovation, organizational creativity should be of greater attention. Organizational creativity is shaped by individual, group, and organizational creativity, or a combination of these three forms of creativity. Thus, issue of organizational creativity needs to be addressed.

Step 2: At this stage, a rich picture representing all the processes, relationships, difficulties and limitations of organizational creativity in the new organizations has been identified by using the results from the questionnaire and receiving the opinions of the experts in the field of organization and organizational creativity. The questions raised to collect information include:

- How do active organizations often work to produce creative outputs?
- What are the causes for organizational creativity?
- Who are the involved people in organizational creativity?
- What internal factors do affect organizational creativity?
- What external factors do affect organizational creativity?
- What is the relationship between the influential internal and external factors?
- What is the process to make creative outputs in the organization?
- What are the limitations of organizational creativity and the people and processes involved in it?
- What can be effective in the progress of organizational creativity?

Table 1. Definitions of CATWOE in Organizational creativity to create a sustainable competitive advantage (Nikghadam Hojati et al., 2017)

CATWOE	Organizational creativity to create a sustainable competitive advantage
Customer: Who are the agents and stakeholders of organizational creativity?	• Clients of the organization: The clients of the organization can be divided into two categories of actual and potential clients. The actual clients' • Needs are constantly changing, and if the organization does not respond to their needs, the organization may lose its actual clients and will be losing its current position on the market. Also, the lack of attention to the expectations and needs of the potential clients and failure to provide products and services and proper marketing by the organization can lead to a loss of potential market share as well as making the competitors stronger. In addition, obvious and hidden needs of the potential clients can be used to create new and unconventional ideas. • Official staff working in the organization have roles in the organization's current activities and are able to engage in innovative processes and influence the organization's performance, existing processes, and the transformation of inputs into outputs by their creative ideas. Official staff can influence the organization by their creative capabilities, knowledge, social influence, and internal motives and are able to create ideas in line with the organization's goals. • Owners of the organization: The needs, desires, thoughts and perspectives of the owner in sole proprietorships, partnerships, joint ventures, limited liability partnerships, and nonprofit businesses can affect the organization's creativity process and support the creative atmosphere of the organization effectively by the influence on goals, strategies and the vision of the organization. • Organizational leaders: Supporting the managers, especially senior executives, is a key factor in organizational creativity. Managers support the transformation of values and norms, risk taking and tolerance of ambiguity in applying their creative ideas properly, and employees, future and opportunities available in the environment, alignment with conditions and realities, independent decision making, growth in productivity which can be effective in organizational creativity. • The organization competitors: The products and services of competitors and their performance in the market, the same as environmental pressure, always affect the organization and the conditions. In addition, information obtained from competitors can be as relevant knowledge to the field of the organization, organizational groups, and employees of the organization and be useful in the process of creativity and providing new ideas. On the other hand, the creative outcomes of the organization also influence conditions and activities of the organization. Therefore, it is necessary to consider the competitors of the organization as the customers of the organizational creativity.
Actor(s): Who are actors and collaborators in organizational creativity?	Staff, the organization's creativity groups, owners of the organization, managers of the organization, including senior managers, middle managers and operational managers, as well as research and development department, HR department, marketing department, production department, and financial department.
Transformation: What turns by organizational creativity? What are inputs and outputs?	Actors and participants' intrinsic motivations in organizational creativity along with knowledge of the relevant field, social influence, individuals' creative behaviors, employees' cognitive abilities, personality of staff, group composition, group processes, and group and environment characteristics transform initial conditions of the organization into creative outputs. The initial conditions of an organization can be defined as processes, products, services, performance levels, productivity, organization status against competitors in the market, knowledge of the organization, systems in the organization, and so on. Innovative outputs of the organization can also be identified by innovative products, services, processes, and methods inspired by the creative idea of employees supported by managers and owners of the organization through knowledge of the relevant field, social influence, creative behaviors, cognitive abilities and individual personality, either individually or collectively, in the processes of creative groups that are influenced by the characteristics of the group and the environment that also affects the entire process.
World view: What is the worldview of organizational creativity?	The ultimate goal of the organizational creativity is organizational survival in the current and future competitive and dynamic environment, which is to preserve the competitive advantage of the organization, improve the organization's performance and productivity, improve the competitive position of the market, and make better use of the limited resources.

continued on following page

Table 1. Continued

CATWOE	Organizational creativity to create a sustainable competitive advantage
Owner: Who is the owner of organizational creativity? Who has the power to stop creativity?	Organization's owners, managers at all levels of management, organization's staff.
Environment: What are the environmental constraints?	• Creativity constraints: Include limits on the lack of a structured design of the organizational creativity. • Employee constraints: Restrictions on the maximum and minimum time employees can be present in the organization, restrictions on the maximum time that employees can devote to a creative idea alongside doing routine duties; limitations of access to organizational resources by employees; limitations of access to information by employees; restriction of employees' access to tacit knowledge of other employees; lack of adequate knowledge of employees about information management systems; employees' unwillingness to accept the process and culture of creative ideas in the organization, negligence of creative ideas when it comes to staff's minds, lack of job satisfaction and lack of empowerment of individual employees for creative ideas. • Restrictions on organizational creativity groups: Absence of knowledge related to the field by individuals participating in organizational creativity groups, lack of sharing unique knowledge of participants in organizational creativity groups, inadequate interaction between participants to share the group's creative ideas, the individuals' unwillingness to share their unconventional ideas in the group because of the fear of being ridiculed by others, the elimination or negligence of many unconventional ideas due to the dominance of convergent thinking of organizational creativity groups, and the lack of proper implementation of divergent thinking in organizational creativity groups. • Managerial constraints: Not familiar with the sources of creativity, the time limit for the implementation of creative organizational climate, the limitation of power to influence the creative organizational climate, the environmental pressures to achieve the organization's goals in the shortest possible time, the lack of managers' risk taking trait in providing creative organizational climate, the lack of managers' risk-taking on financial investment and time devotion on creative ideas for achieving organizational innovations, management inability in planning security providing and privacy of innovative ideas presented up to the time these ideas achieve expected return on investment, holding joint meetings with the managers in a friendly atmosphere. • Restrictions of owners: The owners' unwillingness to invest in creative ideas for their inherent risks, the conflict between short-term interests of owners and long-term gains from organizational creativity plans, limitations of financial resources for implementing sustainable organizational creativity, and insufficient knowledge about accepting the need to implement sustainable organizational creativity. • Organization-specific constraints: the lack of alignment of organizational structure with organizational creativity, lack of organizational resources for implementing organizational creativity, non-flexible organizational rules and guidelines, and a disruptive environment for organizational creativity, the task-orientation of many organizational occupations, non-flexible organizational systems and processes that are inconsistent with organizational creativity, and the non-alignment of organizational tasks with creative ideas.

Step 3. Developing Root Definitions

The basic root definition: Organizational creativity is a function of the creative output of individuals and groups of the organization, which is directly or indirectly influenced by the contextual attributes (such as culture, resource constraints, information and communication technologies), social impact, knowledge, demands of the owners of the organization, the clients' needs, competitors' behavior, market situation and environment.

Root definition of employees: Organizational creativity is a function of the creative output of individuals and groups of the organization, which is influenced directly by the cognitive abilities, personality, knowledge, genetics, creativity and intrinsic motivation of the employees, the contextual features, social influence, and the management style and the directors' leadership. The initial conditions of the organization (influenced by environmental, contextual and social conditions, rivals, clients, etc.) affect the owners' willingness and managers' decisions, resulting in a need for organizational innovation and creativity, as well as encouraged creative behavior in the organization by the managers.

Root definition of organizational creativity groups: Organizational creativity is a function of the creative output of individuals and groups of the organization. In many cases, the organization creates organizational creativity by creative groups whose collective creative behavior is prerequisite. This creative behavior of a group is influenced by creative behavior of employees, the environment, social and institutional implications, and group features and processes. The initial conditions of the organization that are affected by the environmental, contextual and social conditions, rivals, markets, clients and the organization affect the owners' willingness and managers' decisions. Therefore, there is a need for organizational innovation and creativity, making managers to encourage creative behavior in the organization. In this regard, managers support creative activities and behaviors in organizational creativity groups. These groups can be supported by managers and along with other factors using techniques of creating ideas, present creative ideas and behaviors of the groups.

Root definition of managers: Organizational creativity is a function of creative outputs of individuals and groups of the organization, who are influenced by leadership styles, cognitive abilities, personality, knowledge, education, genetics and managers' intrinsic motivation, managers' awareness and motivation, and how they interact with the environment, clients, owners and competitors.

Root definition of owners: Organizational creativity is a function of the creative output of individuals and groups of the organization that respond to the needs of the owners, set new goals, innovative organizational goals and leading organizational strategies. Owners of an organization, in accordance with current status of the organization, the status of competitors, the environmental conditions, and the market, clients' demands, the desire for more profitability, and the desire to improve the organization's performance, require goals and strategies, processes, products, services, or new ideas. They inform the organization's managers about this need for proper planning. Managers of the organization also try to use management methods and tools to enhance the staff's creative behavior and creativity groups of the organization.

Root definition of the organization: The organization affects the creative behavior of the groups of the organization and that of the employees. Organizational information and communication systems, organizational culture, resource constraints, organizational structure, organization's size, and many other contextual factors directly and indirectly affect organizational creativity. Moreover, organizational creativity itself is effective. Organizational creativity, which is present in most ideas, services, products, business processes, and methods, affects the status of the organization in the market, its competitive advantage, its status from the clients' point of view, its opposition to competitors, interaction with the environment and consequently, the survival of the organization.

Figure 1. Conceptual model of organization (Nikghadam Hojati, et al., 2017)

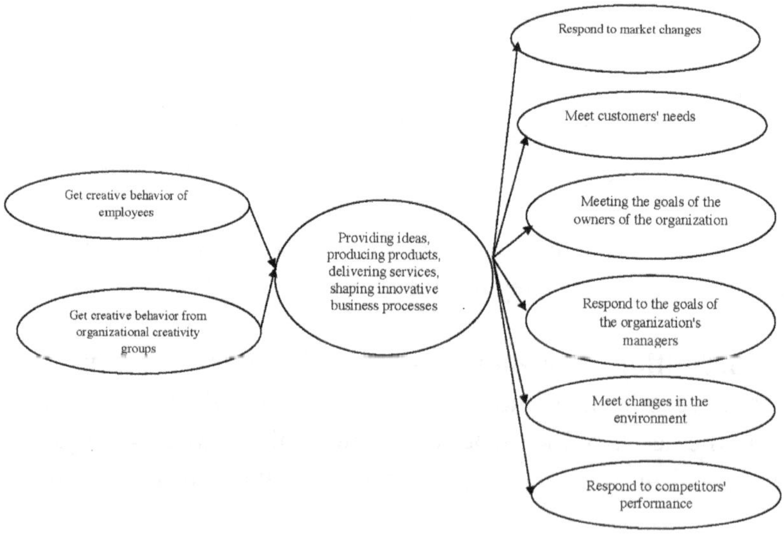

Step 4. Making Conceptual Models

In the fourth stage, root definitions are presented in the form of conceptual models whose main emphasis is on the data conversion into outputs used in the CATWOE components. These models have verbs that are used in root definitions and are ultimately linked to a logical combination. Here's a conceptual model of the organization as described in Figure 1.

SSM IN HRD

The process of optimizing the production and utilization of the workforce is referred to as HRD through which human expertise is developed by developing the organization, training personnel, and making developments to improve performance (Swanson and Holton, 2001). Therefore, HRD as a set of systematic tasks can enrich employees by skills, knowledge, and experiences to meet the current needs and achieve the goals in the future.

Yawson (2012) tried to provide meanings of HRD, emotional intelligence, and social capital as well as their association to organizational productivity; in this context, he argued how system thinking and theory play a central role and how one of the disciplines HRD is borrowed from them. The framework of systems theory causes the integration of content and process components of the existing theories on career development. The long-standing criticisms and questions against career development can be best answered by system theory and thinking, and particularly by soft systems thinking. The utility of the systems approach to return on investment (ROI) measurement in the HRD field can be reflected by regarding the applications.

Due to over reliance on simple systems model of input-output transformation, HRD faced several limitations to be considered as a field of study, resulting

Table 2. Comparison of HRM and HRD (Haslinda, 2009)

HRM	HRD
Definition: HRM refers to a process of human talents management to accomplish the organization's objective.	Definition: HRD is a range of systematically structured activities carried out within a specific time and developed to produce behavioral change.
Process: 1.Recruitment and selection, 2.Compensation and benefits, 3.Labor and Industrial relations, 4. Safety and Health management.	Activities: 1.Training and development, 2.Performance Appraisals Management, 3.Career planning and development, 4. Change Management.

Table 3. Definitions of CATWOE in HRD strategy formulation (Utomo and Yulia, 2018)

CATWOE	HRD strategy formulation
Customer	Entrepreneurs, batik crafters
Actor	Batik crafters, entrepreneurs, universities/Colleges, counselors and mentors
Transformation	Strategy formulation for batik industrial HRD through various programs such as training, mentoring, empowerment, and research.
World view	HRD strategy formulation, knowledge creation, and involvement in planning, controlling, and improving the sustainable HRD.
Owner	Entrepreneurs/companies, local government, bank
Environment	Limited HRD programs and knowledge transfer

Table 4. Activities of the conceptual model and recommendations to change the real-world (Utomo and Yulia, 2018)

Activity	Recommendation
Personal development and Skills training	• University–industry cooperation, • Improve facilities for self-development.
Comparative study	Conducting comparative studies continuously.
Batik exhibition	Local government should support the batik exhibition.
Counseling and mentoring	Local government should organize training and mentoring.
Continuous research	It is essential to perform continuous research for HRD studies.
Company development	Approaches for company development should be promoted.

in the apparent lack of applications of system theory and thinking in HRD practice and research. Besides, the dominant epistemology in the field of HRD is linear epistemology and HRD models have served HRD well but can no longer be the dominant epistemology.

Utomo and Yulia (2018) formulated HRD strategy/ method by using SSM. Some of the problems in the human resource aspects of batik industry are as follows: 1) limited HR development which is highly dependent on skilled batik craftsmen; 2) lack of knowledge management in the batik industry, and 3) the need of continuous training for having a better quality.

After defining the conceptual model and for the purpose of improving production in order to increase income by batik entrepreneurs, the model was compared with the real-world. The results of this comparison is presented in Table 4.

MAINTENANCE OF HUMAN RESOURCES

Human resources management (HRM) is defined as the identification, selection, recruitment, training and development of human resources in order to achieve organizational goals (French, 2006). HRM emphasizes organizational needs to human resources and the role of management in hiring, motivating and developing individuals to sustain these needs (Boxall, 2014). HRM has an impact on sustainable competitive advantage. Human resource maintenance system is one of the main factors of HRM.

According to the experts, the most important aspect of any business is the strike of workers and the sudden departure of work. In fact, the staff and their management abilities are the factors effective on achieving a competitive advantage (Boxall and Purcell, 2011; Pfeffer, 1998; Gratton et al., 1999). Maintenance of human resources has a wider meaning than wage, welfare and safety plans. Meanwhile, employees' expectations are unmatched in all organizations and identifying these expectations seems difficult. In fact, human resource maintenance system is a dependent variable based on preventive activities, medical care, welfare services, retirement measures and insurance activities, which refers to the concept of organizational commitment and employees' job commitment that affects positively the job performance and employee survivability. Therefore, in today's advanced HRM, there is a special view to strategies of HR maintenance. This strategy ensures that the key people stay in the organization, and that the loss of a high and costly employee turnover is based on the analysis of the causes of retention and desertion (Armestrang, 2010).

Harkness and Lea (2001) argued, based on their research findings, that factors such as employee growth and career development with learning, engaging and challenging work, meaningful work and a sense of doing worthwhile works, being part of a group, having good leaders, appreciation of good work and etc. are among the most important reasons for the retention of employees in an organization and preventing their abandonment. Another study of the labor force trend discussed about the imminent shortage of highly skilled workers who have the required knowledge and ability to perform at high levels. This means that failure of organizations to retain high-skilled employees will lead to a loss of valuable and highly skilled, and experienced human capital (Gayathri et al., 2012). In another study, factors such as employee dissatisfaction with the organization, lack of education and development or growth, as well as the lack of appreciation of the organization are among the

Table 5. Definitions of CATWOE in HR maintenance system (Rezayi and Farhadi Mahali, 2014)

CATWOE	HR maintenance system
Customer	Staff and managers
Actor	HR managers, staff
Transformation	Maintaining the competent and qualified people in the organization
World view	Accurate knowledge of the key factors influencing the retention of employees in the organization
Owner	HR Manager, Senior Manager
Environment	Constraints on cultures, different values and requirements of employees, political and economic constraints, employees' economic problems

most important factors for the abandonment of talented employees (Sandhya and Kumar, 2011). Finally, the results indicated that emphasis on staff retention strategies will maintain the best performance and provide opportunities for improvement (Ntshangase and Parumasur, 2013).

Based on SSM and having meetings with HR managers and experts, data was extracted and a rich picture illustrating the current status of the system, its problems and limitations was determined. Then, on the basis of the rich picture, CATWOE components were defined to provide root definitions.

Finally, the root definition of the HR maintenance management system is presented as follows:

"A system administered by the management of the organization and provides the opportunity to provide factors and plans for all employees and managers of the organization to retain in the organization. These plans are provided by HR managers with the participation of employees and other managers. Finally, plans will increase the staff and managers' satisfaction and motivation to a large extent and increase the overall retention of individuals in the organization."

Subsequently, the conceptual models are developed through root definitions, CATWOE components, and the staff's and managers' viewpoints.

KNOWLEDGE WORKER PRODUCTIVITY

The production equipment was considered as the most valuable asset of an organization in the 20th century and for an organization in the 21st century, it was its knowledge workers and their productivity. The knowledge workers are very important for an organization's competitive advantage (Óskarsdóttir and Oddsson, 2013).

There should be present a holistic approach to knowledge worker productivity in order to find methods applicable to manage and improve it. Óskarsdóttir and Oddsson (2013) used a holistic approach using systems to perform a research tackling the knowledge worker productivity. They defined the problem as low knowledge worker productivity from the perspectives of the organization and introduced individual knowledge worker as problem owner and used SSM to define relevant systems. SSM can be beneficial in solving a multi-dimensional problem such as knowledge worker productivity.

The main conclusions obtained from the rich picture with the organization as the problem owner include:

- Communicating organizational objectives and needs by the organization can help the knowledge workers to fulfill value-creating demands and save time by working on the right things.
- Collaboration and knowledge sharing must be promoted in the work environment to provide the knowledge workers with opportunities to contribute to the organizational knowledge base, which brings about the organization competitive advantage. Moreover, the knowledge workers who do not share knowledge and collaborate will be stopped by restricted access to resources.
- The knowledge workers' needs must be fulfilled in the work environment to produce optimum performance; otherwise, the result is underperforming by the knowledge workers.

Table 6. Definitions of CATWOE in a system of knowledge worker productivity (Óskarsdóttir and Oddsson, 2013)

CATWOE	Knowledge worker productivity
Customer	Organization
Actor	Knowledge worker
Transformation	Transformation of knowledge workers' perceived effort to perceived value by the organization
World view	Improving the knowledge worker productivity by supporting the knowledge workers' needs and influencing them to achieve the organizational objectives.
Owner	Organization
Environment	Business environment, industry standards, culture, etc.

As the results indicated, supporting the needs of the knowledge workers in the work environment by the organization can result in improvement in knowledge worker productivity and achieving organizational objectives.

The root definition was defined based on the conclusions of the rich picture and a CATWOE analysis.

The CATWOE analysis showed the benefit of the transformation for the organization. The transformation is executed by the knowledge worker and is from individual knowledge worker's perceived effort to perceived value by the organization. The world view (weltanschauung) is that supporting the knowledge workers' needs and influencing them to achieve organizational objectives results in improved knowledge worker productivity. The root definition is as follows: "An organization-owned system that transforms the knowledge workers' perceived effort to perceived value by the organization through supporting the workers' needs and influencing them to increase their value contribution to the organization in a desirable work environment."

Two main conclusions can be drawn from the rich picture on the problem of low knowledge worker productivity from the perspective of the individual knowledge worker.

The main conclusions from the rich picture with the individual knowledge worker as the problem owner are presented in the followings:

- The individual knowledge worker is expected to manage his personal resources to perform to his full potential. Depleting the personal resources will cause exhaustion and stress that lower the performance.
- The individual knowledge worker is expected to be effective and efficient in doing worthwhile actions.

Table 7. The CATWOE analysis for a system owned by the individual (Óskarsdóttir and Oddsson, 2013)

CATWOE	Knowledge worker productivity
Customer	Organization
Actor	Knowledge worker
Transformation	Transformation of knowledge workers' perceived effort to perceived value by the organization
World view	the knowledge worker's productivity can be improved by managing the personal resources by the worker and hence, increasing effectiveness and efficiency in work
Owner	Individual
Environment	Laws, culture etc.

An individual-owned relevant system was explored by using a CATWOE analysis. There is no change in the transformation, regardless of problem owner, but the world view (weltanschauung) has changed. The perspective is that the knowledge worker's productivity can be improved by managing the personal resources by the worker and hence, increasing effectiveness and efficiency in work.

The root definition of an individual-owned system, defined from the rich picture and the CATWOE analysis is: "An individual-owned system that transforms the individual knowledge worker's perceived effort to perceived value by the organization through managing the personal resources in order to be effective and efficient."

Taking the results from the analysis of the problem situation and creating conceptual models, using SSM, should be the next step in this research. Using logic, the conceptual models explore the needs that have to be fulfilled in order to achieve the purpose defined in the root definitions. These models make it possible to regard intervention points to improve knowledge worker productivity and provide ideas for research opportunities. A change that could be made to improve the real problem situation can occur in intervention points. It can be understood through the rich pictures that possible intervention points could be found in creating the work environment, managing personal resources and communication between organizations and their knowledge workers. These factors can affect positively or negatively on knowledge worker productivity depending on how they are tackled. Deeper exploration of the intervention points and using other tools such as causal loop diagrams can reveal the effect of changes at these points.

CONCLUSION

The challenges from within and outside the system cause evolvement and changes in human resource management (HRM) like other social systems. Independent behavior of acting individuals makes HRM emergent and unstable. HR is a transaction-focused administrative function, which can and should be a strategic partner within the firm. Moreover, being abstracted from the broader social context, much of the data providing the basis for many HRM decisions is meaningless. This difficulty is overcome by soft systems methodology (SSM) as an approach for developing HR-related information.

Various applications of SSM in HRM such as employee participation, group creativity, human resource development (HRD), HR maintenance, and knowledge worker productivity were reviewed in this chapter. The main discussion of this chapter is that SSM can strongly improve inter-subjective understanding vital for effective group development and progress. SSM is particularly helpful in breaking paradigms to enhance group creativity. The issue of current HRD was discussed as it is over-relied on simple systems model of input–output transformation and there is lack of any argument on the central role of SSM in this development. Finally, this chapter provided explanations on the problem situation of low knowledge worker productivity from the perspectives of the organization and also individual knowledge worker as problem owners using SSM.

REFERENCES

Amabile, T. M. (1996). *Creativity in context*. New York, NY: Westview Press.

Armstrong. (2010). *Strategic human resource management: A guide to action*. London: Kogan Page Limited.

Au, E. Y. K. (2016). Employee involvement and participation at work in China (DBA thesis). University of Manchester.

Boxall, P. (2014). The future of employment relations from perspective of human resource management. *The Journal of Industrial Relations*, *54*(6), 578–593. doi:10.1177/0022185614527980

Boxall, P., & Purcell, J. (2011). *Strategy and human resource management* (3rd ed.). New York: Palgrave Macmillan.

Brocklesby, J. (1995). Using soft systems methodology to identify competence requirements in HRM. *International Journal of Manpower*, *16*(5/6), 70–84. doi:10.1108/01437729510095962

Checkland, P. (1993). *Systems thinking, systems practice*. John Wiley & Sons Ltd.

Connell, N. (2001). Evaluating soft OR: Some reflection son an apparently unsuccessful implementation using a soft system methodology (SSM) based approach. *The Journal of the Operational Research Society*, *52*(2), 150–160. doi:10.1057/palgrave.jors.2601054

Cummings, A., & Oldham, G. R. (1997). Enhancing creativity: Managing work contexts for the high potential employee. *California Management Review*, *4*(1), 22–38. doi:10.2307/41165920

French, W. L. (2006). *Human Resources Management* (6th ed.). Boston: Cengage Learning.

Gayathri, R., Kamalambal, R., & Sivaraman, G. (2012). Employee retention strategies in BPO's – An empirical investigation. *Interdisciplinary Journal of Contemporary Research in Business, 3*(12), 573–583.

Gratton, L., Hope-Haily, V., Stiles, P., & Truss, C. (1999). *Strategic human resource management: Corporate rhetoric and human reality*. New York: Oxford University. doi:10.1093/acprof:oso/9780198782049.001.0001

Harkness, J., & Lea, M. (2001). 'Getting it' the making of a dot-comer. *Communication World, 18*(2), 7–9.

Haslinda, A. (2009). Evolving terms of human resource management and development. *The Journal of International Social Research, 2*(9), 180–186.

Leonardi, S. (2015). Employee participation and involvement: The Italian case and trade union issues. *Transfer: European Review of Labour and Research, 22*(1), 81–99. doi:10.1177/1024258915619366

Mackinnon, D. W. (1962). The nature and nurture of creative talent. *The American Psychologist, 17*(7), 484–495. doi:10.1037/h0046541

Molineux, J., & Haslett, T. (2007). The use of soft Systems methodology to enhance group creativity. *Systemic Practice and Action Research, 20*(6), 477–496. doi:10.100711213-007-9078-0

Morgan, D. (1953). Creativity today: A constructive analytic review of certain philosophical and psychological work. *The Journal of Aesthetics and Art Criticism, 12*(1), 1–24. doi:10.2307/426297

Mumford, E. (1996). *Systems design: Ethical tools for ethical change*. London: MacMillan. doi:10.1007/978-1-349-14199-9

Nikghadam Hojati, S., Rajabzadeh Ghatari, A., Alborzi, M., & Hassanzadeh, G. (2017). Representing and structuring the problem of organizational creativity using soft system methodology. *Human Resource Management Resources, 7*(4), 181–203.

Ntshangase, S. C., & Parumasur, S. B. (2013). Using staff retention strategies to secure a happier and more productive workplace. *Corporate Ownership & Control, 10*(3), 413–425. doi:10.22495/cocv10i3c4art1

Oldham, G. R., & Cummings, A. (1996). Employee creativity: Personal and contextual factors at work. *Academy of Management Journal*, *39*(3), 607–634.

Óskarsdóttir, H. G., & Oddsson, G. V. (2017). A soft systems approach to knowledge worker productivity—Analysis of the problem situation. *Economies*, *5*(28), 1–28.

Pfeffer, J. (1998). *The human equation: Building profits by putting people first*. Boston: Harvard Business School Press.

Rezayi, G., & Farhadi Mahali, Al. (2014). Soft system methodology and analytic network process in maintenance of human resources (Case study: Automotive industry). *International Conference on Business Development and Excellence*.

Sandhya, K., & Kumar, D. P. (2011). Employee retention by motivation. *Indian Journal of Science and Technology*, *4*(2), 1778–1782.

Sternberg, R. J., O'Hara, L. A., & Lubart, T. I. (1997). Creativity as investment. *California Management Review*, *40*(1), 8–21. doi:10.2307/41165919

Swanson, R. A., & Holton, E. F. (2001). *Foundations of human resource development* (1st ed.). San Francisco: Berrett-Koehler Publishers, Inc.

Utomo, A., & Yulia, Y. A. (2018). Human resource development strategy model: A case study on small and medium Laweyan Batik industry in Surakart. *Journal of Economics, Business & Accountancy Ventura*, *21*(2), 151–158. doi:10.14414/jebav.v21i2.1436

Yawson, R. M. (2012). Systems theory and thinking as a foundational theory in human resource development—A myth or reality? *Human Resource Development Review*, *12*(1), 53–85. doi:10.1177/1534484312461634

Chapter 9
Project Management:
The Use of Soft Systems Methodology

ABSTRACT

This chapter seeks to explain possible uses of the soft systems methodology (SSM) for project management (PM) when uncertain and sometimes conflicting aims are being pursued. To this end, two topics were considered: (1) application of SSM for funds allocation planning among major development projects and (2) feasibility of industrial projects considering their compliance with principles of sustainable development. The focus of the SSM is on the so-called human activity system (HAS), synergizing all stakeholders towards a single goal. PM, on the other hand, not only deals with the HAS, but also manages organization-wide initiatives participated by a wide variety of stakeholders. In this respect, SSM can contribute to better implementation of the PM initiatives, thereby enhancing the obtained gains.

INTRODUCTION

By definition, a project seeks to achieve a clearly specified objective through a set of activities and tasks that are performed at the cost of resources. It has to be done within a predefined period of time and to particular specifications. According to this definition, a project must be unique, highlighting the variability of project portfolios (Sankaran and Agarwal, 2013). On the other hand, the project management (PM) refers to the process through which the movement toward achieving the project objective(s) is controlled. PM utilizes

DOI: 10.4018/978-1-7998-4504-1.ch009

special tools and techniques to build on the existing infrastructures and resources and hence manage the project in such a way to avoid interrupting the routine activities of the company (Munns and Bjeirmi, 1996). Basically, PM was introduced to evoke an organizational emphasis on the way inevitable changes are encountered by modern-age organizations. Success/failure of a project is largely determined by the way operational and strategic change initiatives are designed and implemented (Cleland and Ireland, 2006).

According to Archibald, a generic project goes through the following life cycle (Archibald, 2003):

- Formulating the concept (initiation, identification, selection),
- Providing the required definitions (feasibility, development, demonstration, prototyping, quantification),
- Execution (implementation, production, and deployment, design/construct/commission, install and test),
- Closure (termination and post-completion evaluation).

These four phases comprise an architecture on which the budgeting, allocation of manpower and resources, and for timing of the project can be based. Details of the phasing may render different among different industries or products, but the basis is the same.

Considering different projects as temporary organizations, Turner and Müller (2003) characterized a project as being unique, associated with large amounts of uncertainty, and in need for much flexibility to address the wide variety of problems that may arise. The project complexity has long been a concern for project managers, and the general increase in the complexity has further added to this concern. Accordingly, it is crucially important to perceive the project complexity appropriately and understand the way it can be addressed by making different before the project goal is attained. Imposing clear impacts on the planning and control of the project, project complexity can interfere with the process through which the goals and objectives are identified and also with the choice of a suitable organizational form, contributing to the final project outcomes (San Cristóbal et al., 2018).

Also called human dimension, the human activity system (HAS) is a component of the PM and refers to initiatives implemented across the organization and participated by various stakeholders. The so-called holistic approach to PM sheds light on the PM based on holistic principles and gets to the HAS early in the course of analysis. For inter-connected projects, one needs a more comprehensive view. Taking such a wider view to the PM highlights the often vague and unstructured nature of the PM, calling for a soft system approach (Siriram, 2017). The introduction of soft system approaches to information systems-related projects for which the success had more to do with people and processes rather than the products and technologies (Sankaran ct al., 2010).

A review on the PM literature highlights the need for further insight into the topic when it comes to systems despite the general increase in the research on the PM in general. Considering the PM, hard and soft components of systems have moved in distinctive directions. The system-related methods and ideas of PM were initially largely associated with hard systems, but then gradually diverged toward softer approaches. Analyses have indicated an increasing trend in the prevalence of soft methodologies and philosophy in the literature, with the subject-matter of management being more and more qualitatively discussed (Costello, 2012).

Sankaran et al. (2010) believed that the PM is closely associated with systems approaches (i.e. systems engineering (SE)) and the operational research, SE and PM had been devised to administer large research and development projects in the field of military science in the mid-90s. The 90s witnessed an evolution in project-based working to help scholars and engineers better adopt complex, innovative, and yet uncertain technologies for developing new weapon systems.

The focus of this chapter is on the application of soft systems methodology (SSM) in PM when uncertain and sometimes conflicting aims are being pursued. It describes two studies about the use of SSM in planning the funds allocation for development projects (Sohrabinejad and Darjazi, 2014) and feasibility study of industrial projects based on sustainable development principles (Shahabi et al., 2013).

SYSTEMS THINKING IN PM

Project managers tend to use systems thinking in PM. This approach points to the need for transparency and a complete understanding of how different parts of the system affect system performance. Traditional project management practices focus on neutralizing the complexity of a project with more careful planning and control over a project. Systems thinking is recognized as a suggested solution to the problem of multi-PM. Understanding the problem-solving process is the starting point for using systems thinking in PM. In this context, the problem is interpreted as a disorder in the status quo and identifying and understanding properly a project problem are the main tasks of project decision makers. Systems thinking in PM provides a holistic approach to problem solving, understanding related phenomena and an interactions network in a project in the form of cause-and-effect processes, and scenario planning and action strategies modeling as an important area of systems thinking. It requires specific behavior such as earning through action, openness and agility in problems management and team approach to the project as well (Kopczyński and Brzozowski, 2015). They considered PM by comparing key spheres of traditional and agile approaches with systems thinking.

SSM AND PM

In 2002, Morris presented the most basic definition for PM describing it as a hybrid of scope management, activity scheduling, and cost and resource management. In the meantime, the control measures differed for various projects depending on the nature of the project, the project manager's role, and the stage in the course of the project life cycle when the project manager was serving.

As a general rule, a member of an organization may expect issues of a broader range if the gap to the definition stage of the project is smaller and/or his/her organizational level is higher. Such issue may arise in different fields including the strategy, finance, organization, technology, control, people and culture, commerce and contracts, community and environment, process and timing, etc. Indeed, SSM has been emerged to address somehow fuzzy issues dealt by PM when uncertain and sometimes conflicting objectives are pursued. The fact that today's organizations are becoming more and more decentralized and flexible further increases the complexity of the problem. Table 2 provides a list of the literature discussing the application of SSM in PM.

Figure 1. Project life cycle that distinguishes projects from other (non-project) activities (Morris, 2002, cited by Costello (2012))

Table 1. PM in traditional, agile, and systems thinking approaches (Kopczyński and Brzozowski, 2015)

	Traditional approach	Agile approach	Systems thinking
Problem solving and project objectives	Project objectives definition with the use of SMART[1] method, Long and short-term objectives cascade by needs analysis.	Define the project outcome in a general and conceptual way, The prime objective of project team is providing values to the customer.	A holistic and comprehensive problem solving, Project problem definition regarding different stakeholders' viewpoints, Objectives mapping considering various aspects of the project.
PM cycle	Linear PM cycle according to structured and well-established phases of the project, Planning on the basis of precise timetable as the basis of PM.	Iterative and incremental PM cycle, Adaptability processes as change is more essential than continuing doing what was planned, Close collaboration with the customers, Processes are absolutely simplified.	Non-linear PM cycle according to cause-effect relationships in a complex context, Interactions network analysis among elements in the project, Alternative project scenarios planning, Developing opportunities for change management, Dynamic change management.
Organizational dimension of a project	Defining detailed work breakdown structure for the work organization, High rate of formalization of the project, Defining organizational structure accurately, Maintaining a balance between the main constraints of the project.	Simplified work organization to a maximum, focusing on flexibility, speed, and adaptability, Low rate of formalization of the project.	Defining work organization focusing on flexibility and efficient functionality of a system, Being able to develope and adapt quickly to dynamic environment because of a high competence of the project team.
Personal aspect and project team	Work based on experts in a narrow field, Members of the project team have high competences regarding their knowledge and experience, Leadership style is democratic and management style is task-oriented.	Work is performed on the basis of self-organized teams, Members of the project team have high competences regarding their knowledge and personal and behavioral inclination, Participative work and decision making, High interactions, Customers are participated in the project to create the final value, Participative leadership and steering rather than controlling.	Work is performed on the basis of interdisciplinary teams, Learning project problems from various viewpoints and holistically, Assuming that the project problem is more complex including many extra elements and relationships, Problem solving in moderated meetings focusing on cause-and effect relations in a problematic situation, Opinions sharing and visualization of dependencies in a project, Creative thinking, Democratic leadership style, Regular meetings.

Table 2. Application areas of SSM in PM, as mentioned in the articles published in IJPM citing Checkland et al. - 1988 to 1998 (Costello, 2012)

SSM Application	References
Problem structuring/ framing/ project definition / modeling	(Davies and Saunders, 1988; Neal, 1995; Yeo, 1995; Chapman, 1998)
Planning / developing / building / evaluating a project management system / IT system	(Robinson, 1989; Yeo, 1990; Saunders, 1992; Yeo, 1992; Yeo, 1995; Lai, 1997; Remenyi and Sherwood-Smith, 1998)
Help with multiple perceptions / application to human behavior	(Daniel, 1990)
Risk management under uncertainty	(Daniel, 1990; Yeo, 1995; Yeo, 1995; Stewart and Fortune, 1995; Ramsay et al., 1996)
Generalization of intellectual and philosophical underpinnings of PM / systems thinking	(Saunders, 1992; Yeo, 1993)
Value management	(Green, 1994)
Organizational problem-solving / change management / learning / business process re-engineering	(Russell-Hodge, 1995; Stewart and Fortune, 1995; Partington, 1996; Sherman et al., 1996; Ramsay et al., 1996; Hsu and Yeo, 1996)

Emes (2018) stipulated that the SSM refers to a 'systemic' approach (as opposed to a 'hard systematic' approach). Development of SSM was partly due to infeasibility of defining clear objectives for mega projects wherein divergence from the original plan is frequently encountered most probably due to changes. Indeed, mega projects are inevitably exposed to various changes and many times the objective(s) of mega projects change during the project life. Therefore, the stakeholders must adopt a systemic approach to examine the feasible and desirability of changes. SSM seeks to develop relationships across projects to lead the decision-making process toward better decisions. Most importantly, SSM provides a 'rich picture' of the situation by which the problem can be perceived deeply by multiple stakeholders, highlighting the sympathies and tensions among various key players. This constitutes a firm basis for the process of requirements management. Based on the rich picture, SSM develops root definitions of relevant systems and further enriches them using the so-called CATWOE framework (Customers, Actors, Transformation process, World view, Owners and Environmental constraints) and the conceptual models to identify rational ways of interpreting and managing the problem.

Winter (2009) focused on how SSM can be used at the front-end. Lifang and Jun (2009) analyzed the use of SSM for risk analysis a construction project risk management. Lockett et al. (2006) showed that the use of SSM is suitable in the information technologies (IT) project of the implementation process of customer relationship management (CRM) applications in small and medium sized enterprises (SMEs). Dressler (2015) applied SSM to a subproject of the Swift Project to determine its ease and effectiveness as a means to describe a situation and suggest future course of actions.

FINANCIAL CONSTRAINTS ON PM

The problems and complexities of the constraints on the PM, such as those related to energy, raw materials, human resources, information and other capital resources, act as barriers against stepping into global markets. Accordingly, choosing the most optimal models for managing the energy consumption, raw materials, and allocation of human and financial resources has always been an objective pursued in the planning process of organizations. When it comes to allocating funds to projects, the most important factors affecting the project timing and hence budgeting include the fundamental policies and the desired level of goal achievement.

Project risks refer to the uncertain events that may or may not trigger complex, long-term, environment-friendly processes (Behrens and Hawranek, 1991). Researchers have made extensive efforts to address financial challenges of PM, with many authors identified several factors that affect the performance of a project, such as rising costs. Behrens and Hawranek (1991) showed that there are different methods of financial valuation in the field of investment.

These methods can be grouped into discounting methods (i.e. net present value (NPV), internal rate of return (IRR), and profitability index (PI)) and simple and easy-to-use non-discounting methods (i.e. payback period and accounting rate of return). Some researchers focused on risk-constrained financial evaluation under uncertainty through break-even analysis, sensitivity analysis, scenario method, theory of games, and decision making theory.

A top executive or decision-maker would be successful if he/she opts for optimal solutions/alternatives by which his/her organization can manage to maximize its benefit despite the existing constraints on financial resources and the wide gap to the desired level of goal achievement. In fact, when resources are limited, the managers must evaluate different alternative projects and allocate the resources to different projects for maximal benefit of the organization. However, resource allocation is not the ultimate goal of the project evaluation; it is rather a mean by which the organization can achieve its goals.

So far, most of the models used for funds allocation and credit distribution have provided planners with an apparently logical solution, but also came with major weaknesses. These models have been generally static, single-purpose, partial, and too simple. In practice, numerous large-scale projects have been selectively funded based on inadequate information or merely political reasons, keeping them from achieving proper economic goals to satisfy the policy-makers.

Focusing on multiple and sometimes conflicting goals, researchers have designed different models and methodologies for allocating very large amounts of credit to major national projects in the framework of development plans. Among others, the problem solving leads individuals toward facing organizational problems by considering not only the problem itself, but also the problematic surrounding environment and conditions.

As a problem-solving method, the SSM has been put forward to address particular social, political, and human issues. In this methodology, the problem is examined as part of a system rather than a standalone identity. The soft system approach provides a way to identify issues in more complicated and ambiguous situations. It uses modeling to structure the topic into a model wherein different conflicting goals, needs, interests and values can be discussed. The SSM considers the system as a whole rather than focusing on individual system components. As a system-based approach to dealing with the real world, SSM enables analysts and participants to understand different perspectives on situations and problems through learning.

In this study, the required data was collected by conducting interviews with key players of funds allocation planning for mega projects in Iran. Based on the acquired data, a rich picture of the current state, processes, problems and constraints of the system was drawn. Using the CATWOE analysis, the ideal system of funds allocation to mega projects was defined (root definition) and a conceptual model was developed to achieve the ideal system. The conceptual model was aimed at mapping the processes and activities that need to be done to achieve optimal planning.

FUNDS ALLOCATION PLANNING FOR DEVELOPMENT PROJECTS

Step 1. Exposure to Problematic Situation

In this research, it is tried to elaborate on funds allocation to broadcasting development projects (*e.g.* procurement of advanced technologies and new

Figure 2. The rich picture of funds allocation planning for broadcasting development projects (Sohrabinejad and darjazi, 2014)

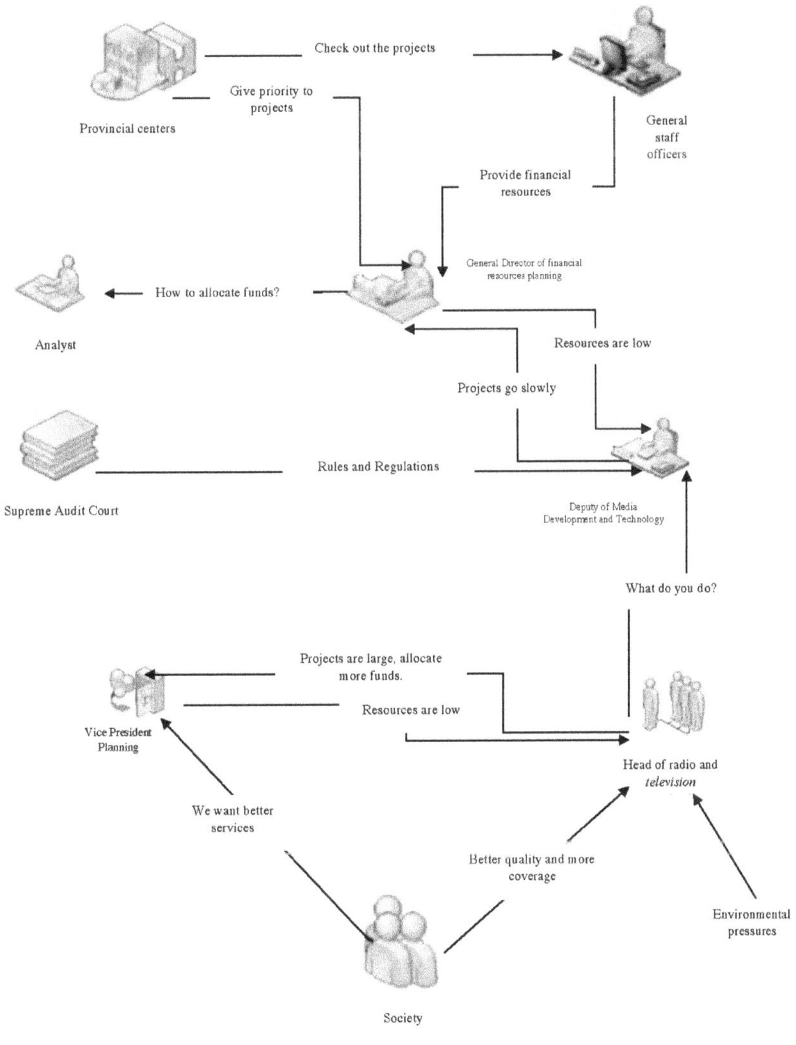

services, construction of television and radio transmitters, extending TV antenna coverage across all parts of the country, upgrading video and audio broadcasting infrastructures, maintenance of organizational resources and assets, and feasibility study of implementing new technologies) in presence of various sources of risk for the system stakeholders under a variety of constraints (*e.g.* organizational and national regulations, political issues, external decisions, and resource scarcity).

The degree to which top managers are satisfied with the outputs imposes direct impacts on the staff's level of motivation and hence the system efficiency and the ultimate project results: the higher the top managers' satisfaction level, the greater the productivity and progress rate of the project.

Step 2. Drawing a Rich Picture

At this point, using the information gathered upon the interviews with experts, a rich picture of the problem was drawn to illustrate the relationships, processes, problems, and constraints.

Step 3. Extracting the Root Definition

In this study, the root definitions were examined from five viewpoints. For each viewpoint, the CATWOE components were expressed before proceeding to the root definition considering its efficacy, efficiency, and effectiveness.

Step 4. Conceptual Model

In this section, root definitions are presented in the form of conceptual models. At this point, the emphasis is on the activities that need to be done to achieve the final and desired product of the system; here the goal is to build a model of desired system rather than the actual problem situation, so as to identify the gap between the ideal situation and the existing reality.

For example, one of the conceptual models is as follows (figure 3):

Figure 3. A Conceptual model (Sohrabinejad and darjazi, 2014)

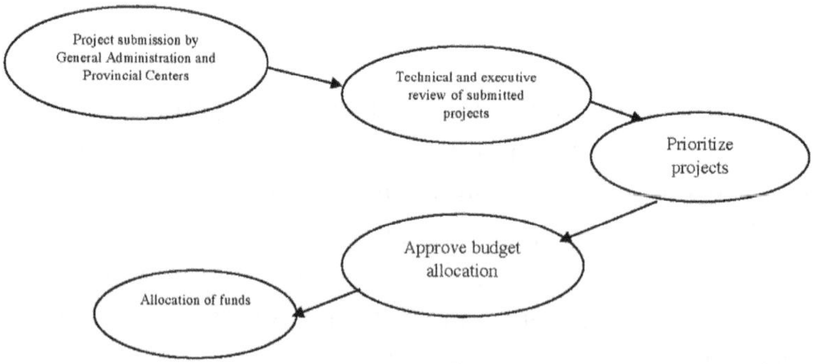

Table 3. CATWOE components from five viewpoints (Sohrabinejad and darjazi, 2014)

CATWOE	General director of financial resources planning	General staff officers	Deputy of media development and technology	Vice president planning	Society
Customer	Deputy of media development and technology, Islamic Republic of Iran Broadcasting (IRIB)	General director of organizational resources planning, Deputy of media development and technology		IRIB and other governmental organizations	People
Actor	General director of financial resources planning, project manager and experts, director and experts of development budget department, general staff officers, and provincial centers	Managers at provincial centers, experts of the relevant general administration		Staff and directors at deputy of presidential planning	Radio and TV organization, vice president planning
Transformation	Funds are allocated to development projects presented and implemented by the general staff officers, and the managers at provincial centers	Present prioritized projects according to the views of the relevant experts at general administration and provincial centers for approval in the project allocation committee	Deputy of presidential planning, IRIB	Due to the policies and prioritization of projects, fund allocation is based on governmental priorities	Provide comments and suggestions to improve the service provided by IRIB
World view	Providing a well-planned and well-executed program that satisfies the general staff officers, and the managers at provincial centers, and thereby enhancing the efficiency of implementation and expediting the completion of projects	Obtain more funding for projects that are prioritized by experts from the general administration and provincial centers	General director of organizational resources planning, general staff officers, and managers at provincial centers	Funds should be allocated to development projects of organizations so that the society gets the most out of the projects and the country can prosper	Optimal, convenient and quality use of the organization's services

continued on following page

Table 3. Continued

CATWOE	General director of financial resources planning	General staff officers	Deputy of media development and technology	Vice president planning	Society
Owner	General director of financial resources planning, deputy of media development and technology, IRIB	General director of financial resources planning, deputy of media development and technology, IRIB	Planning on particular projects to increase the efficiency of the organization and provide the society with the desired services, and reporting based on the mission followed by the organizational and the deputy of presidential planning to attract more funding	Cabinet	Cabinet, IRIB
Environment	Lack of funding against a massive volume of projects, limitations on the expertise required to execute projects, allocation of funds to different departments to complete their projects, completion of incomplete projects from previous tenures, financial debt for previous projects	Implementation of laws and regulations in the organization, lack of funding against a massive volume of projects, limitations on the expertise needed to execute the project, consequences of increased work or increased labor costs in previous projects, previous incomplete projects	Attracting more funds to carry out projects needed to deliver the desired services to the society	Restrictions on financing, state laws, cabinet directives, incomplete projects from previous tenures	Cultural and geographical constraint

Step 5. Comparing the Conceptual Models to the Real-World Situation

In order to compare the conceptual models to the real-world situation, one could use experts' opinions based on interviews or questionnaires used.

Based on the conceptual models developed using the root definitions, the questions were managed to evaluate the satisfaction level of all players across the system. Examples of the questions include:

1) How to integrate the project definition, technical and administrative reviews and resource allocation?
2) How to increase the satisfaction level of the project providers?
3) How to get more funding for projects?
4) How can one minimize the cost of executing projects?

Steps 6 and 7. Implementing Possible and Desirable Changes

Making the change raises two questions:

1) Are potential changes logically desirable?
2) Is it possible to make changes into the organizational culture?

Success is backed by an endless idea of the commitment, and it should be culturally possible to make sure that these potential changes are worth pursuing.

FEASIBILITY STUDY OF INDUSTRIAL PROJECTS BASED ON SUSTAINABLE DEVELOPMENT PRINCIPLES

In general, the feasibility study means analyzing the chances of success of a project or business. In other words, the purpose of a feasibility study is to determine the possibility, applicability, and potential effectiveness of a project. Industrial feasibility study is a controlled process for identifying the costs and benefits of executing a project simultaneously, and describing the conditions in detail. Such a study presents the first step in the decision-making process by investors or managers. Taking this perspective, the feasibility study resembles a turning point in the process of decision-making on project implementation or investment. The answer to the question of "should we implement/invest on this project?" determines the future course of the investor/manager for handling the case.

Ensuring the sustainability of industrial projects, a concept developed by sustainable engineering, is among the most crucial and perhaps the most fundamental issues faced by organizations. The concept of sustainable development has become popular not only among scholars but also among the general public. The sustainable development policies have been regarded much due to the limited possibilities and infinite human needs and desires.

In this context, the key to survive companies in today's competitive environment is to increase the emphasis on the ideal concept of sustainable development. Sustainable development provides for a line of thinking about the future. Industrial feasibility studies is usually conducted prior to the implementation of an industrial investment plan to constitute a foundation on which one cane make decision about investing on the project.

According to the United Nations Industrial Development Organization (UNIDO, 1978), a feasibility study introduces and analyzes the critical components relevant to the production of a specific product and candidate approaches to that production. Such a study is expected to define the production capacity and location, required technologies (considering the raw materials and inputs), the needed investment and associated costs, expected sales, and the resultant return on investment (ROI).

This purpose can be approached through an iterative process composed of feedbacks and inter-linkages to investigate the candidate production plans for minimal investment and production costs. In case a production plan was figured out to be infeasible, one must adjust one or more factors to make the project feasible.

A feasibility study must express this optimization cycle and provide justifications for the underlying assumptions and the proposed solutions while wrapping up the project scope in the form of an integration of the selected partial candidates. Nevertheless, in case no feasible project plan was found, this infeasibility conclusion must be clearly expressed and justified.

Estimated investment requirement and project costs and hence the projected economic profits may deliver some meaning only if the project scope is clearly defined considering all essential parts and associated cost elements. The scope must be supported by drawings and schedules that can be further used as a basis during the project performance.

The basics are the same for most feasibility studies, although there may be significant distinctions in actual orientation and emphasis based on, for example, the nature of the industry, the magnitude and complexity of the production unit, and the required investment and associated costs. In general, a well-done feasibility study is the one where all key components and possible implications of the considered project are carefully taken into account, with any shortfall in this respect declining the utility of the study.

Many times, vendors of technologies or equipment misunderstand the term feasibility study and rather present a proposal biased toward the supply of particular equipment or techniques. There are cases where the experiences on which basis the production or sales estimates are generated are gained in an industrially developed country, with no clue to the conditions encountered in the developing country where the project is planned to be operated. The fact that such studies are only merely related or adapted to the considered local production factors, those may end up misleading the while project toward suboptimal use of resources, as has been frequently practiced in developing countries. A feasibility study must establish links among significant production factors, local market, and production constraints through the analysis of costs and benefits (UNIDO, 1978).

A feasibility study can be based on either the market phenomena (demand level) or material inputs (availability of material or energy). It is not an objective on its own, but rather a tool for finalizing an investment decision that may not necessary be in agreement with the conclusions of the study, as the investors are most frequently not flexible enough to fully admit the results of such a study.

The main components of an industrial feasibility study include the followings (UNIDO, 1978):

- Executive summary,
- Project background and history analysis,
- Analysis of the market and plant capacity,
- Availability of materials and inputs,
- Location and site,
- Project engineering,
- Plant organization and overhead costs,
- Manpower requirements,
- Implementation scheduling, and
- Financial and economic evaluation.

A literature review indicates insufficiency of the application of the principles of sustainability in industrial development, calling for reengineering activities to redesign industrial processes (Chang, 2011). On the other hand, lack of a method to measure and consider compliance of industrial designs with sustainable development has been a weakness to feasibility studies (Behrens and Hawranek, 2003). In the industrial scopes, sustainability issues are managerial problems related to soft systems.

Figure 4. Conceptual model of industrial feasibility study (Shahabi et al., 2013)

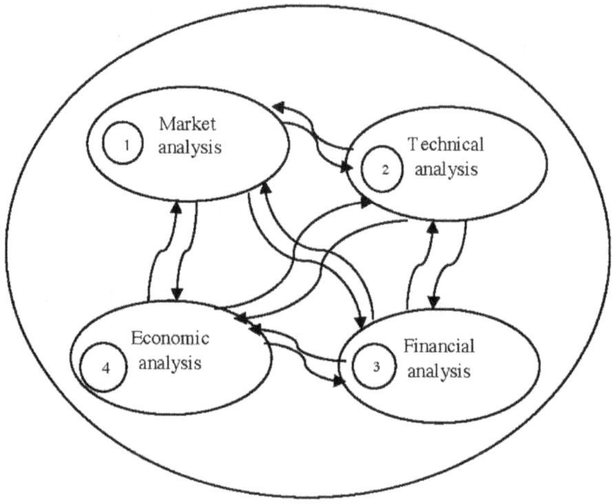

The root definition of industrial feasibility study with an approach to sustainable development is: "a systematic study by an individual or industrial organization based on the principles of sustainable development to ensure economic sustainability of a plan through integrating market, technical, financial and economic analyses. Such a study must provide for setting up or expanding a business or proposing so to a bank."

The integration activity is introduced into the above definition to take into account the factors that would be ignored otherwise. Thus the proposed conceptual model is as follows (figure 5):

In this model, the monitoring activity seeks to ensure the sustainability by evaluating the conformation to the principles of sustainable development. This activity requires a specific and well-defined procedure. For this purpose, a monitoring system was defined as follows:

"a system led by the monitoring team to monitor the activities of the stakeholders to ensure economic sustainability of the plan. The required data is collected upon meeting with expert stakeholders, studying the expressed world views, preparing reporting metrics consistent with the sustainable development principles, completing the SSM process with expert stakeholders, and documenting and submitting suggestions to the control team".

Given its advantages, the PQR formula was used to provide this root definition. The PQR formula provides for a descriptive root definition. In

Figure 5. Conceptual model of industrial feasibility study with the sustainable development approach (Shahabi et al., 2013)

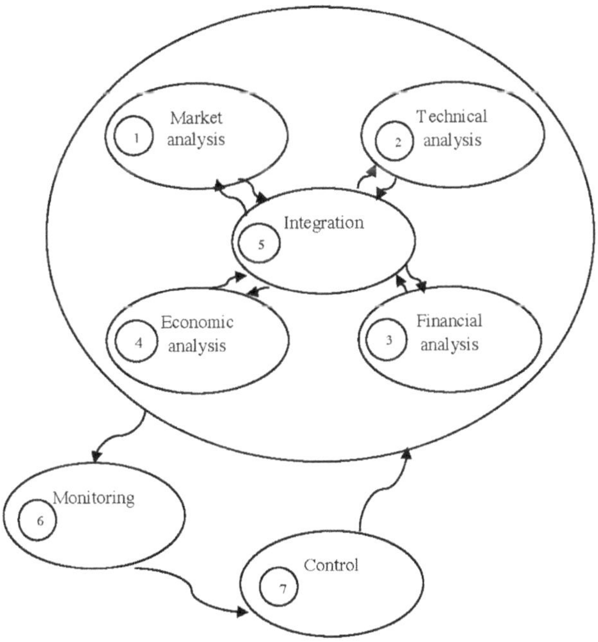

the context of SSM, the PQR formula implies running P (what) through Q (how) to help achieve R (why).

- P signifies what should be done (What): Monitoring of stakeholder activities (market, technical, financial, economic and integration).
- Q defines how to achieve the P under existing constraints (How): Monitoring through the process of meeting with stakeholder teams, preparing reporting metrics consistent with sustainable development principles, charting an SSM process for applying team viewpoints, completing the SSM process with stakeholder teams, and documentation.
- R specifies where we ultimately want to achieve (Why): Monitoring is done to ensure the sustainability of economic plans.

In the monitoring task, meetings were organized with all stakeholders according to the meeting criteria. The stakeholders' world views on the situation were discussed at the meeting and then analyzed by the analyst of the monitoring team. The analyst then developed the criteria for reporting the level of compliance with the principles of sustainable development based on the discussions at the meeting, defined a number of systems based on the expressed world views to complete the SSM process, and developed respective models. Upon reconciling the models with the reality, another meeting was held with stakeholders to re-think about and conclude different views on the model to formulate a series of modifications and suggestions in the form of proposals. To complete the comparative model of the SSM process, questions were asked. Finally, the team reached an agreement on the proposals, which was then documented and reported to the control activity to complete the learning process.

Following the monitoring activity at the first level of the conceptual model, another control activity was undertaken to ensure the sustainability of the plan by controlling the performance of the stakeholders. The control

Figure 6. The 2nd level of the conceptual model for monitoring and control activity (Shahabi et al., 2013)

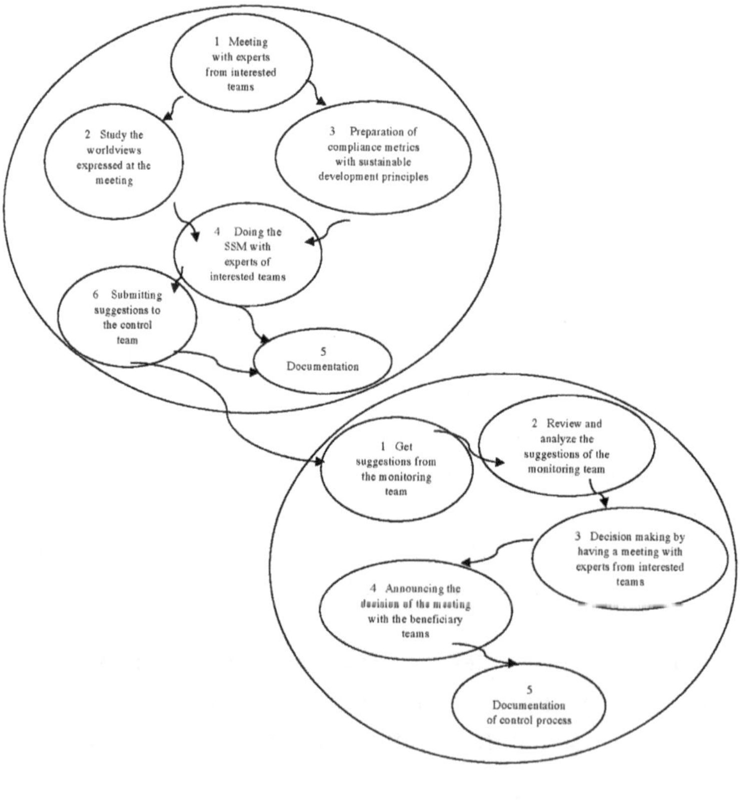

activity represented the executable part of the feasibility study of the model. Feasibility of the proposed changes in the monitoring phase were systematically reviewed for making a final decision, and the results were communicated and documented as guidelines. The analyst's world view determines the definition and execution of new activities by providing or transferring resources. That is, the scope of the model defines the controllable activities that can be decided. Accordingly, the control system can be defined as follows.

"A system administered by the control team, by which the control team can control the performance of the activities undertaken by the stakeholders, ensure sustainability of the economic plan, receive feedbacks from the monitoring team, make decisions by meeting with the stakeholder experts, communicate the decisions made on the meetings to the stakeholders, and document the entire control process".

The second level of the conceptual model for monitoring and control activity is as follows (figure 6):

CONCLUSION

For many companies, projects are being performed on a daily basis and optimal project management (PM) is a major challenge. In this respect, one may refer to organization-wide PM initiatives that are participated by many different stakeholders across the organization. As practical management tools, soft systems methodology (SSM) and PM are used to lead practical actions taken by an organization to manage a particular project. However, PM sees a problem as a set of sub-problems while SSM places an emphasis on problematic conditions.

This chapter sought to explain possible uses of the SSM for PM. To this end, two topics were considered: (1) application of SSM for funds allocation planning among major development projects, and (2) feasibility of industrial projects considering their compliance with principles of sustainable development. The focus of the SSM is on the so-called human activity system (HAS), synergizing all stakeholders towards a single goal, taking every individual equally important with no conflict of power. A rich picture of the situation is drawn to provide for out-of-the-box thinking via CATWOE analysis. This finally leads to better implementation of PM initiatives and hence larger deals of gain.

REFERENCES

Archibald, R. D. (2003). *Managing high-technology programs and projects* (3rd ed.). Wiley.

Behrens, W., & Hawranek, P. M. (1991). *Manual for preparation of industrial feasibility studies. United Nations Industrial Development Organization.* Vienna: UNIDO.

Behrens, W., & Hawranek, P.M. (2003). *Manual for the preparation of industrial feasibility studies*. UNIDO Publication.

Chang, N. B. (2011). *Systems analysis for sustainable engineering: Theory and applications*. New York: McGraw-Hill.

Cleland, D. I., & Ireland, L. R. (2006). *Project management: Strategic design and implementation* (5th ed.). New York: McGraw-Hill.

Costello, K. L. (2012). Building on "soft systems for soft projects": Project management lessons learned (Doctor of Philosophy), University of Technology, Sydney.

Dressler, S. (2015). *Alternative approaches for project definition: An application of soft systems methodology* (Master thesis). Beedie School of Business, Simon Fraser University.

Emes, M. (2018). Systems thinking: How is it used in project management? *Association for Project Management*. Retrieved August 19, 2019, from: https://www.apm.org.uk/media/17308/systems-thinking_final.pdf

Kopczyńsk, T., & Brzozowski, M. (2015). Systems thinking in project management: Theoretical framework and empirical evidence from Polish companies. *Administracja i Zarządzanie*, *34*(107), 79–88.

Lifang, X., & Jun, L. (2009). Case Study on project risk management planning based on soft system methodology. In Y. Shi, S. Wang, Y. Peng, J. Li, & Y. Zeng (Eds.), *Cutting-edge research topics on multiple criteria decision making* (pp. 37–44). Springer. doi:10.1007/978-3-642-02298-2_6

Lockett, N. J., Brown, D. H., & Sissons, A. (2006). Soft systems methodology in IT project management: Implementing CRM in SMEs. In *AMCIS 2006 Proceedings* (pp. 3721-3732). Retrieved February 23, 2020 from https://aisel.aisnet.org/cgi/viewcontent.cgi?article=1995&context=amcis2006

Munns, A. K., & Bjeirmi, B. F. (1996). The role of project management in achieving project success. *International Journal of Project Management, 14*(2), 81–87. doi:10.1016/0263-7863(95)00057-7

San Cristóbal, J. R., Carral, L., Diaz, E., Fraguela, J. A., & Iglesias, G. (2018). Complexity and project management: A general overview. *Complexity*, 1–10. doi:10.1155/2018/4891286

Sankaran, S., & Agarwal, R. (2013). Rethinking project management goals and methods to suit service systems. *Proceedings of the 56th Annual Meeting of the ISSS-2012.*

Sankaran, S., Haslett, T., & Sheffield, J. (2010). *Systems thinking approaches to address complex issues in project management.* Paper presented at PMI® Global Congress 2010—Asia Pacific, Melbourne, Victoria, Australia.

Shahabi, A., Rabani, Y., & Abbasnejad, T. (2013). Development of a methodology for industrial feasibility studies based on Sustainable development principles- integrated approach. *Journal of Economic Development Research, 9*, 117–146.

Siriram, R. (2017). A hybrid (soft and hard) systems approach to project management. *SSRG International Journal of Industrial Engineering, 4*(3), 1-16.

Sohrabinejad, A., & Darjazi, M. (2014). Planning the allocation of financial resources to development projects using soft system methodology. *International Conference on Management in the 20th Century.*

Turner, J. R., & Müller, R. (2003). On the nature of the project as a temporary organization. *International Journal of Project Management, 21*(1), 1–8. doi:10.1016/S0263-7863(02)00020-0

United Nations. (1978). *Manual for the preparation of industrial feasibility studies.* Vienna: United Nations Industrial Development Organization.

Winter, M. (2009). Using soft systems methodology to structure project definition. In T. M. Williams, K. Samset, & K. J. Sunnevag (Eds.), *Making essential choices with scant information* (pp. 125–144). Springer. doi:10.1057/9780230236837_7

ENDNOTE

1 Specific, Measurable, Attainable, Relevant, and Time-Bound.

Chapter 10
Using Soft Systems Methodology for the Analysis of Sustainable Energy Initiatives

ABSTRACT

The chapter is devoted to the energy efficiency analysis as a prerequisite for sustainable use of energy. In this regard, the current study is focused on the application of soft systems methodology (SSM) and its role as a problem structuring approach to analyze the energy efficiency initiatives. For this purpose, four research works were addressed. The mentioned researches employed a combination of multiple-criteria decision analysis (MCDA) and (SSM) to assess the energy efficiency initiatives. The obtained results included the role of key players in rich pictures with a potential interest in a system for energy efficiency initiatives evaluations, the definition of the root, CATWOE components, and a conceptual model. The results of such processes could be applied in the establishment of a sufficiently accurate decision model capable of offering structured support giving rise to a more informed decision in terms of the energy efficiency measures implementation.

DOI: 10.4018/978-1-7998-4504-1.ch010

INTRODUCTION

As stated by Lemaire (2010), sustainable energy refers to the type of energy able to fulfill the requirements of the present generation with no interference with the future generations' ability to supply their own needs. Sustainable energy deals with the discovery of a clean and renewable source of energy instead of the depleting energy sources. In this definition, sustainable energy implies an inexhaustible type of energy that will never be used up or depleted. Sustainable energies can be found in various forms. Besides the most well-known sources (i.e. wind, solar, and water) bioenergy and geothermal energy can be also classified as sustainable energy. Sustainability is also achievable by improving energy conservation and efficiency. Although the common sources of energy (e.g. coal and natural gas) can undoubtedly supply the current energy requirements, they will be burned up leaving nothing for the next generation if we continue to consume them at this rate. Thus the next generations must do what we could already be doing—discovering new methods of energy exploitation.

The success of sustainable energy initiatives is highly probable upon their contribution to other social and economic development objectives (Ahuja and Tatsutani, 2009). It should be noted that the sustainable energy initiatives analysis is based on this assumption that the functions accomplished by people within a society can be sustained through the use of an underlying network involving sustainable energy. Moreover, a complex evolving system can be characterized by a proper balance between the efficiency improvements (in which the system inputs are converted to outputs in the cases of resource scarcity) and a diversification/intensification in the system outputs production (in cases with abundant resources). A complex system refers to a system in which the growing diversity and number of human functions can be reproduced (Labanca, 2017).

The use of soft systems methodology (SSM) in sustainable energy initiatives follows a classic seven-stage procedure involving the analyses to understand the problem condition and derive changes and recommendations to alleviate the problematic condition. Considering sustainable energy initiatives, the relevant stakeholders should be identified prior to the use of SSM. 3 major objectives can be envisaged for the decision-makers: (1) generating knowledge regarding a problematic situation; (2) the use of this knowledge to define the problem, and (3) establishment of a systemic plan. This triple configuration has provided a useful framework to understand the advantages of applying major SSM tools (Coelho et al., 2010).

Energy efficiency can be regarded as an initiative since it can result in sustainable energy. Energy efficiency can be accomplished by grid infrastructure, efficient supply, as well as suitable design, insulation, and retrofit of buildings. Implementation of the renewable self-generation options combined with enhanced efficiency of the consumer appliances and equipment can also contribute to energy efficiency (SEFA, 2012).

Fawkes (2013) discussed about energy management and developed a root definition by the use of SSM to design a model of energy management. The root definition is: for designing a system of management for a company that causes staff and others make a profitable difference to the organization by creating a change, identifying and making use of opportunities to enhance energy effieiciency. The energy management includes three interacting levels in reciprocal influence on other systems in an organization: 1) monitoring and targeting to reduce costs, 2) retrofitting oto buildings and processes, 3) investment in new buildings, processes, and facilities.

Ngai et al. (2012) applied SSM to determine the management support system opportunities to manage energy consumption during a textile manufacturing process. They presented an SSM-based approach for analyzing the complicated development of an efficient energy and utility management support system (EUMSS). Neves et al. (2004) re-established the energy efficiency initiatives analysis by SSM which served as a problem-structuring tool. Their work was aimed at providing the public and private initiative promoters or evaluators with structured support to achieve more informed decisions on taking the energy efficiency measures. The SSM approach requires the determination of all the market players and their relationships, as well as their insight toward the insufficiencies of the current methodologies.

SSM was employed in the compound sustainable energy launching framework (CSEL) in the Iranian household sector by Sirous et al. (2016) to further promote the utilization of solar energy in this sector. Their results revealed that the SSM method could link the CSEL framework to the solar energy application in the Iranian architect environments. Their CSEL multi-methodology framework was not only aimed to resolve the obstacles in energy sustainability but also helped in effective capital investment allocation for such initiatives. Bernardo et al. (2018), introduced a comprehensive problem-structuring approach composed of SSM and value-focused-thinking to address and handle several effective factors influencing the energy efficiency of the school buildings. The major goal of this work was to structure the fundamental objectives for the development of a criterion tree for a multi-criterion classification model which can be used by the managers to rate the overall energy-related function of the school buildings. The mentioned framework can help in addressing the major issues for a holistic energy performance evaluation and its requirements to establish adequate improving policies.

Coelho et al. (2010) tested the application of the SSM method to structure the energy planning issues in an urban environment. To apply this method on a real-world problem, they selected a medium-sized Portuguese and employed the SSM method for a precise definition of the decision problem, identification of the main stakeholders and their relationships, and discerning the relevant criteria for each one. Oliveira et al. (2019) presented a case study about the enhancement of energy efficiency through using SSM to build a multi-criteria decision aiding model to analyze consumer preferences for electric vehicles. Neves et al. (2009) applied SSM to structure a multi-criteria decision analysis (MCDA) model for the purpose of appraising energy efficiency initiatives. They provided some general guides regarding how SSM may contribute the emergence of objectives for MCDA models. The studies clearly indicated that SSM has been often applied in the field of energy efficiency as a crucial factor in energy sustainability. Thus, this chapter is aimed to address the enhancement of energy efficiency through the use of SSM by reviewing the relevant literature.

ENERGY EFICIENCY

Energy efficiency has recently converted to a vital issue in the public policy agenda of the majority of the countries. The significance of energy efficiency as a policy objective is associated with commercial, industrial competitiveness, and energy security benefits. The reduction of carbon dioxide emissions is another important global priority that can be related to energy efficiency (Patterson, 1996). Buildings are responsible for 30% of the total energy consumption which is anticipated to grow by elevation of the life quality standards (Yuan, 2016).

According to Skopek (2013), the building properties (i.e. its age, size, and application of the energy-efficient equipment), energy management and operation practices, and occupants engagement are among the factors with substantial impact on the energy efficiency of the buildings in North America. His study revealed that building size has a higher influence on the overall energy performance of office buildings than its age.

In building the CIBSE-based design (2004), the regional and local climatic conditions, as well as micro-climate, are taken into. Moreover, factors such as topography, landscape, neighboring buildings, and vegetation play a crucial role in locating the building site. On the other hand, The architectural points (e.g. the building shape, its orientation, and windows, as well as its structures) can drastically affect the energy efficiency of a building. The heating, ventilation and air conditioning system (HVAC-system), as well as the electricity and control systems, are intended to provide the occupants with a pleasant indoor condition.

As mentioned by Ebrahimi (2019), concerning the energy efficiency in the residential sector, house-hold applications highly depend on the demographic feature of the occupants. Thus, larger houses will use more energy, in comparison to their smaller counterparts. In terms of energy consumption per capita, however, the smaller houses tend to consume more energy. Regarding the increasing number of small households throughout the Globe, higher per capita energy consumption is anticipated. In the United States, the energy consumption rate of the older single individuals (60 years old and older) at home is greater than the other singles, considering both heating and home appliances. The low-income elderlies, however, consume lower amounts of energy than the others. This implies that energy consumption has a direct positive correlation with income. Furthermore, household composition can influence the energy consumption. They also indicated the impact of culture and public policies on energy consumption, by varying the people's residence and lifestyle and considering the migration patterns, social impacts, working hours, and tax relief on the mortgage interests.

SSM IN THE ANALYSIS OF ENERGY EFFICIENCY

SSM has been employed for gaining insight into the problematic situations. In this case, the problematic concept of the energy efficiency initiatives needed further understanding (Neves et al., 2004). SSM employs four approaches to find about a problematic condition: creating rich pictures and following three types of inquiry namely Analyses One, Two and Three (Checkland and Scholes, 2000). The mentioned analyses can offer other frameworks that can be helpful in gaining a rich overview of the problem (Checkland, 2000).

Analysis One considers the aspects of the intervention as its subject and determines the "client", "intervention-commissioned individuals", and "situation improving facilitator". During this process, the facilitator tries to identify the "stakeholders". By stakeholder, we mean the people with an interest in or those who could be affected by the situation. This information can serve as a starting point to gather other information. Analysis Two deals with the social setting of the problematic situation and tries to identify the social roles and their expected behavioral norms. Analysis Three is responsible for uncovering the power relationships within the situation (i.e., how the power is manifested, distributed, applied, attained, and delegated). This requires exploring the official structure of the power as well as the informally-offered or accepted leadership. This analysis provides the facilitator with the required power issues during the later stages of the SSM process. In the most basic form, the three analyses could be merged as an analytical tool: the selection of the involved individuals, identification of their power type and scope, and describing their contextual immersion (Georgiou, 2008).

Neves et al. (2004) determined all the agents in the market, who can be promoted or influenced by the energy efficiency initiatives. Their corresponding roles and the relations of power were also addressed:

- An energy agency, which is responsible for managing the public funds devoted to predicting the energy efficiency, by its own initiatives or financing the third parties. Moreover, the energy market regulator is aimed at fostering the efficiency (not only economically, but also in terms of energy), by use of the tariff mechanisms; in such a situation the mentioned regulator should apply a proper approach to assess the initiatives suggested by the regulated company. The energy agency and the regulator are public entities that are authorized by the government to address the energy market. The government's economic analyses may affect the national budget, social welfare, and the environment.
- The energy companies work in 4 distinct realms: generation, transmission, distribution, and retail. Each of these companies has different points of view on energy efficiency initiatives. They consider energy efficiency as a cost-reducing measure.
- The Energy Service Companies (ESCOs) are involved in energy efficiency.
- The end-use equipment manufacturers who can be obligated to present efficiency to the market through the proper standards or mandatory labeling. Moreover, they can exploit the energy efficiency as a marketing benefit. These manufacturers could also apply for financing to increase the pace of the new technologies introduction to the market. They are aimed at maximizing their sales while reducing their costs.
- Consumers, environmentalists, and society: these groups are capable of affecting the decisions taken by all the major actors; thus their

concerns must be considered. The consumers respond to the initiatives in accordance with the barriers. They have a limited analysis capacity. The environmentalists assess the environmental effects of the policies; while the society examines the economic, environmental, welfare, and employment condition (almost all the external influences of the energy use).

Neves et al. (2004) used a root definition to define a system for evaluating the advantages of the promoter initiatives for the end-uses energy efficiency fostering by taking the promoter's advantages and disadvantages into account. The CATWOE mnemonic resulted in the definitions listed in Table 1.

The conceptual model resulted from the system in Figure 1 together with a sub-system is essential for the modeling phase.

Activity 1 involves collecting all the data relevant to the initiative definition, for instance, its objectives, goals, implementing agents, estimated costs, and achievements.

Activity 2 is responsible for determining the entities under the influence of the initiative to elucidate their possible reactions.

These reactions will be assessed in activity 4, this process requires an estimation of the initiative success, based on the potential "participation" level of consumers attained in activity 3. The mentioned input is also required for

Table 1. Definitions of CATWOE to evaluate the energy efficiency initiatives (Neves et al., 2004)

CATWOE elements	Definitions
Customer	The initiative promoters, the external sponsors if any existed, the beneficiaries (the consumers who are benefited from the initiative, the society and its concerns on the environmental status and other benefits, the manufacturers and the sellers of the improved equipments) and the victims (energy companies whose sales are dropped or the manufacturers of the substituted equipments).
Actors (Decision Maker(DM))	The promoters of the initiatives, or those responsible for its evaluation, according to a contract. One of the following six entities: Energy Agencies, Energy Market Regulators, the Government, Energy Companies, Energy Service Companies, and Equipment Manufacturers.
Transformation	Initiative with unclear interests → known interests
Weltanschauung	An initiative will be implemented only if its advantages for the promoter overrules its drawbacks, the consequences of the interaction with other affected entities should be also included.
Owner (Decision Maker)	Someone at the highest hierarchal position (e.g. the Government as the power above the Agency or the Regulator).
Environment	The capability of attaining the relevant data; estimating the initiative success (potential adherence of end-users); budget; international agreements and directives.

the correct assessment of all the initiative effects which will be conducted by activity 6.

The available budget for implementation or sponsorship of the initiative might be a significant issue in some cases. Budget evaluation in activity 5 can provide valuable information to activity 7.

The system is aimed to "compare" all the benefits and drawbacks which will be conducted in activity 7.

The general monitoring and control measures in any SSM model involve the determination of some criteria to assess: 1) Efficacy: Is the system capable of correct identification of the valid energy efficiency initiatives? 2) Efficiency: Does the system operate with minimal resources? And 3) Effectiveness: Are the initiatives well categorized by the actually-implemented system?

A set of evaluation criteria should be first established to assess the cons and pros of energy efficiency initiatives. This requires to consider a new subsystem (shown as 6.x in Figure 1)

Figure 1. Conceptual model of the analysis system (Neves et al., 2004)

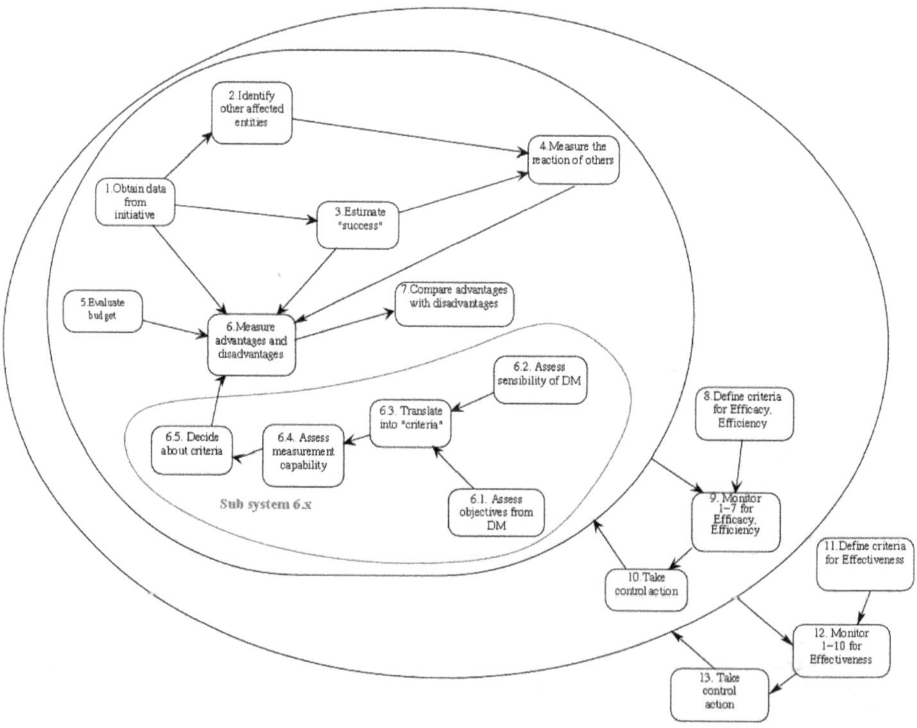

Sirous et al. (2016) applied SSM in the CSEL framework to not only eliminate the energy sustainability barriers but also establish an efficient capital investment allocation for such initiatives. CSEL framework satisfies three following principles:

1. Analysis of the sustainable energy initiatives attractiveness, including the use of solar energy as a renewable form of energy, in specific society considering its special cultural features.
2. Identification of the energy sustainability obstacles, demonstrating the energy sustainability gaps and definition of the corresponding roles and responsibilities of the relevant organizations or entities to resolve the obstacles.
3. Efficient budget allocation.

They introduced a rich picture illustrating the major entities and their interactions, which can have a direct or indirect influence on the solar energy application in the Iranian buildings:

- Government and legislation represent a class of entities responsible for Energy Demand Reduction (EDR) and implementation of the sustainable energy measures under Resistance Economy strategies and other long-term or periodic energy strategies.
- The Construction Engineering Organization (a nongovernmental organization) categorizes the engineers and experts and train them to cope with the construction challenges. This entity is authorized to grant different permissions at different construction stages. So that they could play a decisive role in solar energy application in the Iranian buildings.
- The contractors work in close contact with Construction Engineering Organization and the supervisor engineers. In addition to the construction supervisors, the energy managers and engineers are also supervising the energy management measures in the buildings.
- The Energy Service Companies (ESCOs) and renewable energy organizations are commercial or non-profit businesses in charge of developing, designing, implementing and funding the energy-saving and retrofitting projects (which ca decline the costs associated with energy, operations, and maintenance). ESCOs often develop the project in terms of energy conservation considering its potential technical and operation risks. Such companies are highly required in Iran; the

Table 2. CATWOE definitions for facilitating energy sustainability and deployment (Sirous et al., 2016)

CATWOE elements	Definitions
Customer	The Iranian government, ESCOs, or Construction Engineering Organization.
Actors	the system analysts or project developers probably from ESCOs or a universities
Transformation	CSEL framework to deploy solar energy in the Iranian Buildings.
Weltanschauung	SSM which can be helpful in adapting the CSEL framework for facilitating energy sustainability and deploying the solar energy in the Iranian buildings.
Owner	Government, ESCO, or universities
Environment	Iran is rapidly growing with an urge for economic improvement under the policy of the resistance economy.

already-existing ones should work at their highest possible efficiency, with sufficient knowledge, experience, and skilled experts. One of the ESCO departments deals with the implementation of the energy management measures in a construction environment within the CSEL framework.

- Employers play a significant role in launching sustainable energy measures. Upon the employer's tendency to deploy the energy efficiency measures and solar energy components, (particularly in Iran), a huge part of obstacles will be removed and budget allocation will easily occur with high effectiveness.
- Under the influence of the media, the customers could become more sensitive to sustainability in the field of construction; so they may ask for an inexpensive sustainable source of energy.

System root definition could be applied in SSM application for facilitating the launch of solar energy systems in the Iranian buildings with the help of systems analysts and project developers, regarding the urgent demands for improving the Iranian economy. The CATWOE mnemonic resulted in the definitions represented in Table 2.

A conceptual model will be resulted which involves the following activities in combination with a sub-system.

Activity 1: Responsible for deciding on the surveying groups for their classification

Activity 2: Responsible for definition of the high-priority decision-making criteria,

Activity 3: Responsible for determining the alternatives for the surveying groups,
Activity 4: Responsible for deciding on the application of an analytical approach for the interest analysis,
Activity 5: Responsible for determining the crucial solar energy deployment obstacles,
Activity 6: Responsible for classification of these challenges and identifying the stakeholders' roles,
Activity 7: Responsible for efficient assignment of the capital investment.

The sub-activities are represented by 7.X. format:

7.1: Responsible for defining the energy cost centers in the buildings,
7.2: Responsible for determination of the best possible solution for each center,
7.3: Responsible for the investment planning for profitability analysis of the projected investment
7.4: Responsible for deciding on the total amount of capital invested in solar energy initiatives

The sub-activities can provide the data for rational analysis. The results of activity 7 can help the decision-maker in an efficient budget assignment in solar energy solutions.

Bernardo et al. (2018) used the SSM to address the energy performance of the Portuguese school buildings. Their rich picture was formed through an inquiry process namely, Analyses One, Two and three. The major stakeholders and their roles were determined as follows:

- **International institutions** can affect the major directions in the field of energy policy by defining the standards and directives to promote the use of energy efficiency improvement plans and measures (e.g., European Commission).
- **National government** puts the international directives into action to develop a national regulatory and policy framework regarding the energy and environment, establish some targets to decline the energy consumption and greenhouse gas emission and promote the market transformation to further spread the application of the energy efficiency initiatives. It is also in charge of financing the school operation and legislation to succeed in the improvement of energy efficiency and

indoor air quality. The national government also pays the required fees (to buildings management company) for the modernization programs.

- **School management company** plans, manages, develops, and implements the modernization programs in the public schools administrated by the national government (Ministry of Education). It is an independent state-owned company, which functions as a private sector company. In cooperation with the schools' management board, this company implements the energy efficiency projects, through national and international programs or an energy performance contract with the ESCOs.
- **Energy supply companies** are in close commercial relationships with consumers and provide their energy demands. This research was focused on electrical energy and natural gas retail companies in a liberalized market. These companies are aimed at lowering the costs and increasing the revenues, supply reliability, and compatibility with the already-available energy infrastructures. The popularity of energy infrastructure improvements will be incremented by the extensive use of smart grids and smart energy management devices.
- **Energy services companies (ESCO)** supply energy services and put the energy efficiency measures into action while avoiding or decreasing the operational costs and environmental consequences on the school facilities. Their business model relies on the energy performance contract.
- **Equipment manufacturers and retailers** present the equipment and systems capable of enhancing the energy performance of the buildings. Appropriate standards or mandatory labeling schemes could be used to guide the manufacturers/retailers to provide the market with more energy-efficient equipment. Moreover, the energy efficiency issue can be exploited as a marketing tool to enhance their sales rate.
- **Facility management companies** are responsible for providing the services relevant to the integrated technical management, planning, operation, and maintenance, to support and improve the efficiency of the building's facilities and infrastructures.
- **School** implies the school building and its facilities and encompasses the management board as well. Schools should provide proper indoor conditions which often result in enhanced energy consumption and energy costs. For declining the operational costs while maintaining a sufficiently proper indoor condition, the organizations have to manage their buildings considering the energy efficiency issues.

- As the school building occupants, the **students and staff** could benefit or be the victims of the indoor environmental condition offered by the building's facilities.
- **Local community** consists of the students' and staff's families and neighbors. They may learn and adapt these implemented practices to decrease their energy bills and attain more and better energy services at their houses.

The root definition can be defined as a classification system for the school buildings grouping them in terms of their energy performance. This system considers multiple energy-related and non-energy issues to help the School Management Company in improving energy management by defining some energy policies and energy-related investments.

Table 3 lists the CATWOE mnemonic definitions for the analyzed situation.

Following the root definition step, the next stage deals with modeling the activities of the system. A conceptual model was developed to classify the school buildings in terms of their performance as follows:

Activity 1: Responsible for collecting and analyzing the energy bills, typical occupancy data, and other relevant variables (e.g. number of the served meals). These analyses also include the architectural and engineering plans of the buildings and their corresponding energy systems (heating, ventilation and air conditioning - HVAC, pumps, lighting, and domestic hot water).

Table 3. The elements of a CATWOE for energy performance assessment (Bernardo et al., 2018)

CATWOE elements	Definitions
Customer	School, students, and staff, local community and national economy.
Actors	International institutions, national government, school buildings management company, energy supply companies, energy service companies, equipment manufacturers and retailers, facilities management companies, school, students and staff, local community.
Transformation	Understanding the energy performance of the school to improve the energy management and determination of the energy policies and energy-related investment.
Weltanschauung	There are several energy-related and non-energy decisions that can affect or be influenced by the energy performance of the school buildings. These decisions have to consider the stakeholders' priorities.
Owner	Schools Management Company, as the representative of the national government
Environment	Ability to collect all the relevant information, challenge the existing plans and operations; funding and technological limitations; legislation and directives.

Activity 2: Responsible for the building facilities inspection to assess the systems and provide an answer to the questions introduced in the preliminary review.

Activity 3: Responsible for communicating with the major stakeholders to provide a common understanding of the building facilities, their management norms, and comfort conditions during and after visiting the site.

Activity 4: Responsible for the identification and collection of the other relevant information applicable in the classification process.

Activity 5: Responsible for monitoring energy consumption status. Through this activity, it is possible to quantify the energy flow and energy load profile and assess the energy performance of the facilities. In combination with the measured energy data, the indoor environmental quality data allows for incorporating the comfort issues of the evaluation model.

Activity 6: Responsible for collecting all the relevant energy and non-energy data to be used in the energy performance classification system. During this stage, the values of the stakeholders will be converted into objectives considering all the evaluation-related quantitative and qualitative information.

Activity 7: Responsible for classifying the school buildings in terms of their performance. This process highlights the urge for a multi-criterion method which incorporates the objectives and values of the decision-maker and other stakeholders into the decision process.

The conceptual model should also include a monitoring and control procedure to establish the performance measures. Monitoring and control will be defined in terms of efficacy, efficiency, and effectiveness ("3Es").

Coelho et al. (2010) employed SSM for energy planning in a medium-sized Portuguese city. According to the interview-based information, the following stakeholders, with different interests and priorities, were determined:

- **International institutions** can affect energy policy directions and establish legislative rules to properly finance through sources or programs.
- The project financing will be referred to **the national government.** It may accept or reject the applications. Moreover, it is responsible for providing a regulatory and policy framework for other stakeholders in local energy planning to operate, demanding for secure energy supply, energy savings and reasonable energy consumption, and

the environment protection as well as analyzing the international competitiveness of the energy sector.

- **Financial institutions**: provides financial support for the local producers (for investing in renewable sources), the consumers (for investing in efficient technologies/appliance), and the local government (for supporting the new plans).
- **Energy agency**: asks to be involved in the planning processes. It also provides information, promotes the initiatives and monitors compliance with the implemented measures.
- **Environmentalists**: analyze the consequences of the alternatives on the environmental and social welfare. Although they do not participate in the legislation process, they can put pressure on the legislator board.
- **Local government**: asks for secure energy supply, energy saving, reasonable energy consumption, and the environment protection, it is authorized to stop any project, demand more involvement in the planning procedure; establish relevant rules and legislation. It also provides a market for the new technology, encourages the local energy producers, approves the construction plan for new houses and infrastructures. It operates according to the national energy policies. It is also a prominent decision-maker.
- **Consumers**: have some concerns about energy costs, environment protection, and reliable supply. The consumers may respond to new infrastructures and technologies and are capable of influencing the stakeholders' decisions.
- **Manufacturers**: are in charge of technical assistance. They usually accept to implement some consumption reducing measures to optimize their sales. By specific standards or mandatory labeling, they can be also obliged to present more efficient products to the market.
- **Technical officers**: provide information for the decision-makers and consult them. Their duty is to observe the national and local rules and norms.
- **Energy companies**: are aimed to lower the costs and increase the revenues, supply reliability, and compatibility with the available energy infrastructures. The improvement of energy infrastructures can dramatically affect the final decision.
- **Local producers**: contribute to the energy supply systems their objective is a durable and feasible control of the production system.

The CATWOE mnemonic results in the following definitions (Table 4).

Table 4. The elements of a CATWOE for energy planning (Coelho et al., 2010)

CATWOE elements	Definitions
Customer	could be the system victims or beneficiaries. The beneficiaries will be benefited from the low price of reliably-supplied energy. Moreover, they are free to choose. Manufacturers could be also benefited from sales enhancement due to the use of renewable energy technologies/equipment. The society also have some concerns about sustainable energy and national energy dependence. The victims: the energy companies whose sales rate is declined; the producers of the substituted technologies/equipment.
Actors	The local planning committee whose members are the urban planners, developers and consultants and energy companies' managers.
Transformation	Transformation of the existing sectoral energy-related urban plans into an integrated urban energy plan with well-defined targets, policies, and procedures to adjust the future demands and supply in a sustainable manner in the medium term.
Weltanschauung	Integrated urban energy planning aimed at improving the decisionmaking process through the involved actors or those influenced by local energy planning by a selection of a proper mix of energy technologies to develop the infrastructures.
Owner	The Municipality
Environment	Difficulty in access to the information and the capability of challenging the available plans; economic, environmental, and technological limitations; international agreements and directives.

The following root definition results in the following CATWOE: "a system aimed at helping the Municipality in deciding on the sustainable development framework designed to implement by a local planning committee including scenarios for energy demand and identification of a portfolio of options with influence on the local energy systems (regarding an overall concept of energy consumption) to be assessed based on multiple axes of evaluation".

The conceptual model was constructed based on the root definition. The corresponding diagrams illustrate the modeling procedure involving 7 major activities as well as the performance-monitoring and controlling activities of the transformation stage.

Activity 1: Responsible for identifying all the essential information,

Activity 2: Responsible for collecting the information including local availability of the renewable source of energy; accessible energy carriers, energy converting techniques; opportunities to improve energy efficiency, clean transport technology, existing energy infrastructures, and legislative laws.

Activity 3: Responsible for determining all the constraints relevant to the urban energy system encompassing the legislative, environmental, economic and technical constraints as well as those related to energy resource availability and capacity.

Activity 4: Responsible for evaluating the consequences of technology in terms of investment and maintenance costs, performance and reliability, confidence, acceptance, and applicability.

Activity 5: Responsible for analyzing the energy infrastructure alternatives. This stage requires the information attained through activities 2, 3, and 4.

Activity 6: Responsible for the assessment of the consequences of the energy infrastructure options.

Activity 7: Responsible for evaluating the energy infrastructure options with an emphasis on the need for a multi-criterion approach.

Monitoring and control also include 3 activities: defining the Efficacy, Efficiency, and Effectiveness (three Es) criteria, monitoring the activities according to the metrics mentioned for the three Es; and controlling through these metrics.

DISCUSSION

In this chapter, four studies were reviewed which have similarities in terms of using SSM as a problem structuring tool, encompassing the development of a decision support based on a Multi-Criteria Decision Analysis (MCDA) in the assessment of energy efficiency initiatives. Problem structuring for MCDA has gained increasing interests over the last two decades form both the conceptual and the practical points of view (Marttunen et al., 2017). The integrated use of SSM, as a problem structuring method (PSM), and MCDA was explored in various studies such as Kuang and Fan (2009) in the public crisis management, and Fan and Kuang (2013) on the social systems.

Belton and Stewart (2010) examined 5 principal methods of problem structuring (Strategic Options Development and Analysis (SODA), SSM, Strategic Choice Approach (SCA), Robustness Analysis, and Drama Theory). The former three methods - SODA, SSM, and SCA – are the most commonly used ones as they could be employed for surface ideas and structured thinking concerning any broadly-defined issue. Robustness Analysis is particularly focused on future uncertainty; while the Drama theory emphasizes the tensions resulting in the potential cooperation or conflict among the involved parties. The major characteristics of these principal approaches as well as their potential to be integrated with MCDA are listed in Table 5.

Oliveira et al. (2019) adapted general guides for the use of SSM to show MCDA objectives which is presented in Table 6.

Table 5. Problem Structuring approaches and their connection with MCDA (Belton and Stewart, 2010)

Method	Major properties	Potential integration with MCDA
SODA	It begins by the idea generation and attempts to capture and structure the issue complexity manifested by several perspectives.	Able to be flexibly employed with MCDA, either as a precursor or in an integrated manner. benefited from facile incorporation and comprehensive prioritization.
SSM	Employing the rich pictures, CATWOE, root definitions, and conceptual models it explores the issue from various aspects.	Able to be flexibly employed with MCDA, either as a precursor or through an integrated manner.
SCA	Involving four modes: Shaping, Designing, Comparing, and Choosing. It emphasizes the major uncertainties (about relevant areas, environments, and values) and analyzes the interconnected decision alternatives.	It can be used in parallel with MCDA. Shaping and designing are focused on the key options; while comparing evaluates them by a simple form of multi-criteria evaluation.
Robustness Analysis	It is concentrated on the identification of the options capable of good performance in all possible future scenarios	Works in complementary to MCDA; it is focused on different aspects of an issue
Drama Theory	Works well in multi-party conditions, where the outcomes depended on the interdependent activities of the parties; it tries to determine the stable options.	Drama theory requires ranking of the possible futures in terms of their preference in a holistic manner.

CONCLUSION

This chapter was focused on the use of soft systems methodology (SSM) as a problem structuring tool for the analysis of sustainable energy initiatives which can be achieved through improved energy efficiency. Four studies have been reviewed which applied SSM in the field of energy efficiency as one of the aspects of sustainable energy. All of these studies encompass a combination of multiple-criteria decision analysis (MCDA) and SSM to assess the energy efficiency initiatives. Aligned with the purpose of this study, the method should be sufficiently flexible to adapt to the various concerns of the private and public parties; its outcomes must be evident and significant for the decisionmakers. SSM applies the rich pictures, CATWOE analysis, root definitions, and conceptual models to examine the different aspects of the issue. It can be flexibly employed in combination with MCDA, either as a precursor or in an integrated manner. Two of the review studies (Bernardo et al. (2018) and Coelho et al. (2010)) referred to the work carried out by Neves et al. (2004). Thus, this chapter first addressed the study of Neves et al. (2004).

The presented results include actors playing roles in rich pictures with a potential interest in a system to analyze the energy efficiency initiatives, root

Table 6. General guides for the use of SSM to show MCDA objectives (Oliveira et al., 2019)

Questions	Support in answering
The phase of finding out	
Why is the situation under consideration problematic?	Objectives that have not yet been satisfactorily achieved.
What are the objectives of each actor?	Objectives of each actor
What are the behavioral norms of each actor?	Norms and social limitations of stakeholders' objectives
What makes a good performance for each actor?	Objectives of each actor
What things do manifest power? How are they acquired, maintained, and passed on?	The political nature objectives obout power distribution and control.
The phase of system definition	
Customer: What are the benefits and disadvantages?	Objectives to maximize benefits and minimize disadvantages.
Actors: What defines a good role?	Objectives of each actor
What is the Weltanschauung?	Restrictions or objectives which can be relabled as objectives.
Owner: Why become an activity, successful, promoted and worthless?	Owner's objectives
What are the environmental restrictions?	Restrictions which can be relabled as objectives.
Which criteria can be used to measure effectiveness, efficacy, and efficiency?	Objectives regarding effectiveness, efficacy, and efficiency
Why is the activity important?	Objectives followed by the activity.
The phase of system comparison	
Is each difference between the real world activities and the models a negative or positive aspect and why?	Objectives that their achievements degree would change.
Why is each change desirable or undesirable?	Objectives that their achievements degree would change.

definitions, CATWOE components, and a conceptual model. The outcomes of this process can be employed in the establishment of a decision model with higher accuracy. In this way, it will provide the decision-makers of different parties with structured support to reach more informed decisions on the implementation of energy efficiency measures.

REFERENCES

Ahuja, D., & Tatsutani, M. (2009). Sustainable energy for developing countries. *S.A.P.I.EN.S*, *2*(1). Retrieved June 30, 2019, from https://journals.openedition.org/sapiens/823

Belton, V., & Stewart, T. (2010). Problem structuring and MCDA. In M. Ehrgott, J. R. Figueira, & S. Greco (Eds.), *Trends in multiple criteria decision analysis* (pp. 209–223). Springer. doi:10.1007/978-1-4419-5904-1_8

Bernardo, H., Gaspar, A., & Antunes, C. H. (2018). A combined value focused thinking-soft systems methodology approach to structure decision support for energy performance assessment of school buildings. *Sustainability*, *10*(2295), 1–19. doi:10.3390u10072295

Checkland, P. (2000). Soft systems methodology: A thirty years retrospective. *Systems Research and Behavioral Science*, *17*(S1), S11–S58. doi:10.1002/1099-1743(200011)17:1+<::AID-SRES374>3.0.CO;2-O

Checkland, P., & Scholes, J. (2000). *Soft systems methodology in action.* Chichester: Wiley.

CIBSE. (2004). *CIBSE guide F. Energy efficiency in buildings.* Norwich: Page Bros Ltd.

Coelho, D., Antunes, C. H., & Martins, A. G. (2010). Using SSM for structuring decision support in urban energy planning. *Technological and Economic Development of Economy*, *16*(4), 641–653. doi:10.3846/tede.2010.39

Ebrahimi, M. (2019). Enhancing residential energy efficiency enhancement: Through the use of system dynamics. *International Journal of Sustainable Society*, *11*(3), 162–185. doi:10.1504/IJSSOC.2019.103694

Fan, D. P., & Kuang, Y. Y. (2013). A Study on management methodology for the complexity of social system— The combination of MCDM and SSM. *International Journal of Operations Research*, *10*(2), 49–55.

Fawkes, S. (2013). *Energy efficiency: The definitive guide to the cheapest, cleanest, fastest source of energy* (1st ed.). Routledge.

Georgiou, I. (2008). Making decisions in the absence of clear facts. *European Journal of Operational Research*, *185*(1), 299–321. doi:10.1016/j.ejor.2006.12.038

Kuang, Y., & Fan, D. (2009). MCDM and SSM in the public crisis management: from the systemic point of view. In Cutting-edge research topics on multiple criteria decision making (pp. 661-668). Springer. doi:10.1007/978-3-642-02298-2_98

Labanca, N. Energy and complex systems dynamics. In N. Labanca (Ed.), *Complex systems and social practices in energy transitions, green energy and technology* (pp. 29–57). Springer.

Lemaire, X. (2010). *Glossary of terms in sustainable energy regulation.* REEEP / Sustainable Energy Regulation Network. Retrieved June 30, 2019, from: https://www.reeep.org/sites/default/files/Glossary%20of%20Terms%20in%20Sustainable%20Energy%20Regulation.pdf

Marttunen, M., Lienert, J., & Belton, V. (2017). Structuring problems for multi-criteria decision analysis in practice: A literature review of method combinations. *European Journal of Operational Research*, *263*(1), 1–17. doi:10.1016/j.ejor.2017.04.041

Neves, L. M. P., Martins, A. G., Antunes, C. H., & Dias, L. C. (2004). Using SSM to rethink the analysis of energy efficiency initiatives. *The Journal of the Operational Research Society*, *55*(9), 968–975. doi:10.1057/palgrave.jors.2601763

Neves, L. P., Dias, L. C., Antunes, C. H., & Martins, A. G. (2009). Structuring an MCDA model using SSM: A case study in energy efficiency. *Operations Research*, *199*(3), 834–845.

Ngai, E. W. T., To, C. K. M., Ching, V. S. M., Chan, L. K., Lee, M. C. M., Choi, Y. S., & Chai, P. Y. F. (2012). Development of the conceptual model of energy and utility management in textile processing: A soft systems approach. *International Journal of Production Economics*, *135*(2), 607–617. doi:10.1016/j.ijpe.2011.05.016

Oliveira, G., Dias, L. C., & Neves, L. (2019). Preference elicitation approaches for energy decisions. In M. Lopes, C. H. Antunes, & K.B. Janda (Eds.), Energy and behaviour, Towards a low carbon future (pp. 353-388). Elsevier.

Patterson, M. G. (1996). What is energy efficiency? Concepts, indicators and methodological issues. *Energy Policy*, *24*(5), 377–390. doi:10.1016/0301-4215(96)00017-1

SEFA. (2012). *Sustainable energy for all, a global action agenda, pathways for concerted action toward sustainable energy for all.* The Secretary-General's High-Level Group on Sustainable Energy for All. Retrieved July 02, 2019, from: https://www.seforall.org/sites/default/files/SEFA-Action-Agenda-Final.pdf

Sirous, R., Lopes, R., & Sirous, S. H. (2016). Application of soft systems methodology to trigger solar energy in iranian buildings. *Journal of Solar Energy Research*, *1*(1), 35–43.

Skopek, J. (2013). Factors affecting building performance. Central Europe towards Sustainable Building, Prague.

Yuan, L., Ruan, Y., Yang, G., Feng, F., & Li, Z. (2016). Analysis of factors influencing the energy consumption of government office buildings in Qingdao. *Energy Procedia*, *104*, 263–268. doi:10.1016/j.egypro.2016.12.045

About the Author

Maryam Ebrahimi currently is an independent researcher in Germany. Her post-doctoral research was in the area of Information Systems Management funded by the Alexander von Humboldt Foundation, Germany. She has oriented her studies towards the application of modeling and simulation methodologies especially system dynamics and agent-based modeling for the purpose of policymaking. A few of her publications are 'hybrid simulation approach for technological innovation policymaking in developing countries' and 'modeling and simulation techniques for improved business processes'.

Index

T

www.ingramcontent.com/pod-product-compliance
Lightning Source LLC
LaVergne TN
LVHW081323300926
849161LV00008B/1863
* 9 7 8 1 7 9 9 8 4 5 0 4 1 *